THE CLASSICS OF WESTERN SPIRITUALITY

THE CLASSICS OF WESTERN SPIRITUALITY
A Library of the Great Spiritual Masters

President and Publisher
Kevin A. Lynch, C.S.P.

EDITORIAL BOARD

GEORGE HERBERT
The Country Parson, The Temple

EDITED, WITH AN INTRODUCTION
BY
JOHN N. WALL, JR.

PREFACE
BY
A. M. ALLCHIN

PAULIST PRESS
NEW YORK • RAMSEY • TORONTO

6499

Cover Art
The artist, WILL HARMUTH, is a professional artist and illustrator who lives in Bernardsville, New Jersey. A graduate of Newark School of Fine/Industrial Arts, Mr. Harmuth attended the Arts Students League. In his rendition of Herbert he attempted to convey the man's "intensity and depth, along with the flavor of early seventeenth-century England."

Publisher's Note:
The spacing of the stanzas of poetry in this edition differs at times from that of the 1633 edition of Herbert's works.

Design: Barbini, Pesce & Noble, Inc.

Library of Congress
Catalog Card Number: 81-80287

ISBN: 0-8091-0317-6 (Cloth)
       0-8091-2298-7 (Paper)

Published by Paulist Press
545 Island Road, Ramsey, N.J. 07446

Printed and bound in the
United States of America

CONTENTS

Editor of the Volume

JOHN NELSON WALL, JR. is currently engaged in a study of the relationships between Christianity and literature in the English Renaissance. His special fields of interest include medieval, Renaissance, and modern literature and culture, but he is also concerned with the history of Christian worship and thought. An Episcopal priest as well as an English professor, he has published essays on the history of the English Reformation and edited Erasmus' *Paraphrases* of the Gospels and Acts. Professor Wall's publications on English literature include *A Guide to Prose Fiction in* THE TATLER *and* THE SPECTATOR and essays on Donne, Hooker, Shakespeare, and Milton in *Studies in Philology, Seventeenth-Century News, Shakespeare Quarterly,* and *Milton Studies.* After studying at the University of North Carolina and Duke University, he received his theological education at the Episcopal Theological School and his doctorate in English literature at Harvard University. He has held post-doctoral fellowships at the National Humanities Center and Duke University. He is at present Associate Professor of English at North Carolina State University. He lives in Raleigh with his wife Terry and their two daughters, Sarah and Frances.

Author of the Preface

ARTHUR MACDONALD ALLCHIN is a Residentiary Canon of
Canterbury Cathedral. Born in London in 1930, he was educated at
Christ Church, Oxford and Cuddesdon Theological College. Ordained
Deacon in 1956 and Priest in 1957, he was appointed to the staff of Pu-
sey House, Oxford in 1960. In 1967 he became Warden of the Sisters of
the Love of God, an Anglican contemplative community at Fairacres
in Oxford. Since 1973 he has been based in Canterbury.

Concerned with the question of Christian unity since school days,
he studied the Eastern Orthodox tradition in Greece in the year before
ordination. He is Chairman of the Council of the Fellowship of St. Al-
ban and St. Sergius and for sixteen years edited its journal *Sobornost*.
He holds an Honorary Doctorate from the Theological Institute in Bu-
charest. In 1967 and 1968 he was Visiting Lecturer in Ascetical Theology in the General Theological Seminary in New York. He has served
on a number of Commissions in the Church of England and is at present a member of the Advisory Council on Religious Communities and
the International Anglican Orthodox Commission.

Publications include *The Rediscovery of Newman* (with John Coul-
son), a study of the eighteenth-century Welsh hymn writer Ann Grif-
fiths, and two collections of studies of theological and spiritual
subjects, *The World Is a Wedding*, and *The Kingdom of Love and Knowledge*. In 1981 he is publishing a book *The Dynamic of Tradition*, which
contains a chapter devoted to the period of which George Herbert was
a part.

PREFACE

The current revival of interest in spirituality began with a strong tendency to turn toward the traditions of the further East. Only gradually did people come to suspect that we might have spiritual resources nearer home, treasures hidden in our own backyard. George Herbert, whose place in the development of English literature in the seventeenth century is secure, is one who deserves to be much more widely known and appreciated as a significant contributor to the development of the spiritual heritage of the English speaking world. He is part of our own neglected tradition of inner life and experience, of exploration into God.

George Herbert's works come to us from the first half of the seventeenth century, a very special moment in the history of the post-Reformation Church of England. It was the period in which a distinctively Anglican position began to emerge, not only in matters of theology and Church order, but also in terms of spirituality and devotion. T. S. Eliot describes this moment very well in his essay on Lancelot Andrewes, published in 1928 in the little book which first announced his adherence to the Christian faith.[1] It is an essay which can tell us much of what attracted him, as a man of the twentieth century, to these seventeenth century writers, and why it was that he found them helpful in his own struggle to find a way of thinking, living and praying that faith in our own complicated century.

In the men of this period, Eliot found a remarkable combination of qualities. There was a willingness to question, joined to a deep power of affirmation; there was a sense of the uniqueness of the individual together with an appreciation of the value of what is corporate and traditional; there was an intuitive understanding that Christian life is not either inward *or* outward; it is inescapably both. In his own words,

---

1. T. S. Eliot, *For Lancelot Andrewes* (London, 1928), pp. 17–18.

PREFACE

they were men who spoke "with the old authority and the new culture." They were men who lived on our side of the Renaissance and the Reformation. The critical questions which the new learning had raised were familiar to them. The heightened awareness of individual responsibility and guilt, the inner anguish of the Reformers, was theirs also. But at the same time they were conscious of belonging to an older and larger tradition. Their horizons were not bounded by the controversies of the sixteenth century. The massive effort to recover something of the balance and openness of the first Christian centuries, to be seen alike in Richard Hooker and Lancelot Andrewes, largely presupposed in George Herbert, had rendered them remarkably independent of the stereotyped controversies of their day.

Richard Hooker, for example, begins his great work on *The Laws of Ecclesiastical Polity* with a tribute to Mr. Calvin, "whom, for mine own part, I think incomparably the wisest man that the French Church did enjoy since the hour it enjoyed him." But he at once goes on to indicate the places where he parts company with Calvin, and concludes, "but wise men are men, and the truth is truth". Andrewes, for his part, constantly quotes the Fathers of the Church in his sermons, and is not averse to citing medieval writers such as Bernard of Clairvaux. We look in vain in his preaching for references to Luther or Calvin. It was in such a school of thought, which sought to escape from the increasing rigidity of current controversies by an appeal to the method and spirit of the early Christian centuries, that George Herbert was formed. It helps us to understand the fusion of prayer and thought, of feeling and intelligence, of heart and head, which everywhere marks his poems. In the words of the patristic adage, "a theologian is one who prays truly; one who prays truly is a theologian."

Although all this seventeenth century development had a strong historical dimension, it had urgently contemporary intentions. It was not at all a matter of antiquarianism. It was part of a desire to find ways of unity and agreement in an age of divisions and disagreements. It was marked by what Eliot describes as a "determination to stick to essentials, an awareness of the needs of the time, a desire for clarity and precision on matters of importance, and an indifference to matters indifferent." Much of this, too, we find in Herbert with the intensely Christocentric quality of his thought and devotion, and his remarkable capacity to hold together things often believed to be separable or opposed to one another.

PREFACE

The most immediately evident thing about Herbert's poems is that they record his deeply personal struggle with God. He himself says we are to find in them "a picture of the many spiritual conflicts that have past betwixt God and my soul, before I could subject mine to the will of Jesus, my Master." Herbert makes no attempt to disguise the element of conflict in this relationship with God, the frequent changes of mood and understanding which marked it. He does not hide his moments of rebellion, the temptations to doubt, the periods of dryness and deadness. As the great Puritan divine of the later seventeenth century, Richard Baxter, put it, "Herbert speaks to God like one that really believeth in God, and whose business in the world is most with God. *Heart-work* and *Heaven-work* make up his book."

But all this inner activity is placed within the context of the life and prayer of the Church as a whole. The very arrangement of the poems makes this clear. And when we read Izaak Walton's *Life* we may be surprised to see how great a stress Herbert put on the proper understanding of the Church's ordered round of worship in his instruction of his village congregation. "The texts for all his future sermons . . . were constantly taken out of the Gospel for the day; and he did as constantly declare why the Church did appoint that portion of Scripture to be that day read; and in what manner the collect for every Sunday does refer to the Gospel or to the Epistle then read to them." In his exposition of the liturgy he went on to unfold the meaning of the Church's year, the constant round of feasts and fasts which initiates us into the understanding of the different articles of faith. All this is a necessary part of the context of his inner pilgrimage.

There is a similar combination of things too often separated in Herbert's attitude to the Bible and the sacraments. There is no limit for his reverence for Scripture as the Word of God. "Next God, he loved that which God hath magnified above all things, that is, his Word; so as he hath been heard to make solemn protestation, that he would not part with one leaf thereof for the whole world, if it were offered him in exchange." Hence it is that he himself declares "the country parson preacheth constantly; the pulpit is his joy and his throne." But this regard for the ministry of the Word goes hand in hand with a similar regard for the ministry of the sacrament, which is no less a handling of the things of God. "The country parson being to administer the sacraments is at a stand with himself, how or what behaviour to assume for so holy things. Especially at Communion times he is in great

PREFACE

confusion, as being not only to receive God, but to break and administer Him." So in his poem called "The Priesthood" he can write:

> But th'holy men of God such vessels are,
> As serve him up, who all the world commands:
> When God vouchsafeth to become our fare,
> Their hands convey him, who conveys their hands.
> Oh what pure things, most pure must those things be,
> Who bring my God to me!

This matter of the priesthood is one which recurs often in Herbert's verse, and for intimately personal reasons. We know that it was
not without much struggle that he renounced possibilities of political
and academic advancement and decided to enter the Church's ministry. One of the most remarkable of all his poems is called simply "Aaron." It combines two apparently conflicting affirmations in one clear but
complex statement. On the one side there is the Reformation affirmation of man's total dependence on God's grace for his salvation, and of
the total dependence of all Christian ministry on the one and only
priesthood of Christ. On the other side there is an equally clear affirmation of the social and sacramental nature of ministry within the
Church. As a recent commentator has noted, "The picture of Aaron
standing robed before the people of God acts as a ruling conceit organizing all the material of the poem, shaping the poet's exposition of his
own experience of priesthood. With that image goes one unavoidable
affirmation, that priesthood is a social institution, a form through
which people are related to one another as well as to God. . . . The cli-
max of the poem is not merely 'Aaron's drest,' but 'Come people, Aaron's drest.' . . . The priest's calling is to represent to mankind at large
those things which are considered most vital to the life of a man, those
truths which are saving truths because they are sacred and sacred because they are saving."[2] Here as in other places in Herbert's writing
the dichotomies of Evangelical and Catholic are transcended. The affirmations are wholly Catholic because wholly Evangelical, wholly Evangelical because wholly Catholic. Here is no disjunction of word and
sign, of inner and outer, but rather a steadfast attempt to hold them together in a rich if precarious fullness.

------

2. Kenneth Mason, *George Herbert, Priest and Poet* (Oxford, 1980), p. 18.

PREFACE

So alike in his poetry and his prose Herbert discovers the sacramental quality of all life, of the whole creation:

> Teach me, my God and King,
>   In all things thee to see
> And what I do in anything
>   To do it as to thee.

All things share in God's life. We are reminded of Hooker's great assertion, "All things that are of God (and only sin is not) have God in them and he them in himself likewise." All things may be known as ways in which God comes to us and speaks with us. Nothing is excluded. So in his chapter on "The Parson Catechising" Herbert insists on the importance of using the very homeliest illustrations to illuminate divine truth, and notes that this is how God himself proceeds. "Doubtless the Holy Scripture intends this much, when it condescends to the naming of a plough, a hatchet, a bushel, leaven, boys piping and dancing; showing that things of ordinary use are not only to serve in the way of drudgery, but to be washed and cleansed, and serve for lights even of heavenly truths."

Hence it is that in his poetry Herbert is able to use an extraordinary variety of images, bringing together old and new, traditional and innovative, inner and outer, earthly and heavenly in a single moving but unified picture. If we consider for a moment the sonnet entitled simply "Prayer," we shall discover images from the Bible, from the Christian tradition, from the classical world, from Herbert's own creative heart and mind. All are brought together into one statement of great richness and, in the end, great simplicity. There is one long sentence consisting of a series of illuminative images and metaphors; and here one suspects is a place which reveals that Herbert was not altogether ignorant of the older language of his native land, for he employs one of the classical techniques of Welsh poetry, *dyfalu*.

This unity of vision allows him constantly to make use of surprisingly concrete, earthy images for the most subtle of interior experiences, as he writes, for instance, in "The Flower":

> Who could have thought my shrivelled heart
> Could have recovered greenness? It was gone
>   Quite underground; as flowers depart
> To see their mother-root, when they have blown;

PREFACE

Where they together
All the hard weather,
Dead to the world, keep house unknown.

If the use of this kind of startling imagery is one of the things which makes his poetry difficult, it is also one of the things which makes for its continued vitality. These are poems that wear well. They do not reveal their secrets all at once. We need to come back to them, time and again, and as we do so we shall always find new things in them. Only gradually do they yield up all the richness of meaning and experience contained within them.

Perhaps we have already suggested some of the reasons why George Herbert's work is important for us today. He lived in a time of change and disruption, of rapid expansion of knowledge, not altogether unlike our own. Without evading the complexity of things, without glossing over the fragility and brokenness of man's experience of life in time, he managed to reaffirm the great unities of Christian faith and prayer. These are unities which draw together the separated strands in the Christian heritage, which draw together past and present in a living and creative appropriation of tradition, which bring together creation and redemption, outer life and inner life into a single, complex but fruitful whole.

We have said that Herbert is representative of a crucial period in the history of Anglicanism, and this is certainly true. But he is something more than that, and he can speak more widely than that statement might suggest. Richard Baxter in the seventeenth century, John Wesley in the eighteenth century, S. T. Coleridge in the nineteenth century, and in our own time T. S. Eliot or Simone Weil—all have borne witness to the power of his verse. His life and his work is part of the spiritual heritage of Christians across the globe. At his greatest he soars up through the complexities of his art into statements of complete simplicity which, we may believe, had cost not less than everything. These are statements which can speak directly to us today, across all the frontiers of culture and tradition. They are statements which come from the heart of a life which did indeed partake of the unity and joy which comes to us from God.

Come, my Way, my Truth, my Life:
Such a Way, as gives us breath:

PREFACE

Such a Truth, as ends all strife:
Such a Life, as killeth death.

Come, my Light, my Feast, my Strength:
Such a Light, as shows a Feast:
Such a Feast, as mends at length:
Such a Strength, as makes his guest.

Come, my Joy, my Love, my Heart:
Such a Joy as none can move:
Such a Love, as none can part:
Such a Heart, as joys in love.

A. M. Allchin

FOREWORD

This volume, *George Herbert*, contains *The Country Parson*, a prose treatise on the conduct of a rural Anglican ministry, and *The Temple*, a substantial anthology of religious poetry organized by Herbert into three sections: "The Church Porch," "The Church" and "The Church Militant." It also includes a few other poems by Herbert, drawn either from Izaak Walton's *Life* or from an early manuscript of *The Temple* collection. As such, it offers all of Herbert's major writings in an edition based on the earliest printed versions. The texts have, however, been conservatively modernized in spelling and punctuation in an attempt to preserve the full experience of what Herbert wrote while making him accessible to the reader unfamiliar with seventeenth-century English.

George Herbert (1593–1633) was born into an aristocratic English family which had distinguished itself in service to the English crown in its native Montgomeryshire on the Welsh border. After attending Westminster School and Cambridge University, he was appointed University Orator in 1620. In 1624, after serving briefly in Parliament as a representative from Montgomeryshire, he was ordained a deacon in the Church of England. In 1629, he married Jane Danvers; the following year, he was named the rector of the parish church of Fugglestone St. Peter and the chapel of Bemerton St. Andrew and was ordained to the Anglican priesthood at Salisbury Cathedral. He died on the first of March, 1633, in his rectory at Bemerton.

Neither *The Country Parson* nor *The Temple* was published during Herbert's lifetime, although we can be fairly certain that he worked on both, and especially on the poems, over a considerable number of his all-too-brief forty years of life. *The Temple* was, however, published in 1633, within a few months of Herbert's death, in an edition seen through the press by Nicholas Ferrar, a friend of Herbert better known for his establishment of an Anglican religious community at Little Gidding. *The Country Parson* was published in 1652, in an edition

FOREWORD

of Herbert's *Remains,* compiled by Barnabas Oley, a Fellow of Claire Hall, Cambridge.

The two major works contained in this volume are best seen as complimentary presentations of an argument for the Christian life, as George Herbert experienced it. The distinctive quality of seventeenth-century Anglicanism is its devotion to the worship of God through observance of the Daily Offices of Morning and Evening Prayer and regular administration of Baptism and Holy Communion, as made possible by the Book of Common Prayer. Growing from this round of worship, and enabled by it, is the practice of active charity towards one's neighbor. In *The Country Parson,* Herbert presents the rural priest as the one responsible for making worship the center of life in his parish, and charity its underlying motivation. He also makes clear that the devoted practice of this life is the best way to persuade others to take it up.

The Temple, therefore, must be seen as both presentation and apologetic. On the one hand, it explores for us the experience of Christian living in a long series of poems notable both for their poetic excellence and for their Christian candor. On the other, it dramatizes that experience for us in such a way that we are drawn, through Herbert's guidance, to make it our own.

ACKNOWLEDGEMENTS

In the course of preparing this volume, I have become indebted in large ways and small to a great many people and institutions, only some of whom can be mentioned here. A grant from the Andrew W. Mellon Foundation made possible a year of postdoctoral study at Duke University during which much of my research on Herbert and his text was carried out. Duke's Humanities Council, under the able leadership of John Oates, made my stay especially enjoyable. The librarians and staff of Duke's Perkins Library and the D. H. Hill Library at North Carolina State University provided invaluable assistance in locating various materials. The Department of English at North Carolina State University provided funds for preparation of the manuscript; Charlene Turner, in her usual splendid way, typed it in all of its various forms.

John Creasey, the Librarian of Dr. Williams's Library, Gordon Square, London, has graciously consented to my use of the manuscript

FOREWORD

copy of Herbert's *The Temple* in the possession of that library as copy-text for the six poems not found in the 1633 edition. W. H. Bond, the Librarian of the Houghton Library, Harvard University, has made this a richer volume by permitting the reproduction of the Robert White sketch of Herbert now on display in Cambridge, Massachusetts.

George Walton Williams of Duke University and Gwynne Blakemore Evans of Harvard University taught me what I know about editing; J. Max Patrick of the University of Wisconsin at Milwaukee graciously shared with me his views on Herbert's text and the best way to treat it for an edition such as this one. More important, the editions prepared by these men over the years have set standards of scholarly excellence and meticulous attention to detail, which I can hope only to have approximated. In pursuit of a common goal, to make what an author wrote available to the modern reader, many editors may disagree as to appropriate means; I take full responsibility for all decisions regarding Herbert's text in this volume, and try to justify them in the textual introduction.

O. B. Hardison, Jr., then of the University of North Carolina at Chapel Hill and now director of the Folger Shakespeare Library, first introduced me to the study of seventeenth-century literature; Herschel Baker of Harvard University called my attention to its religious dimensions. The Very Reverend Harvey Guthrie and the Reverend Lloyd Patterson of the Episcopal Divinity School guided me in the study of Christian spirituality; even more by their example than by their instruction, they have made the spirit of Anglicanism a living tradition. The Reverend John Booty, also of the Episcopal Divinity School, taught me what I know about the English Reformation; his kind attention to my work over the years, including an early version of the Introduction to this volume, has always been of the greatest helpfulness. His edition of the Elizabethan Prayer Book should be a constant companion for any reader of George Herbert.

M. Thomas Hester and Antony Harrison, my colleagues at North Carolina State University, have also read drafts of the Introduction with careful attention and greatly needed encouragement. The Reverend Keith J. Reeve, rector of Saint Mark's Episcopal Church, Raleigh, North Carolina, and an exemplary parish priest very much in the mold of Herbert's Country Parson, has also given support to this project in a variety of ways, including helpful suggestions for the Introduction.

The good qualities of this volume owe much to all these men; the faults, as always, are but my own. I am grateful to them for sustaining support through a long and difficult process.

My greatest debts, however, are to my daughters, Sarah and Frances, and to Terry, my wife: "Ladies, look here; this is the thankful glass/That mends the lookers' eyes."

INTRODUCTION

"Thus he lived and thus he died like a Saint, unspotted of the World, full of Alms' deeds, full of Humility, and all the examples of a virtuous life": So Izaak Walton, his most famous biographer, summed up the earthly career of George Herbert, seventeenth-century Anglican priest, poet, and essayist of the parson's life.[1] Even if, in recent years, we have come to question Walton's accuracy in recounting some of the details of Herbert's biography,[2] we still have every reason to accept the justness of his overall assessment. For, after all, he was not the first to make it; Nicholas Ferrar, in introducing the volume of Herbert's religious poems he saw through the press shortly after Herbert's death, noted that Herbert's "faithful discharge [of his priestly calling] was such, as may make him justly a companion to the primitive Saints, and a pattern or more for the age he lived in."[3] To Henry Vaughan, Herbert was "a most glorious true *Saint,*" whose "holy *life* and *verse* gained many pious *Converts,*" of whom, Vaughan wrote, "I am the least."[4] From a very different perspective, Richard Crashaw, who subordinated one of his own volumes of poetry to Herbert's by entitling it *Steps to the Temple,* found "Divinest love" in Herbert's verse:

> When your hands untie these strings,
> Think you have an Angel by th' wings.
> One that gladly will be nigh,

---

1. In his *Life of George Herbert* (1670; reprinted Oxford: Oxford Univ. Press, 1973), p. 319. Hereafter referred to as *Life.* As with all quotations from primary sources in this book, I have taken the liberty of modernizing spelling according to the principles followed in the texts of Herbert's writings, outlined on p. 47 of this volume.
2. See especially Amy Charles, *A Life of George Herbert* (Ithaca, N.Y.: Cornell Univ. Press, 1977), and David Novarr, *The Making of Walton's Lives* (Ithaca, N.Y.: Cornell Univ. Press, 1958) for assessments of the accuracy of Walton's portrait of Herbert.
3. Reprinted in *The English Poems of George Herbert,* ed. C. A. Patrides (London: Dent, 1974), pp. 30–31.
4. In *The Works of Henry Vaughan,* ed. L. C. Martin, 2nd ed. (Oxford: Clarendon, 1957), pp. 186, 391.

1

INTRODUCTION

To wait upon each morning sigh.
To flutter in the balmy air,
Of your well-perfumed prayer.
These white plumes of his he'll lend you,
Which every day to heaven will send you:
To take acquaintance of the sphere,
And all the smooth faced kindred there.[5]

What is clear is that from the very first Herbert has been seen as an exemplary figure, one who for his fellow Anglicans exhibited a normative conduct of the priestly life and sketched out a pattern for others' emulation. As such, he can bring us to the very heart of early seventeenth-century Anglicanism if we can locate in his life and work those qualities that his contemporaries found so worthy of the highest praise.

In this endeavor, Nicholas Ferrar's Preface to the 1633 edition of *The Temple* will serve as our guide. Ferrar notes five ways in which he finds Herbert's conduct of his priestly office to be exemplary. Among all the things Ferrar might have praised, he chooses to comment on the path Herbert took to the priesthood, his independence in the conduct of his office, his devotion to the Bible and the discipline of the Church, and his humility in carrying out his priestly duties. Since, as we will see, Ferrar shared with Herbert a pattern of life that led them from the center of English political and social life in London and its Houses of Parliament to rural Christian community and devotion to observation of the Prayer Book services, Ferrar's points about Herbert's life and ministry seem especially worthy of our attention.

Ferrar's first observation is that Herbert, although he had opportunities for worldy advancement, chose instead the office of country parson: "Quitting both his deserts and all the opportunities that he had for worldly preferment, he betook himself to the Sanctuary and Temple of God, choosing rather to serve at God's Altar, than to seek the honor of State-employments." As we now know, Ferrar here radically simplifies and abbreviates what was for Herbert a long and arduous journey toward the priesthood. Although in 1616 he began the course of study at Cambridge that would, in the ordinary course of things, lead to the degree of Bachelor of Divinity and ordination before 1623, Herbert was not ordained deacon until 1624 and did not advance to the

---

5. From "On *Mr.* G. Herberts *booke, The Temple,*" in *The Complete Poetry of Richard Crashaw*, ed. George Walton Williams (Garden City, N.Y.: Anchor, 1970), p. 68.

priesthood until 1630.[6] Yet, in the end, Ferrar is probably right that for Herbert, "As God enabled him, so he accounted him meet not only to be called, but to be compelled to this service." Our review of Herbert's life will suggest that Herbert's progress toward holy orders was, for all its seeming tranquility at the end, filled with peaks and valleys, with what Walton has Herbert call "the many spiritual Conflicts that have past betwixt God and my Soul."[77] Yet the sense of confidence in one's calling that Herbert exhibits in *The Country Parson* holds out hope to those caught up in such conflicts that it is still possible "to subject mine to the will of Jesus my Master."

Ferrar's second point concerns Herbert's "independency upon all others," which he demonstrates by recalling that Herbert "used in his ordinary speech, when he made mention of the blessed name of our Lord and Savior Jesus Christ, to add, *My Master.*" In an age in which the Church was being torn apart by controversies over order, ceremony, and doctrine, one's stand on such issues could often be colored by political considerations. The English Civil War, which broke out in the 1640s, dramatically demonstrates the close connections in seventeenth-century England between religion and politics. In our review of Herbert's church practices and theological statements, we can use Ferrar's comment as a perspective from which to indicate that Herbert's positions were his own, uncolored by external political or ecclesiastical loyalties. In all, Herbert's goal was service to God, in spite of what might be advantageous to him in terms of secular or ecclesiastical advancement. Ferrar's point here is that Herbert's choice of a country parish declared his loyalty to Christ and his independence of the social and ecclesiastical value systems of his day. Herbert's stance in this regard may have cost him a courtly career like that of his elder brother Edward, Lord Herbert of Cherbury, or an ecclesiastical position like those of his friends Lancelot Andrewes or John Donne. The parish church in Bemerton was, after all, far from the centers of religious or political life in Stuart England. On the other hand, Herbert thus gained for himself an authority in speech that only personal integrity can provide.

Third, Ferrar notes that Herbert "next God, . . . loved that which God himself hath magnified above all things, that is, his Word." In dis-

---

6. I am indebted chiefly to Amy Charles's biography for guiding me through the details of Herbert's life.

7. *Life*, p. 314.

cussing Herbert's prose and verse, we will note his devotion to the Bible and his sense of the value of the proclaimed Word. We will find that Herbert borrowed from the Bible not only subject matter but also style, form, genre, and language. Always subordinating his own efforts with words to the claims of biblical language, Herbert sought to engage God's Word in dialogue, to dramatize his own encounter with the Word made flesh, so as to point his audience beyond his own words to the source of whatever power and authority they might have. As Ferrar notes, Herbert "hath been heard to make solemn protestation, that he would not part with one leaf thereof for the whole world."

Ferrar's fourth point is that Herbert's "obedience and conformity to the Church and the discipline thereof was singularly remarkable." In seeking to understand the aims of Herbert's verse, we will need to grasp Herbert's sense of the importance of the Church, not as a mystical company known only to God, but as the outward and visible company of believers. Although Herbert was aware of and interested in developing the inner life, he held to the ancient Christian view that personal and private devotion was subordinate to the corporate worship life of God's people gathered together in prayer and thanksgiving, to hear God's Word read and preached and to celebrate his bounteous goodness through sacramental action. As Ferrar notes, "Though he abounded in private devotions, yet went he every morning and evening with his family to the Church; and by his example, exhortations, and encouragements drew the greater part of his parishioners to accompany him daily in the public celebration of Divine Service." In discussing Herbert's image of the priestly life, we will note his devotion to the daily round of prayer and Bible reading provided for in the Offices of daily Morning and Evening Prayer in the Book of Common Prayer, as well as his stress on the importance of regular attendance at the sacraments of Baptism and Holy Communion. In examining his poems, we will discover that he constantly locates his exploration of the spiritual life in the context of the Church's ongoing round of corporate worship. By direct reference, by allusion, by verbal echo, we are never allowed to forget that whatever meaning his poems have, they take it from their relationship to the Prayer-Book worship of the English Church.

Ferrar's final point about Herbert in his Preface concerns the humility of his subject. Ferrar notes that Herbert once tried to give up "an Ecclesiastical dignity," since identified as the Prebendary of

INTRODUCTION

Leighton Bromswold in Huntingdonshire, only a few miles from Little Gidding. The church building at that place had been in disrepair for some years, rendering it unfit for public worship.[8] Ferrar states that "God permitted not the accomplishment of this desire [to give up the post], having ordained him his instrument for reedifying of the Church." Herbert did set in motion a project to repair the building; on being reminded of it on his deathbed, Herbert said, according to Ferrar, "It is a good work, if it be sprinkled with the blood of Christ." For Herbert, Ferrar notes, "otherwise than in this respect he could find nothing to glory or comfort himself with, neither in this, nor in any other thing." What seems clear is that Herbert, who turned from any chance for either secular or ecclesiastical advancement, wished to accept no credit for any achievement in this life; instead, in all things, he affirmed that the glory was God's and not his. Ferrar's sketch of Herbert concludes on the same note by reminding us of Herbert's motto, "with which he used to conclude all things that might seem to tend any way to his own honor; *Less than the least of God's mercies.*"

Ferrar's stress on Herbert's humility suggests that for the leader of the community at Little Gidding, Herbert was an exemplary figure in every respect because of the way in which he understood the relative importance of things. Placing God's Word and service to his people gathered in public worship before all other considerations, Herbert could stand apart from interest in worldly advancement as well as from involvement in the religious and social controversies of his day. What Ferrar is getting at, as we will come to see, is that for his contemporaries, and perhaps for us as well, Herbert's value as an exemplary Christian and Christian priest is in terms of his devotion to the proclamation of God's word and the ongoing work of God's people in the world, the task of building up what he saw as Christ's earthly body, which is the Church. In the midst of an age fraught with religious controversy, Herbert represented for his contemporaries a clear point of reference, a voice honest about the complexities of the Christian life yet affirming its central tasks. As such, Herbert would serve as a reminder of the essentials of Christian living, as well as an example of one who would not be swayed from his devotion to them. In his humble devotion to the proclamation of God's Word in the context of

---

8. On Herbert's efforts to repair this church, see Charles, pp. 121–31, 150–52, 174–75.

5

Prayer-Book worship and to the calling of mankind to respond to that Word through the Prayer Book's language of prayer and praise, Herbert expresses the essential spirit of seventeenth-century Anglicanism.

THE LIFE

The George Herbert who stands before us in *The Temple* and in *The Country Parson* is a man of the Church, the public and visible sign of God's presence in the world. Although his poems frequently explore the spiritual life of the inner man, they always put that dimension of religious experience into the context of man's corporate worship of God. As Herbert says in "Perirrhanterium," the first poem in *The Temple*, "Though private prayer be a brave design, / Yet public hath more promises, more love."[9] The very title of his book of poems, *The Temple*, evokes the image of the Church as the proper context of man's religious life. His poems presuppose as their setting and context the ongoing public worship of God, conducted according to the Anglican use, as prescribed in the Book of Common Prayer. This round of services, including daily Morning and Evening Prayer and regular celebration of Holy Communion, the major feasts and fasts, including Christmas, Easter, Whitsunday, Trinity Sunday, and Lent, the reading of Scripture, reciting of Psalms, and preaching of sermons—all the public acts of worship in the Church provide occasions for Herbert's verse. Even the physical features of the Church building—the floor, the altar, the windows, the monuments—appear in his poems.

Herbert's prose treatise, *A Priest to the Temple, or, The Country Parson*, again makes clear Herbert's primary emphasis on the active life of the visible Church. Here, the chief functions of the priest are defined in terms of his service to the people of God; he is, Herbert says, "the Deputy of Christ for the reducing of Man to the Obedience of God."[10] All the actions of the priest, whether by himself or with his congregation, are aimed at providing for others a model of the Christian life and moving them to emulate it. To this end, the priest misses no opportunity to preach, to catechize, to instruct informally, using "all possible art" to achieve his ends. Public conduct of worship is so much the center of all that the priest does, according to Herbert, that his discussion

---

9. See below, p. 135.
10. See below, p. 55.

of "The Parson Praying" is devoted entirely to reflection on conducting the services of the Prayer Book: Private prayer is not mentioned at this point in his argument.

According to Walton, Herbert's own conduct of his duties as rector of Bemerton reflects the same devotion to the ongoing life of the visible Church:

> *Mr. Herbert*'s own practice . . . was, to appear constantly with his Wife, and three Nieces (the daughters of a deceased Sister) and his whole Family, twice every day at the Church-prayers, in the Chapel which does almost join to his Parsonage-house. And for the time of his appearing, it was strictly at the Canonical hours of 10 and 4; and then and there, he lifted up pure and charitable hands to God in the midst of the Congregation. And he would joy to have spent that time in that place, where the honor of his *Master Jesus* dwelleth.[11]

While Walton is probably idealizing his portrait of Herbert here (as he does elsewhere), what comes through this description is the same element we noted in Ferrar's account—the high value Herbert placed on the public and corporate prayer-life of his Church.

In conducting the reading of the daily Offices with such rigor, Herbert was simply living out the vows he took on being ordained deacon in 1624 and continuing a practice he actually had begun participating in much earlier at home and at school. Yet the very fact that he did so publicly and encouraged his parishioners to do the same suggests that Herbert saw this basic devotional practice in its corporate and public aspects as the center of all Christian spirituality. Walton says that the effect Herbert's efforts had on his parishioners was remarkable: Herbert's example "brought most of his Parishioners, and many Gentlemen in the Neighborhood, constantly to make a part of his Congregation twice a day." Even those in the fields unable to attend Herbert's daily recitation of the Offices "would let their Plow rest when Mr. *Herbert's Saints' Bell* rung to Prayers, and they might also offer their devotions to God with him."

Herbert's emphasis on the place of the visible Church in the religious life of individual Christians may seem unexceptional; it is not, however, when viewed against the background either of general reli-

---

11. *Life*, p. 302.

gious tendencies in Herbert's time or of specific developments within the Church of England. C. J. Stranks has noted that "[t]he growth of individual religion, which was so marked a feature of the later Middle Ages, was greatly stimulated by the Reformation with its increased emphasis on the responsibility of each soul before God."[12] This tendency, with its implicit denial of the importance of visible, public religious institutions, was beginning to make itself felt in Herbert's day in a variety of ways. The Puritan wing of the Anglican Church, that body of English Christians most heavily influenced by the continental Reformation, would eventually collapse as a united movement because of its leaders' inability to reconcile the claims of individual relationships with God with the demands for uniformity of practice necessary for the maintenance of a state church. During the reign of Elizabeth, Puritans rallied around the Geneva model of presbyterian church organization; later, under Charles I, they would unite in resistance to Archbishop Laud's attempts to achieve uniformity of practice throughout England. Once in power, however, they would be unable to establish a viable nonepiscopal form of Church polity, and could only acquiesce to the reestablishment of Anglicanism in 1660.

Puritan Calvinists, stressing the importance of divine election as the true test of Church membership, encouraged individuals to evaluate their lives for signs of divine favor. The fragmenting results of such an emphasis are visible throughout England in the seventeenth century. For instance, John Cotton, the Puritan rector of Saint Botolph's Church in Boston, England, for twenty years before he emigrated to America to become the minister at the First Church of Boston, Massachusetts, overtly rejected the claims of the visible congregation to be the true Church; instead, he stressed the authenticity of the invisible company of the elect and formed a separate "church" within his parish, made up of those who could meet his standards for inclusion.[13]

But the fragmenting of the faithful was not limited to such varieties of orthodoxy in the seventeenth century. Herbert's own eldest brother, Edward, Lord Herbert of Cherbury, devised his own theology, one that anticipates in many ways the Deist movement of the

---

12. C. J. Stranks, *Anglican Devotion: Studies in the Spiritual Life of the Church of England between the Reformation and the Oxford Movement* (London: SCM Press, 1961), p. 13.

13. For Cotton's image of the visible church as a garden filled with both flowers and thorns, see his *A Brief Exposition of the Whole Book of Canticles* (London: 1648), p. 62.

eighteenth century.[14] John Milton summed up for many the overall tendency of the period when he made the goal of his *Paradise Lost* the search for a "paradise within."[15] John Bunyan, his later contemporary, in writing what was to become after the Bible the single most popular Christian document, would juxtapose the solitary way of his *Pilgrim's Progress* toward heaven over against the "vanity fair" of human society.

The mainstream of Anglicanism, however, had always been in opposition to this tendency. The English Reformation under Henry VIII and especially under Edward VI was sponsored by men who saw their age as one of great opportunity for the recreation of community, for the establishment of a true Christian commonwealth.[16] Their stress was on public worship, organized through use of the Book of Common Prayer, on mass education of the people through reading of the Bible in the vernacular and preaching of set homilies that define the Christian life as one of active charity toward one's neighbor and service to one's God through devotion to English society and its king. The thrust of the English Reformation was not toward the Church, as an end in itself, but on the reformation of society through the agency of the Church. John Booty, in his eloquent description of the Elizabethan Prayer Book, strikes just the right note: "In the parish churches and in the cathedrals the nation was at prayer, the commonwealth was being realized, and God, in whose hands the destinies of all were lodged, was worshipped in spirit and in truth."[17]

In the reign of Elizabeth, the essential documents of the Edwardian reformation were picked up, revised, augmented, and again put to use. The thrust of Anglicanism was still outward, toward society, seeking to encompass the total life of the nation in its political and social as well as its religious dimension. The life of the Church was again subsumed within the national life; Anglicans could still look to religious leadership from lay persons such as Queen Elizabeth, while the Earl of

---

14. See *The Life of Edward Lord Herbert of Cherbury Written by Himself*, ed. Horace Walpole (London: Printed for J. Dodsley, 1770).

15. See *Paradise Lost*, Bk. XII, 1, 587. For a study of the literary history of this motif, see Louis L. Martz, *The Paradise Within: Studies in Vaughan, Traherne, and Milton* (New Haven: Yale University Press, 1964).

16. See my article, "The Book of Homilies of 1547 and the Continuity of English Humanism in the Sixteenth Century," *Anglican Theological Review* 58 (1976): 75–87.

17. In *The Book of Common Prayer, 1559: The Elizabethan Prayer Book* (Charlottesville: University Press of Virginia, 1976), p. vi.

Leicester and Sir Philip Sidney could aspire to the creation of a united Protestant Europe.[18] Richard Hooker could respond to the Puritan challenge not with a pointed attack, but with that magisterial and all-encompassing treatise *Of the Laws of Ecclesiastical Polity.*

The quintessential Anglican poet of the Elizabethan age is Edmund Spenser, whose first volume of *The Faerie Queene* appeared in 1590, just three years before Herbert's birth. Overt in its didacticism, aimed at the same sort of moral reformation of English society aspired to by the Edwardian reformation, Spenser's epic romance begins in its first book with an exposition of the devout life. The hero of that book is the Red-Cross Knight, who is called on to defeat the world, the flesh, and the devil; to do so, he must be instructed in moral virtue. Yet the point of Spenser's poem is that Red-Cross is no special paragon of holiness. Instead, he is an Elizabethan Everyman whose path to victory is open to all who would follow it. Spenser's focus is on the role of Elizabethan England in the Christian history of salvation; the individual Englishman who would take his place in that history and obtain citizenship in the New Jerusalem must first locate himself in the building up of Gloriana's Court, that earthly city Spenser refers to as Cleopolis. This affirmation of a societal context for the Christian life lies at the heart of Elizabethan religion.

In response to the renewed vigor of the Puritan challenge, the Stuart Church began to turn inward, to clarify its institutional structure and refine its theological position. Throughout the reigns of James I and Charles I, the Church of England exhibited a hardening of party lines, a choosing up of sides before the great conflict that was to tear the Church and the nation apart in the middle of the seventeenth century. With no room left on either side for generosity, the tone of debate became more rancorous; its subject, the very nature of the Church itself.[19] One of the catalysts for revolution would be Archbishop Laud's attempt to enforce doctrinal and liturgical uniformity. A poem of *The Faerie Queene*'s inclusiveness is unthinkable in the seventeenth century; more typical is John Donne's Holy Sonnet "Show me dear Christ, thy

---

18. For a discussion of Sidney's role in plans for the unification of Protestant Europe see James Osborne, *Young Philip Sidney, 1572–74* (New Haven: Yale University Press, 1972).

19. For an account of the Anglican stress on moral behavior in the seventeenth century, see J. Sears McGee, *The Godly Man in Stuart England: Anglicans, Puritans, and the Two Tables, 1620–1670* (New Haven: Yale University Press, 1976).

spouse, so bright and clear,"[20] in which the speaker's concern is with identifying which of several options is the true "mild Dove" of God.

Herbert did not live to see the Civil War; had he done so, he would have observed Anglican poetry merging with the broader emphasis on individual salvation. The Commonwealth, for a time, disbanded the Anglican Church, ironically forcing its adherents closer to the Puritan experience of the Christian life. Later in the seventeenth century Anglican poets like Thomas Traherne and Henry Vaughan, Herbert's chief poetic imitator, would also stress the interior search for a "paradise within," and document the religious life of the individual Christian, apart from the visible and earthly community of believers. Vaughan, too, wrote a poem on the British Church; it notes

> The Soldiers here
> Cast in their lots again,
> That seamless coat
> The Jews touch'd not,
> These dare divide, and stain.[21]

Herbert's stress on the Church as the primary arena for exploring the Christian life, therefore, must be seen in part as a reflection of developments in English church and society early in the seventeenth century. Herbert's stress on the role of the visible Church represents to some extent a shift within Anglicanism away from a focus on society as the arena for Christian living and toward a greater emphasis on the value of corporate religious life for its own sake. We must remember that in the early seventeenth century, the Church of England was the only religious option. Coterminous with English society, the Anglican Church not only ministered to the spiritual needs of the entire nation but also defined, through universal baptism, the meaning of citizenship in the body politic. What Herbert reflects in his stress on the Church is not a shift in audience, but a change in the terms in which that audience is defined. Yet to account for the fact that Herbert chose, finally, to make that emphasis so central not only to his writings but also to the

---

20. From *Divine Poems*, ed. Helen Gardner (Oxford: Oxford University Press, 1952), p. 15.

21. See *Works*, ed. L. C. Martin, 2nd ed. (Oxford: Oxford University Press, 1957), p. 410.

conduct of his life requires a more detailed investigation of Herbert's life and his involvement in the social and political events of his day.

We can assume that Herbert inherited from the age of Elizabeth that era's emphasis on the social context of the Christian life; he might easily have done so, not only through his involvement in the religious and educational institutions shaped during her reign but also through his close contact with the Sidney family.[22] We can also assume that Herbert, in choosing to emphasize the role of the Church, was adhering to the heart of the English Reformation's stress on the Church as the vehicle for social reform. What we need to explore is Herbert's involvement in the Parliament of 1624, which seems to have marked a turning point in Herbert's life. Before Herbert took his seat in that Parliament, he had delayed his ordination to the diaconate; after that Parliament, he hastened to ordination through special dispensation of the Archbishop of Canterbury. What will become clear is that Herbert became so disillusioned during the Parliament of 1624 with the possibilities for pursuing the Christian life through lay involvement in government that he sought ordination because active participation in the life of the Church seemed to him the only way still open for furthering the moral reformation of English society.[23]

Before exploring the events surrounding the Parliament of 1624, however, it is necessary to recount briefly the main events of Herbert's life.[24] Born the seventh of ten children, and the fifth of seven sons, to Richard and Magdalene Herbert, George Herbert first entered this life on April 3, 1593, at Black Hall, the Herbert family home in Montgomeryshire, on the border between England and Wales. Herbert's father, the eldest son of Sir Edward Herbert, had, like *his* father, served the Tudor crown for many years in the ongoing English efforts to subdue the Welsh and make that country a part of the larger English nation. Herbert's life has a certain symmetry; the early years spent in rural western England balance the final years spent in rural southern En-

---

22. See Joseph H. Summers, *George Herbert: His Religion and Art* (Cambridge: Harvard University Press, 1968), p. 31, for a discussion of Herbert's family ties to the Sidneys.

23. In taking this position, I am following arguments put forth by Summers and by Marchette Chute (*Two Gentle Men: The Lives of George Herbert and Robert Herrick* [London: Secker & Warburg, 1960]) and expanding their implications.

24. For the details of Herbert's life, I am especially grateful to the work of Amy M. Charles, who in her *A Life of George Herbert* has recorded a herculean labor in unscrambling and ordering what we know of Herbert.

INTRODUCTION

gland. But Richard Herbert's death in 1596, while Magdalene was still carrying their last child, meant that the middle years of Herbert's life would be spent much closer to the center of English national life. Shortly after her husband's death, Magdalene moved her family to Oxford, where Edward, her eldest son, later to be Lord Herbert of Cherbury, was attending the university.

In 1601, she moved again, this time to London. George Herbert was eight years old when his mother established her household at Charing Cross;[25] three years later, he became a day student at Westminster School, just at the end of Lancelot Andrewes' tenure as dean of the Abbey. The next year, in 1605, he was elected a scholar at Westminster School, where he became one of that ancient institution's most illustrious students. From there, he proceeded to Trinity College, Cambridge, as King's scholar, again distinguishing himself academically. He received his Bachelor of Arts in 1613, and his Master of Arts in 1616, in each instance ranking near the top of his class. After completing this basic training, Herbert continued at Cambridge in a program of study leading to the degree of Bachelor of Divinity. At the same time, he was chosen a Major Fellow of Trinity, a post that carried with it tutorial responsibilities. In 1618, he was chosen to deliver university-wide lectures in rhetoric; in 1620, he was elected Public Orator for the University, a post essentially of public relations, of addressing noble visitors and writing letters to present and potential benefactors of the university.

In the normal course of things, Herbert would have been ordained by 1623; instead he delayed ordination to the diaconate until late in 1624. In the interim, he served in Parliament as a representative from Montgomeryshire, a point to which we shall return. Even after ordination, however, Herbert did not immediately take up a clerical position. Herbert was ordained deacon by John Williams, Bishop of Lincoln, who presented him a portion of the living at Llandinam, Montgomeryshire, on December 6, 1624, but it was not until July 5, 1626, that he was installed as a canon of Lincoln Cathedral and given the living of Leighton Bromswold. Nor did he proceed with ordination to the priesthood until some months after he was presented with the living of Fugglestone with Bemerton in April of 1630. In the interim, Herbert

---

25. In the various biographies of Herbert, from Walton to Charles, the figure of Lady Magdalene Herbert always threatens to overwhelm that of her son; I have tried to avoid that imbalance. For more about this grand Stuart lady, see Charles, pp. 36–65.

seems to have been traveling for his health and staying with family and friends in various country retreats.

Herbert's mother had remarried in 1609; her new husband was Sir John Danvers, a man some years her junior. Her death in June of 1627 and the breakup of the family home on Danvers' remarriage in 1628 seem to have precipitated Herbert's entry into active ministry. After living with the Earl of Danby in Dauntesey, Wiltshire, from 1628–1629, Herbert married Jane Danvers, a local girl of noble family and the cousin of Sir John Danvers, on March 5, 1629. On April 26, 1630, Herbert was finally installed as the rector of Bemerton and shortly thereafter his family took up residence in Bemerton rectory. His ordination to the priesthood took place at Salisbury Cathedral on September 19, 1630. His process to the priesthood, and to ecclesiastical employment, begun so many years previously, had finally reached its conclusion.

Herbert lived at Bemerton and served as rector of Saint Andrew's Church for less than three years; he died there on March 1, 1633. Yet the popular image of Herbert stresses this period of his life, and ties to it both his *Temple* poems and his prose discussion of the priestly role in *The Country Parson*. Such an image is valid to the extent that Herbert probably put both works into the form in which we now have them during his tenure at Bemerton. Neither was published during his lifetime; in fact, Walton's *Life* contains a touching description of Herbert's sending Nicholas Ferrar a "little Book" from his deathbed that contained "*a picture of the many spiritual Conflicts that have passed betwixt God and my Soul, before I could subject mine to the will of* Jesus my Master."[26] According to Walton, Herbert instructed Ferrar to publish the book, "*if he can think it may turn to the advantage of any dejected poor Soul.*" Walton says this "little Book" was *The Temple,* although his claim has been disputed.[27] Whether or not Walton is right on this point, we are on solid ground in believing that Herbert spent at least some of his time at Bemerton revising his two accounts of life in the Church.

But only *revising,* for there is strong evidence that Herbert arrived at his view of the Church as the appropriate context for living out the Christian life substantially before the end of his life. Herbert himself

---

26. Walton, *Life,* p. 314.
27. For a discussion of this episode, see J. Max Patrick, "Critical Problems in Editing George Herbert's *The Temple,*" in *The Editor as Critic and the Critic as Editor,* ed. Murray Krieger (Los Angeles: Clark Library, 1973), pp. 4–12.

tells us in his brief preface to *The Country Parson*, dated 1632, that in this volume he has "resolved to set down the Form and Character of a true Pastor, that I may have a Mark to aim at."[28] What he gives us of the true pastor's activities is thus more of an ideal portrait than an actual description of his practice at Bemerton. The tone of Herbert's introduction suggests the work was composed in *anticipation* of taking up the duties outlined in the work, and not written while those duties were actually being carried out.

In addition, in the case of *The Temple*, we have quite specific evidence that Herbert was at work on the individual poems in his collection some years before he became rector of Bemerton. We know, for example, that his interest in specifically religious poetry was of long standing. In 1610, Herbert sent two sonnets to his mother, the first of which contains these lines:

> My God, where is that ancient heat toward thee,
> Wherewith whole shoals of *Martyrs* once did burn,
> Besides their other flames? Doth Poetry
> Wear *Venus'* livery? only serve her turn?
> Why are not Sonnets made of thee? and lays
> Upon thine Altar burnt? Cannot thy love
> Heighten a spirit to sound out thy praise
> As well as any she? Cannot thy *Dove*
> Outstrip their *Cupid* easily in flight?
> Or, since thy ways are deep, and still the same,
> Will not a verse run smooth that bears thy name?[29]

Herbert is reacting here to the vogue for secular love sonnets at the turn of the century; having made this appeal for specifically religious poetry in 1610, however, waiting twenty years to respond to it on his own seems overlong. Nor would we expect even a man of Herbert's poetic gifts to write such mature poetry at Bemerton without a long period of apprenticeship. This, in addition to the fact that if Herbert had waited to write all the poems found in *The Temple* until he reached Bemerton, he would hardly have had time to be the attentive country parson he proposed for himself in *The Country Parson* and as Walton describes him in the *Life*.[30]

---

28. See below, p. 54.
29. See below, p. 332.
30. See Charles, p. 81, for a fuller discussion of this point.

In addition, the recent rediscovery of a manuscript of Herbert's two poems to Elizabeth Stuart, daughter of James I and Queen of Bohemia, helps us to date Herbert's early work on the last section in *The Temple*, "The Church Militant." Scholars have long noted the verbal similarities between these poems;[31] Ted-Larry Pebworth's dating of the poems to Elizabeth from the years 1621–1622 would seem to apply to "The Church Militant" as well.[32]

If, therefore, Herbert was at work on individual poems that would eventually take their place in *The Temple* by 1622 (and some critics argue a date as early as 1613–1615 for "The Church Porch"),[33] when did the specifically church-related structure of *The Temple* come to mind? What follows can only be conjecture, but it is based on evidence as solid as circumstantial evidence can be. There exists a manuscript of *The Temple* that clearly represents a version earlier than the one we have in the printed version of 1633.[34] This manuscript, referred to as *W* by scholars because it finally wound up in Dr. Williams's Library in London, contains seventy-nine poems, including the two poems in "The Church Porch" section of the 1633 text (although in *W* the title "Perirrhanterium" is given to the first stanza of the poem entitled "Superliminary" in 1633) and the long poem called "The Church Militant," which bracket the grouping of shorter poems in the *Church* section. Although the number of poems in *W* is significantly fewer than the 1633 text (79 poems vs. 173), the principle of organization is the same. Six of the poems in the *W* manuscript do not appear in the final version of Herbert's collection; other poems exhibit signs of heavy revision.

While we cannot date this manuscript version of *The Temple*, it suggests two important considerations for understanding Herbert's process of arriving at the shape of his poem collection. First, we may surmise that Herbert worked on *The Temple* collection over a number of years, adding some poems to it, revising others, and deleting still others, until the whole collection reached the state of completion reflected in the 1633 version. Second, we may conclude that long before

31. See K. A. Hovey, "George Herbert's Authorship of 'To the Queene of Bohemia,'" *Renaissance Quarterly* 30 (1977): 47.

32. In "George Herbert's Poems to the Queen of Bohemia: A Rediscovered Text and a New Edition," *English Literary Renaissance* 9 (1979): 108–20.

33. For a summary of this argument, see Charles, pp. 82–84.

34. This manuscript of *The Temple* is now generally available in the facsimile edition of Amy M. Charles, published by Scholars' Facsimiles & Reprints, Delmar, New York, 1977.

INTRODUCTION

Herbert had written the great bulk of the shorter poems on which much of *The Temple*'s reputation rests, he had already conceived the overall shape of the entire collection. As in the early manuscript, so in the final version, the collection begins with an introductory section entitled "The Church Porch" and ends with a long poem entitled "The Church Militant." Arranged between these two is a lengthy series of much shorter poems in a section entitled "The Church." Whenever Herbert began to write religious verse in response to his own call for poems to be "upon thine altar burnt," he eventually developed a scheme for organizing a large body of his religious verse; the *W* manuscript represents an intermediate version of that scheme, while the text of the 1633 edition represents Herbert's final realization.

A further point can now be made. The poems found in the *W* manuscript make up the bulk of those poems in the 1633 text that treat events in the life of the Church. Among them are poems for Good Friday and Easter, for Whitsunday and Trinity Sunday, for Matins and Holy Communion, for Christmas and Lent. Let us remember that the three sections of *The Temple*, at least from the time of the *W* manuscript, call our attention immediately to the Church. "The Church Porch" section serves as an entryway into the "Church" section proper; the concluding "Church Militant" section gives a longer view of that institution by summarizing the history of its experience in the world. This, coupled with the fact that so many of the poems in the "Church" section that take as their occasion specific events in the life of the Church—days or seasons of special observance, services for use on those occasions—are already present in the *W* manuscript of *The Temple*, strongly suggests that Herbert conceived of the organizational emphasis of his poetry collection after some of his poems were written but before he had composed most of them. Having once formulated the concept of a collection of religious verse that would explore the realities of the Christian life specifically within the context of the Church, the earthly, visible community of God's people, Herbert then brought into this frame poems written earlier; he continued to revise earlier poems and to add new ones to the collection until it reached the state of completion represented by the edition of 1633.

Yet the question remains as to when Herbert conceived of structuring his poems according to an extended reference to the life of the Church. The evidence points to sometime after 1621–1622, when, as we have already seen, Herbert probably wrote "The Church Militant." In addition, many scholars have had difficulties understanding how "The Church Militant" fits into the overall scheme of *The Temple* collection.[35]

The image of *The Temple* provided by Walton's account that Herbert called it as "a picture of the many spiritual conflicts that have passed betwixt God and my Soul" fits very nicely with the poems in the "Church" section, but not with the long historical narrative Herbert gives us in "The Church Militant." In addition, in the *W* manuscript, five blank pages intervene between the text of the last poem in the "Church" section and the text of "The Church Militant." Although Herbert did finally integrate "The Church Militant" into the overall frame of *The Temple*, the evidence suggests Herbert composed "The Church Militant" before he devised the scheme that would ultimately unify the whole sequence of poems. The blank pages in the *W* manuscript suggest signs of a work in progress, of problems with integration of different parts into a whole, of space left in a working manuscript to provide room for modification. Occuring just before "The Church Militant," these blank pages indicate just where Herbert was having problems bringing material written earlier into a larger overall scheme.

Having brought this admittedly speculative line of reasoning to the point of concluding that Herbert conceived of the emphasis on the Church context of his poems sometime after 1621–1622, we must now survey in more detail certain incidents in Herbert's life after that date to suggest when and why he arrived at the vision of Christian life centered in the ongoing life of the Church as the unifying scheme of his *Temple* collection and the focus of *The Country Parson*. Central to my argument is the belief that Herbert underwent a period of struggle with his religious vocation in the period 1616–1624. As a result, instead of proceeding as he had promised in 1616 to ordination before 1623, Herbert stood for election to Parliament from Montgomeryshire and served in the Parliament that met in the winter and spring months of 1624. Yet something happened at that Parliament; after it, Herbert, who had delayed ordination when he had years to arrange it, hastened into orders before the end of 1624 by means of a special dispensation from the Archbishop of Canterbury. Herbert's final acceptance of holy

---

35. For a summary of these arguments, see Stanley E. Fish, *The Living Temple: George Herbert and Catechizing* (Berkeley: University of California Press, 1978), pp. 137–54.

orders thus seems a decision to reject secular office and to embrace the Church as an alternative course of action. From these events emerges the decisive and shaping emphasis in Herbert's writing. In this light, the events at the Parliament of 1624 become crucial in importance.

Entering the Church was an appropriate choice of career for a younger son of a noble family in the seventeenth century, as it had been for many centuries. Herbert initially pursued such a career with enthusiasm. After receiving his Master of Arts from Trinity College in 1616, Herbert set out on the course of study that would eventually lead to the degree of Bachelor of Divinity and a career in the Church. He plunged into his studies with a clear sense of direction; a letter to Sir John Danvers, his stepfather, dated March 18, 1618, requests additional funds to purchase needed books. "I want Books extremely," he writes, "You know, Sir, how I am now setting foot into Divinity, to lay the platform of my future life, and shall I then be fain always to borrow Books, and build on another's foundation?"[36] Another letter of that year, to his brother Henry in Paris, suggests urgency: "The disease which I am troubled with now is the shortness of time."[37]

Yet by 1619, Herbert was pursuing the post of Public Orator for the University, a position that had led others to major positions in government. Sir Francis Nethersole, Herbert's predecessor in that post, questioned Herbert's interest in the office because it could serve as a diversion from the path of divinity. Herbert justified his quest in a letter, again to his stepfather:

> I understand by Sir *Francis Nethersole*'s letter, that he fears I have not fully resolved of the matter, since this place (the post of Public Orator) being civil may divert me too much from Divinity, at which, not without cause, he thinks, I aim; but, I have wrote him back, that this dignity, hath no such earthiness in it, but it may very well be joined with Heaven.[38]

In spite of Herbert's reassurances, however, he did not proceed to ordination in 1623; instead, he was in London in 1624, serving in Parliament.

I believe Marchette Chute and Joseph Summers, two of Herbert's

---

36. Reprinted in *Works*, ed. F. E. Hutchinson (Oxford: Oxford University Press, 1941), pp. 364–65.
37. Ibid., pp. 365–66.
38. Ibid., pp. 370–71.

recent biographers, are right in seeing Herbert's decision to serve in Parliament not as a sharp break with his earlier desire to serve God, but as merely a shift in the arena of service.[39] Such a view accords with concepts of the Christian life Herbert would have inherited from the Age of Elizabeth; as we noted earlier, the official documents of the Tudor Reformation proclaimed all of English society as the proper context for living out the Christian life, and service to the crown as the chief means of doing God's will in this world. Herbert grew up on these documents, for his mother led her household in morning and evening devotions and set an example by attending the daily Offices of Morning and Evening Prayer after she moved her family to Charing Cross. While at Westminster School, Herbert was caught up in the great round of Anglican services in the Abbey, as well as special devotions provided for the students. At Trinity, he again participated in the daily round of Morning Prayer, Holy Communion, and Evening Prayer, with additional private prayers and public readings from the Scriptures. While it is true that the idealism of the Edwardian period of the English Reformation waned somewhat during the long reign of Elizabeth, all the documents were still in place and in use. It is not at all hard to imagine Herbert's being captured and fired by the image of Church reforming society that those documents reinterate over and over again.

In addition, Herbert had at least one direct personal link with the great age of civic religion in Elizabeth's day; the close connections between the Herbert family and the Sidneys would have meant that Herbert would have been very familiar with the legacy of Sir Philip Sidney's heroic image as the true Christian knight, serving God through serving his Queen.[40] Sidney had enunciated in his *Defense of Poetry* that doctrine of poetry which Herbert later paraphrased in the opening lines of his "Church Porch." Herbert had said that "a verse may find him, who a sermon flies"; Sidney had written that poets "do merely make to imitate, and imitate both to delight and teach: and delight to move men to take that goodness in hand, which without delight they would fly as from a stranger."[41]

---

39. See Chute, pp. 68–84, and Summers, pp. 39–43.
40. For an account of Sidney's involvement in the efforts at creating a united Protestant Europe, see James M. Osborn, *Young Philip Sydney*, 1572–77 (New Haven: Yale University Press, 1972).
41. Sidney, *Defense of Poetry*, in *Miscellaneous Prose*, ed. K. Duncan-Jones and J. Van Dorsten (Oxford: Clarendon, 1973), p. 81.

INTRODUCTION

Although he would have rejected Sidney's militarism, Herbert could hardly have questioned the validity of Sidney's approach to Christian service through service to the crown; in addition, 1623 might well have appeared to him an appropriate time to explore it for himself. Herbert had grown up in a noble household, frequented by those close to royalty and the national government. By 1623, two of his brothers, Edward and Henry, had distinguished themselves as ambassadors; three others, Richard, William, and Thomas, had followed nautical or military careers, which had cost Richard and William their lives. With Charles, his sixth brother, dead since 1617, Herbert may well have felt that the way was clearer for a younger son to follow a public career. Herbert had also begun to make friends in high places. His service as Public Orator had brought him the praise of King James and the opportunity to correspond with Sir Francis Bacon and Bishop Lancelot Andrewes. Herbert also was on good terms with two of James's favorite courtiers, the Duke of Lennox and the Marquis of Hamilton.

In addition, a crisis in the relationship between England and Spain that occurred in 1623 may well have given Herbert additional motivation to enter public service. In an attempt to cement his relationship with Spain, James had sent his son Charles to marry a Spanish princess. This romantic mission ended in failure, however, threatening the peace. Chute and Summers have argued that Herbert was drawn toward service in London because he was a man of peace and saw in the King a like-minded monarch. One of the facts that James was proudest of was that he had kept England at peace throughout his reign; in 1619, when Herbert was seeking the post of University Orator, James, with the help of Bishop Andrewes, had written a pamphlet entitled *The Peacemaker*, in which he had argued that England was a blessed haven from the "perpetual deluge of blood and enmity" that engulfed the rest of the world.[42]

Herbert had written, earlier, a Latin poem, *"Triumphus Mortis"* (the triumph of death), sharply attacking man's growing ability to destroy his fellowman.[43] In 1623, having just lost one brother in combat, Herbert may have felt that his king needed a man equally devoted to peace in a position of public trust. It was well known that Prince Charles had returned from Spain and his failure to secure a Spanish

---

42. Quoted in Chute, pp. 75–76.
43. See *Works*, ed. Hutchinson, pp. 418–21.

bride eager to go to war. Herbert's oration on the occasion of the Prince's return may well be an opening response to that desire, for, in the midst of that oration, Herbert again attacks the costs and ravages of armed combat.[44] Herbert's devotion to James is also clear; his praise of James attached to the end of his *Musae Responsoriae*, a treatise defending the use of the Book of Common Prayer against Puritan attack, refers to the English monarch in glowing terms as a great shepherd of his flock who had kept England and her Church on the true middle way.[45]

It is not unlikely, therefore, that George Herbert, as he approached the time of decision about ordination to the diaconate in 1623, might well have felt that service to God could as well be conducted in public service to such a monarch, especially when he needed men to defend the peace, as in public service to that monarch's church. Herbert thus stood for election from Montgomeryshire, and took his seat in Parliament when it met in London in February 1624. Yet the events of that session were enough to disillusion even the most devoted believer in service to God through work toward peace in the secular arena. In the Parliament of 1624, Prince Charles and Buckingham, his close friend and aide, worked tirelessly for war; caught in the middle, James finally capitulated and dissolved the treaty of peace with Spain on March 23, 1624.

The pace of Herbert's life, usually slow and steady, suddenly picked up. Parliament adjourned on the twenty-ninth of May; by the eleventh of June, Herbert had obtained from the Cambridge Senate a six-month leave from his duties as Public Orator. On November 3 of that year, the Archbishop of Canterbury granted a special dispensation allowing John Williams, Bishop of Lincoln, to ordain Herbert deacon. Williams granted Herbert a portion of the living at Llandinam, Montgomeryshire, on December 6, 1624, leading most scholars to date Herbert's ordination to the diaconate as taking place sometime between early November and early December of 1624.[46]

Herbert was not the only member of the Parliament of 1624 to be moved to take orders as a result of that body's legislative actions. Nicholas Ferrar, a friend of Herbert from their days together at Cambridge, saw the charter of his Virginia Company revoked by the crown in

---

44. Ibid., pp. 444–55.
45. Ibid., pp. 401–02.
46. Thus John E. Booty, "George Herbert: *The Temple* and *The Book of Common Prayer*," *Mosaic* 12 (1979): 76–77.

INTRODUCTION

April of 1624, in spite of heroic efforts by Ferrar and over one hundred members of the company who were also members of that Parliament. Here, the lives of the two young men follow such parallel paths that the one illuminates the other. Ferrar was ordained deacon by Bishop Laud in 1626; he moved quickly to establish his Anglican community at Little Gidding.[47]

Herbert was to comment later, in *The Country Parson*, that there was "no School to a Parliament." What I am suggesting is that Herbert's idealistic visions of insuring the peace through service to the crown were dashed by the warmongering of Prince Charles in the Parliament of 1624; this, along with the fate of his friend Nicholas Ferrar's Virginia Company, hastened the departure of both men from the seat of government, never to return. To hold to one's idealism in the face of such realities could for Herbert be achieved only by returning to the source of that idealism, the Church. This course of action, parallel to that taken by Nicholas Ferrar, meant a return not so much to earlier hopes of ecclesiastical employment, but to the life of the Christian community, marked in Stuart England by devotion to the round of prayer and Bible reading embodied in the services of Morning and Evening Prayer. When he was ordained deacon, Herbert promised to repeat these Offices every day, until his death; if we are to believe Walton's portrait of Herbert at Bemerton, this discipline formed the center of his daily life. At Little Gidding, Ferrar's community expressed similar devotion to the round of Offices; there, to ensure that the Psalter was recited all the way through every day, members took turns with this task into the night, only to begin again the next morning.

Herbert, at the same time, became involved in a similar devotional practice, but with a larger and more scattered group. From July 5, 1626, when Herbert was installed, apparently by proxy, as a canon of Lincoln Cathedral, he took on the responsibility of repeating Psalms 31 and 32 privately each day. Joined with the other canons of the Cathedral, who bore similar responsibilities for the other Psalms, Herbert thus also participated in the devotional practice of reading daily through the Psalter. John Williams, the Bishop of Lincoln, provides another link between Herbert and Ferrar. Williams ordained Herbert deacon and made him a canon of Lincoln Cathedral; he also three times

---

47. For a detailed account of Ferrar's response to the Parliament of 1624, see A. L. Maycock, *Nicholas Ferrar of Little Gidding* (London: SPCK, 1938), pp. 97–122.

visited Little Gidding, which was located in his diocese, and served as ecclesiastical protector for Ferrar's community.

We know that Herbert and Ferrar were friends before either took orders; we also know that they kept in close contact by letter after the climactic events of 1624. Amy Charles, Herbert's recent biographer, argues convincingly that Herbert must have visited Little Gidding in 1626.[48] It was to Ferrar that Herbert entrusted the manuscripts of both *The Temple* and *The Country Parson*.[49] The similarity of their responses to the Parliament of 1624 suggests that both men saw in a renewed devotion to the round of services that mark the passage of time in the life of the Church an appropriate response to a government turned hostile to their ideals.

At the same time, Herbert was engaged in the process of rebuilding the damaged fabric of the stone church at Leighton Bromswold, which Bishop Williams had put under his care. Herbert never actually took up residence near this church, but he did undertake a fund-raising campaign to restore it.[50] Herbert's actions here again parallel those of Ferrar, who undertook a similar restoration of the church at Little Gidding.

Herbert's actions at this stage in his life suggest why he would now begin to shape his occasional religious poetry into a larger scheme stressing the life of the Church rather than English society as the proper arena for exploring the nature of the Christian life. Even as he worked to repair the visible church at Leighton Bromswold, so he would build up a collection of poems exploring and encouraging the life to be lived in the Church. I must therefore conclude that the *W* manuscript of *The Temple* dates from late in the period 1625–1630, after Herbert had taken orders and before he assumed the time-consuming responsibilities as rector of Bemerton. In this work, Herbert would not describe the Church as an ideal, but would affirm his choice of that institution in the ordinary conduct of its liturgical and devotional practices as the appropriate context for living out the Christian life.

Yet Herbert was not to settle for a situation like that established by Ferrar at Little Gidding. To be true, finally, to the idealism at the heart of Herbert's Anglicanism meant to do more than simply keep the round of church services either alone or in the company of a few like-

---

48. Charles, pp. 122–27.
49. Thus Patrick, pp. 9–14.
50. Charles, pp. 128–30.

minded friends. The thrust of Herbert's scheme in *The Temple*, as he evolved it in those years, could only lead him to take a more active role in the life of the larger Church. After five years as a deacon, Herbert finally sought a larger community with which to develop the ideals of communion and community embodied in the worship books he knew so well. In preparation for assuming this new role, he sketched out for himself an image of the country parson, a figure he must have come to know well in his years of retreat after the Parliament of 1624. We have that image, embodied in *The Country Parson*. While the death of his mother in 1627 and the final breakup of his family household with the remarriage of his stepfather in 1628 may have contributed to Herbert's final decision to seek ecclesiastical employment, it was, I suspect, his desire to fulfill his vocation that ultimately led him to Bemerton, a rural parish far from London.

There, Herbert would devote all his energies, all his skills with language, all his persuasive powers, to move his congregation toward that ideal of community which the Church taught was the goal of human life on earth. At least, such is the theme of *The Country Parson*. At the same time, Herbert would use "all possible art," including poetry, to achieve such ends. At Bemerton, I would argue, Herbert gave final form to his collection of poems and created what we know as *The Temple*. The central theme of this work is the Christian life on earth, viewed in the context of the ongoing life of the Church as the source of meaning and definition for the lives of its individual members. As we read these poems, we are confronted with ourselves, judged against high standards of Christian conduct, and found wanting. At the same time, we are told that to be judged is part of the process of entering fully into the life of the Church, which takes its vitality not from its individual members but from the life of its risen Lord, whose earthly body it represents to the world. In Herbert's view, an individual's relationship with God is never an end in itself, but is always grounded in the experience of God received by the corporate community of the faithful.

Herbert's *Temple* thus represents one stage in the development of religious poetry in the English Renaissance. In the reign of Elizabeth, religious poetry was not overtly religious at all; taking all of Tudor society as the arena for living out the Christian life, it defines Christian living primarily in terms of moral and ethical conduct aimed at the reformation of society into an image of the true Christian commonwealth. Herbert might have taken that direction had he not been disillusioned by the events of the Parliament of 1624; in retreat from that world, however, he returned to the Church as the institution through which he could appropriately express his energies and his devotion.

Anglican poets after Herbert, who saw destroyed the very institution Herbert knew as the source of idealism in national life, found the inner life of the individual to be the proper arena for exploring man's relationship with God. For Vaughan and Traherne, the Church exists more as an idea than as a living, visible presence. But for Herbert, the ongoing life of the Christian community, expressed through the disciplines of the Book of Common Prayer, is that context in which men and women must find themselves and their God. What we will explore in the remaining sections of this Introduction are the ways in which Herbert seeks to encounter us, his readers, to confront us and to draw us into the life of that institution. For it is in the life of the Church in its simplest manifestation, the rural parish, that Herbert finally found the avenue for his talents, the proper arena for his idealism, the context for full expression of his own relationship with God.

THE WORKS

To stress Herbert's humility, his devotion to God's Word and to the institution that mediates that Word to the world, is not to argue for his simplicity. Although Herbert has traditionally been viewed as a poet of simple pieties, the voice that actually confronts us in *The Temple* is one of great variety and range, of broad as well as subtle variations in mood and tone, of richness in imagery and complexity of poetic strategy. In fact, one of the major contributions of modern scholarship to our knowledge and appreciation of Herbert has been the recovery of a sense of his poetic genius.[51] What does reflect Herbert's devotion to his calling in *The Temple* is not a simplicity of faith but a unity of purpose. Herbert makes clear in *The Country Parson* that the chief role of the priest is his didactic function. Everything the priest does, according to

---

51. Studies of Herbert that focus on his poetic craftsmanship include Arnold Stein, *George Herbert's Lyrics* (Baltimore: Johns Hopkins Press, 1968); Mary Ellen Rickey, *Utmost Art: Complexity in the Verse of George Herbert* (Lexington: University of Kentucky Press, 1966); Coburn Freer, *Music for a King: George Herbert's Style and the Metrical Psalms* (Baltimore: Johns Hopkins Press, 1972), and Helen Vendler, *The Poetry of George Herbert* (Cambridge: Harvard University Press, 1975).

INTRODUCTION

Herbert, acts out one central task: "A Pastor is the Deputy of Christ for the reducing of Man to the Obedience of God." Teaching, for Herbert, is not a static offering of truths, but a dynamic impinging on the members of his congregation to move them toward behavior in accord with the divine will.

In *The Country Parson*, Herbert sketches the various ways in which the parish priest should act out his calling. All the parson's activities are intended to teach, either directly through preaching, catechizing, and conducting public worship, or through example, in the organization of the parson's household, in his public and private conduct, and in the sense of values he expresses through his choice of wife, the way he spends his money, and the conduct of his conversation. The priesthood, as Herbert presents it, is a teaching office, aimed at moving all members of the congregation toward composing "themselves to order . . . in frame," enclosing all into the earthly body of Christ, the Church.

No less in his poems than in his preaching, Herbert seeks to procure "attention by all possible art," to achieve his didactic ends. The initial aim of all Herbert's poems is toward us, his readers, to impinge on our lives, and to change us, so that we will be different people as a result of reading his works. To read *The Temple* is to find ourselves judged and found wanting, and to be pointed toward him from whom all help comes. Herbert assumes a variety of poses, or roles, to achieve this end. In "The Church Porch," the first section of *The Temple*, his stance is clearly instructive, providing clear choices for the conduct of our lives and mapping out the consequences of each alternative. In the many short poems of "The Church" section, his teaching is more by example, offering us a profusion of models to help us find ourselves and to move beyond where we are to a deeper knowledge of our relationship with God. In "The Church Militant," he takes a longer view, recounting the history of the Church and locating it in the working out of God's history of salvation. Here, his tone is that of exhortation, calling us to faithfulness to the one who is working his purposes out, even in the events of Herbert's own day. Yet, even here is Herbert's humility displayed, for he makes clear over and over that the effectiveness of his own work comes not from him, but from the one whose work in the world he has set out to do.

In reviewing in necessarily brief form the contents of *The Country Parson* and *The Temple*, our purpose will be to note the extent to which Herbert's didactic understanding of the priestly life underlies the contents of each work. In discussing *The Country Parson*, we will stress Herbert's descriptions of how his ideal priest carries out the teaching of his congregation. In describing *The Temple*, we will notice how these various strategies of didacticism are actually acted out in the 175 poems of his collection. We will also note how Herbert, in building a verbal temple, constantly refers us to the actual, visible Church as the place in which he believes we must live out the Christian life he would move us to participate in.

A Priest to the Temple, or, The Country Parson

Herbert's prose treatise on the life of the country parson is, as we have suggested earlier, not so much an actual description of Herbert's pastoral practice as it is an idealized description of that practice, "a mark to aim at" both for Herbert and all those who read it. Organized into thirty-seven sections, the work surveys almost everything a country parson might need advice about. Early sections give overall guidance about the general conduct of life and necessary preparation for the rural parish priesthood. Sections VI through VIII focus on the conduct of public worship and the behavior of the priest on Sundays after public worship is completed. Sections IX through XIII provide guidance for the regulation of the priest's personal life, his household, his behavior toward his parishioners, and the maintenance of his church building. Sections XIV through XXXVII survey the broader context of the parson's ministry—his attentiveness to the needs of his congregation legally, medically, and economically, as well as spiritually.

The life of the country parson is clearly, for Herbert, one that touches the lives of his parishioners at every point and on every day of the week. Nothing they do is outside his concern; nothing he does is free of opportunity for instruction. He is, in fact, called to place himself at the center of their lives, to show them that doing God's will involves ordering the entire conduct of their existence toward him. In this context, Herbert's emphasis on calling all to join him in the Church's daily round of prayer and praise is especially significant.

In examining what Herbert says about how the parson goes about the conduct of his duties, we need to remember that all his writings, both his prose and his poems, are products of a rhetorical age. This is an important fact to hold on to, because it forces us to question readings of Herbert that see his works as static, objectifiable accounts of a man's (presumably Herbert's) spiritual journey.[52] The aim of rhetorical discourse is always to be dynamic, to impinge on the world of the reader, to encounter him where he is, and to move him toward some place the speaker of the discourse would like him to be. Education at the university level in both Tudor and Stuart England heavily emphasized the study of rhetoric. Always an integral part of the *trivium* of logic, rhetoric, and grammar, the basic curriculum of the medieval university, stress on rhetoric was given added emphasis in the sixteenth century, which made of it the chief ingredient in a university education.[53] Everywhere in Tudor culture, the stress on rhetoric is clear, especially in discussions of poetry and poetic method.[54] As we have already noted, Sir Philip Sidney made the Ciceronian paradigm of teaching, delighting, and moving the heart of his definition, and defense, of poetry, an argument echoed and amplified in that other great Tudor work of poetic theory, George Puttenham's *The Art of English Poesy*.[55] If Tudor and Stuart religious poets and preachers had needed any justification for their using classical rhetoric as a model for Christian discourse, they had recourse to the authority of Saint Augustine, another Churchman schooled in classical rhetoric, who gave the aims of preaching as *"docere, delectare, et movere."*[56]

---

52. For readings of Herbert's poems as accounts of a personal spiritual journey see Joseph H. Summers, *George Herbert: His Religion and Art* (Cambridge: Harvard University Press, 1954); Rosemond Tuve, *A Reading of George Herbert* (Chicago: University of Chicago Press, 1952); Louis L. Martz, *The Poetry of Meditation* (New Haven: Yale University Press, 1962); William H. Halewood, *The Poetry of Grace: Reformation Themes in English Seventeenth-Century Poetry* (New Haven: Yale University Press, 1972); Sister Maria Thekla, *George Herbert: Idea and Image* (Buckinghamshire, England: Greek Orthodox Monastery of the Assumption, Filgrave, Newport Pagnell, 1974); and Barbara K. Lewalski, *Protestant Poetics and the Seventeenth-Century Religious Lyric* (Princeton: Princeton University Press, 1979).

53. See Joan Simon, *Education and Society in Tudor England* (Cambridge: Cambridge University Press, 1966); and Lisa Jardine, "The Place of Dialectic Teaching in Sixteenth-Century Cambridge," *Studies in the Renaissance* 21 (1974): 31–62, for a discussion of the changing shape of the university curriculum in response to humanism's renewed interest in rhetoric.

54. For discussions of rhetoric in English renaissance art and culture, see, among other works, W. G. Crane, *Wit and Rhetoric in the Renaissance* (New York: Columbia University Press, 1937); Walter J. Ong, S. J., *Ramus, Method, and the Decay of Dialogue* (Cambridge: Harvard University Press, 1958); Rosemond Tuve, *Elizabethan and Metaphysical Imagery* (Chicago: University of Chicago Press, 1947); Thomas O. Sloan and Raymond B. Waddington, eds., *The Rhetoric of Renaissance Poetry* (Berkeley: University of California Press, 1974), and Joel B. Altman, *The Tudor Play of Mind: Rhetorical Inquiry and the Development of Elizabethan Drama* (Berkeley: University of California Press, 1978).

55. 1589; reprinted Kent, Ohio: Kent State University Press, 1970.

56. In *De Doctrina Christiana*, lib. IV, cap. xvii, in *Patrologiae Latini*, 34 (1861): 103.

29

INTRODUCTION

It is important to remember, in this context, that George Herbert not only received intensive training in rhetoric at Trinity College, Cambridge, but that he did sufficiently well in it to be elected to offer university-wide lectures in the subject. In addition, Herbert obtained his greatest fame during his lifetime as Public Orator. In *The Country Parson*, we find that Herbert sees many of his priestly functions precisely in terms of effective use of language, as that would be understood in rhetorical circles. His description of "The Parson Preaching" is cast in rhetorical terms:

> When he preacheth, he procures attention by all possible art, both by earnestness of speech, it being natural to men to think, that where is much earnestness, there is somewhat worth hearing; and by a diligent, and busy cast of his eye on his auditors, with letting them know, that he observes who marks, and who not; and with particularizing of his speech now to the younger sort, then to the elder, now to the poor, and now to the rich.

Herbert here makes three points; first, attention is achieved through setting a good example. Throughout *The Country Parson*, Herbert labors to make clear that the parson's first teaching device is his own conduct, as a model for his parishioners. The touchstones of the Country Parson's life are "Patience" and "Mortification," precisely because these are "the two highest points of Life, wherein a Christian is most *seen*" (emphasis mine). The Country Parson acts as a positive *exemplum;* he is also careful to avoid that behavior which his parishioners will find most suspect, such as "coveteousness," "Luxury," and breaking his word of trust. In a rhetorical context, the example set by the priest is one of "earnestness," his personal conviction of the importance of his subject, which will move his audience to attentiveness.

Herbert's second point is that the parson must pay close attention to the response of his parishioners, and let them know of his attentiveness. This monitoring of his parishioners is the touchstone of the parson's daily conduct. Herbert asserts that the Country Parson spends weekday afternoons "in Circuit," observing his flock "most naturally as they are," praising their good conduct and reproving their errors. For, "the Country Parson, where ever he is, keeps God's watch; that is, there is nothing spoken, or done in the Company where he is, but comes under his Test and censure." In reproof, however, he also is

30

careful to apply that sort of admonition which will do the most good, depending on the state of the one to be admonished:

> Those that the Parson finds idle, or ill employed, he chides not at first, for that were neither civil, nor profitable; but always in the close, before he departs from them: yet in this he distinguisheth; for if he be a plain countryman, he reproves him plainly; for they are not sensible of fineness; but if they be of higher quality, they commonly are quick, and sensible, and very tender of reproof: and therefore he lays his discourse so, that he comes to the point very leisurely, and oftentimes, as *Nathan* did, in the person of another, making them to reprove themselves.

This approach of letting the kind of reproof fit the station of the one to be disciplined brings us to the third point Herbert makes about the parson's preaching, that he varies his speech to fit the specific requirements of his audience. Herbert does not see, as did John Cotton, his older contemporary, any distinction between any members of his congregation in terms of their ultimate destiny before God; all are called, equally, to the same Church and the same altar. The task of the priest, in Herbert's terms, is to find each parishioner where he is and move him from that place toward fuller involvement in the Christian life.

Herbert thus describes the life of the Country Parson almost totally in didactic and rhetorical terms. For him, "a Pastor is the Deputy of Christ for the reducing of Man to the Obedience of God." All the Parson's activities are bent in this direction, from the smallest detail of the operation of his household to the most significant detail of the conduct of public worship. His role is a teaching office, aimed at moving all members of the congregation toward composing "themselves to order . . . in frame," enclosing all into the earthly body of Christ, the Church. This is where Herbert begins his description of the Country Parson, and how he understands the role. To make this clear, Herbert resorts to a quotation from Saint Paul:

> And therefore Saint *Paul* in the beginning of his Epistles, professeth this: and in the first to the *Colossians* plainly avoucheth, that he *fills up that which is behind of the afflictions of Christ in his flesh, for his Body's sake, which is the Church.* Wherein

is contained the complete definition of a Minister. Out of this Charter of the Priesthood may be plainly gathered both the Dignity thereof, and the Duty: The Dignity, in that a Priest may do that which Christ did, and by his authority, and as his Viceregent. The Duty, in that a Priest is to do that which Christ did, and after his manner, both for Doctrine and Life.

The priest's task in the Church is to minister to the Church, which is both the means and the goal of his activities. As the corporate body of the faithful, it is that group which must be moved; as the earthly Body of Christ, it is that toward which they must be moved. This paradoxical view of the concrete, earthly institution is implicit in Herbert's comments on the administration of Holy Communion:

> The Country Parson . . . at Communion times . . . is in a great confusion, as being not only to receive God, but to break, and administer him. Neither finds he any issue in this, but to throw himself down at the throne of grace, saying, Lord, thou knowest what thou didst, when thou appointest it to be done thus; therefore do thou fulfill what thou didst appoint; for thou art not only the feast, but the way to it.

Herbert makes the essentially didactic role of the Priest clearer still in his description of "The Parson Catechizing."[57] Here, he defines the task of the Priest precisely in terms of moving the congregation:

> The Country Parson values Catechizing highly: for there being three points of his duty, the one, to infuse a competent knowledge of salvation in every one of his Flock; the other, to multiply, and build up this knowledge to a spiritual Temple; the third, to enflame this knowledge, to press, and drive it to practice, turning it to reformation of life, by pithy and lively exhortations; Catechizing is the first point, and but by Catechizing, the other cannot be attained.

Herbert contrasts Catechizing with preaching; the latter is better for "Inflaming," while the former is better for "Informing." In his discus-

---

57. Stanley E. Fish has recently stressed the importance of this section of *The Country Parson* for our understanding of Herbert's poetry. See his *The Living Temple: George Herbert and Catechizing* (Berkeley: University of California Press, 1978).

sion of catechizing, Herbert applies the same principles of adjusting the discourse to the hearer he puts forth in his discussion of sermon technique. Having first used the set form of Catechism authorized by the Church, "partly for obedience to Authority, partly for uniformity sake, that the same common truths may be every where professed," Herbert says that varying the set text with a Socratic method of asking leading questions is an effective way of proceeding.

> This order being used to one, would be a little varied to another. And this is an admirable way of teaching, wherein the Catechized will at length find delight, and by which the Catechizer, if he once get the skill of it, will draw out of ignorant and silly souls, even the dark and deep points of Religion.

This method of catechizing employs but three techniques:

> First, an aim and mark of the whole discourse, whither to drive the Answerer, which the Questionist must have in his mind before any question be propounded, upon which and to which the questions are to be chained. Secondly, a most plain and easy framing the question, even containing in virtue the answer also, especially to the more ignorant. Thirdly, when the answerer sticks, an illustrating the thing by something else, which he knows, making what he knows to serve him in that which he knows not.

I have quoted Herbert on this subject to make three points. First, Herbert's description of pastoral technique shows how much the didactic intent informs all his duties as a priest. Second, this discussion reveals the extent to which the essentially rhetorical stance of the speaker underlies not only preaching, but other of his pastoral duties as well. Third, Herbert's stress, as in his description of the act of preaching, is on encountering the hearer to teach him about himself and moving him toward the speaker's preordained goal: "This is the Practice which the Parson so much commends to all his fellow laborers; the secret of whose good consists in this, that at Sermons and Prayers, men may sleep or wander; but when one is asked a question, he must discover what he is."

My final point about Herbert the Catechist is his description of the audience for such activity, which includes not only his parishioners, but the priest himself: "In Catechizing there is an humbleness very suitable to Christian regeneration, which exceedingly delights him as by way of exercise upon himself, and by way of preaching to himself, for the advancement of his own mortification; for in preaching to others, he forgets not himself, but is first a Sermon to himself, and then to others; growing with the growth of his Parish." The goal of all priestly activity is growth, not only of the congregation, but of their priest as well. This understanding will help us tie together, in our consideration of *The Temple*, the various roles Herbert will take in his religious poems. He is poet-priest, using "all possible art" to move his audience; subject, using his own experience of the Christian life as one source for the content of his poems; and audience, using his own poems as part of his own process of growth in the Christian life. Herbert can thus exemplify for us in his poems all three parts of the paradigm of communication—author, subject, and audience—and instruct us in our own reading and responding to his poetic creations.

We might want to remember at this point that Herbert says, in his preliminary comments to the reader, that he wrote *The Country Parson* initially for himself, "that I may have a Mark to aim at." He now provides it for others to aim at, in full awareness that he does not offer here a complete portrait. Instead, he prays, "The Lord prosper the intention to myself, and others, who may not despise my poor labors, but add to those points, which I have observed, until the Book grow to a complete Pastoral." Whatever trace of spiritual autobiography Herbert included in *The Temple* must be seen as one among many resources for religious poetry incorporated into, and subjected to, the overarching didactic intent of the whole collection. Herbert is as critical of himself in *The Temple*, in all his priestly functions, as he is of us in our functions as readers. He joins us in *The Temple* as guide and mentor but also as fellow wayfarer in corporate journey toward God. What we must note here is the open-endedness of the work, a book set forth to instigate change, yet a work incomplete without the efforts of others to live out its precepts and add to it.

This quality of open-endedness applies to all the activities of *The Country Parson*. Herbert is clear, in his discussion of the audience for catechizing, that "all" are required to be present, for different reasons:

First, for the authority of the work; Secondly, that Parents, and Masters, as they hear the answers prove, may when they come home, either commend or reprove, either reward or punish. Thirdly, that those of the elder sort, who are not well grounded, may then by an honorable way take occasion to be better instructed. Fourthly, that those who are well grown in the knowledge of Religion, may examine their grounds, renew their vows, and by occasion of both, enlarge their meditations.

In Herbert's view, each parishioner will benefit from the same instruction, but in differing ways, depending on where in the process of Christian living he may find himself encountered by Herbert's didactic technique. Thus the role of the teaching minister, whether preaching to his congregation or instructing them in the catechism, involves the use of a strategy that will involve all in growth toward that goal of all ministry which is to make the means of salvation—the Church—into the goal of salvation—the Church.

Herbert thus poses for the would-be country parson the goal of achieving a truly didactic life, a life that in every particular exhorts and inspires his congregation toward greater growth in the Christian life. That life, lived out in response to God's saving Word, has as its context the ongoing life of the Church, within which God's Word is heard and responded to in prayer and praise. The humility with which Herbert accepted that vocation, and the integrity with which he enunciated it and lived it out, would make him an exemplary figure for his contemporaries, and perhaps for us as well.

The Temple

Implicit in the foregoing discussion of *The Country Parson* is the belief that Herbert's poetic strategies in *The Temple* are analogous to those he prescribes for the priest in carrying out his didactic vocation. Herbert's collection of religious poems shares with all Herbert's priestly activities the same didactic intent and rhetorical method, the use of "all possible art" to impinge upon the world of its readers, and to move them toward fuller participation in the Christian life. In his poems, as in his priestly duties, Herbert understands his role as that of "the Deputy of Christ for the reducing of Man to the Obedience of God." This means to provide knowledge of salvation, to build up this knowledge "to a spiritual temple," and "to enflame this knowledge, to press, and drive it to practice, turning it to reformation of life." In the poems, as in catechizing and preaching, Herbert enacts the various roles of poet, subject, and audience, aware of the goal of the Christian life, aware of how to achieve that goal, and also aware that he, too, is still growing, still in need of the same encouragement he provides his wider audience. In the poems, his concern is always for that wider audience, seeking in a multitude of ways to meet his audience where it is, to teach us who we are by helping us discover for ourselves where we are in the Christian life and moving us further down the road toward our common goal. He employs a variety of strategies and languages, of styles and techniques, knowing that we are a various lot and will respond at various times to differing approaches. Some of us will accept "plain reproof"; others of us are of higher quality and "very tender of reproof," and so will require more subtle approaches. On occasion, the direction of his strategy is outward, to teach directly, to show us he knows where we are, knows of our tendency to "sleep or wander." On other occasions, his thrust is upward, toward the God from whom all our help comes. On yet other occasions, his direction is inward, to provide examples both of success and failure in knowledge or practice. On yet other occasions, his approach is indirect, so "that he comes to the point very leisurely, and oftentimes . . . in the person of another, making [us] to reprove [ourselves]." In each case, however, his emphasis is on encounter with his audience: "None goes out of Church as he came in, but either better, or worse."

In every case, the common ground of all his approaches is the Church, which is the context of all Herbert's explorations of the Christian life because it is the intersection of all movement toward and from God—downward in judgment and reconciliation, upward in praise and intercession, outward in love and compassion, inward in attention and growth. The Church, for Herbert, is both that which is to be moved—the body of the faithful that "groaneth to be . . . holy, pure, and clear"—and that which is to be achieved—the "spiritual Temple," the Body of Christ. The visible Church, that institution into which all Englishmen in Herbert's day were required by law to be baptized, is at once the company of fallen men and women and the community of grace, the source of God's reconciling love. While, for a Puritan like John Cotton, the fullness of time will reveal God's elect "flowers" within the garden of fallen humanity, for Herbert the eschatological moment will entail instead the completion of God's reconciling work among all the faithful. In this heavenly work, man has a task in bringing about the full revelation of God's love for his creatures. It is to the furthering of that task that Herbert set himself in his poetic activities no less than in his priestly duties.

In this context, it is important to point out that Herbert believed firmly that whatever he achieved, the glory and power were God's and not his. As he says in the "Dedication" to *The Temple*, "Lord, my first fruits present themselves to thee; / Yet not mine neither: for from thee they came, / And must return." Herbert takes great pains in *The Temple* to make clear that God is the great poet of the universe. Herbert's poems are but "brittle crazy glass"; only when God makes them part of his story of man's salvation, "Making thy life to shine within . . . then the light and glory / More rev'rend grows, and more doth win" ("The Windows," 11.2, 7–9). Throughout *The Temple*, whatever achievement in poetry or in spiritual growth Herbert records—and the two are closely related—is constantly undercut by the affirmation that God is its source, that God has in fact already achieved it through his "full, perfect, and suffcient sacrifice." The story of man's salvation is not Herbert's, but God's story, the record of the activities of the one who was, who is, and who is to come.

A major theme in Herbert's poems, therefore, is the relationship between God's perception of man and man's perception of himself. Bound by the limitations of his temporal existence and fallen perceptions of the world, man sees his salvation as something to be achieved, something yet to be accomplished. From God's eternal perspective, however, man's salvation is already achieved through God's eternal reconciling action in Jesus Christ. Incorporation into God's salvation history for an individual is for him a temporal discovery of God's eternal view of him; it is a "letting go" of man's time-bound sense of reality.[58] To make that discovery is to make an offering of one's life to the God who promises to make that life new. Since Herbert's poetic method reflects his themes, his poems become in themselves a kind of offering, the same offering he urges us to make of ourselves.

Since one of Herbert's chief concerns is the proclamation of God's Word, it is especially appropriate that he chose the Bible as his chief model for religious poetry. The influence of the Bible on *The Temple* is all-pervasive, providing examples of different types of address to the

---

58. The term is that of Stanley Fish; see his "Letting Go: The Dialectic of the Self in Herbert's Poetry," in *Self-Consuming Artifacts: The Experience of Seventeenth-Century Literature* (Berkeley: University of California Press, 1972), pp. 156–223.

divine, images of the relationship between man and God, vocabulary with which to express and explore that relationship, as well as the central proclamation about that relationship which is the subject of Herbert's poetry. A brief review of the notes appended to this edition of *The Temple* will demonstrate the extent of Herbert's debt; hardly a poem lacks its own direct echoes of one or another biblical passage.

Each section of *The Temple* has its appropriate biblical analogue. "The Church Porch," with its detailed prescriptions for living out the Christian life, echoes the prescriptive language of Proverbs and Ecclesiastes. "The Church," with its extensive and rich collection of lyrics, is indebted to the dialogue form of The Song of Solomon as well as to the many and various stances of prayer and divine address exhibited in the Psalms.[59] The recounting of the history of the Church in "The Church Militant" has its analogues in the narrative books of the Old Testament as well as in the theology of history expounded in the Prophets.

Yet, for Herbert, the Old Testament models have their value only in light of New Testament proclamation. The Song of Solomon, seen in Herbert's day as an allegory of the relationship between Christ and his Church, can serve as a model for his own poetry only because of that fact. The Christian reading of the Song opens to Herbert the possibility of using it as a means of exploring a loving relationship between God and his speaker. The Christian reading of the Psalms renders them useful as examples of differing stances of address to the divine as well as precedents for incorporating certain states of feeling or experience into his verse. In the same way, the Christian belief that the promises God makes to his people in the Old Testament are fulfilled in the New opens the way to incorporating into Herbert's verse Old Testament forms of instruction and Old Testament understandings of what God's people are to expect in this world.

Herbert's poems always point us beyond and through themselves to the God whose Word is the standard for all Herbert's words, a Word that judges, but that accepts us in love for our caring response to that judgment. The most obvious source for that Word is, as we have seen, the Bible, "joy's handsell [where] heav'n lies flat" ("The Holy Scriptures I," 1. 13). Yet, for Herbert, that is only one source. Herbert

---

59. I am indebted here to Barbara K. Lewalski's major study, *Protestant Poetics and the Seventeenth-Century Religious Lyric.* See especially pp. 283–316 for a fuller discussion of Herbert's use of biblical poetics.

points us primarily to the Word made flesh, to God's act of love in Jesus Christ, and to the Church, which is his earthly body. For Herbert, a devoted and exemplary user of the Book of Common Prayer, the Church is the context for Bible reading.[60] The regular progression through the Bible set forth in the two calendars of the Prayer Book, one for the daily Offices of Morning and Evening Prayer, the other for celebration of Holy Communion, a procedure we know Herbert was devoted to, must be seen as the setting for Herbert's use of the Bible in his poems.

What becomes clear, as we read *The Temple*, is that for Herbert the Church is a living extension of God's Word, a continuation of his saving actions, even as it is the continuing context for the Bible, the story of God's actions, to be read. To be clear about the significance of this for Herbert's poems, we need to understand how the Bible was viewed in Herbert's day, as an account of universal history, and as a source for readings, as well as for "reading," or understanding, events in the present moment of the reader's experience. The Bible is, first of all, a narrative of God's saving encounters with man. As Eric Auerbach has pointed out, the Bible exerts the absolute claim on its readers that the story it relates is the essential story for understanding all of human history.[61] The Bible contains two sorts of material, the narrative itself, and various attempts to understand the significance of that narrative. So long as the biblical narrative is seen as open and applicable to events in the reader's day, the interpretive element in the Bible is constantly open to updating, to revision in light of more recent events. This is what happens in the New Testament, in which the writers use Old Testament language to show the significance of the life, death and resurrection of Jesus Christ. To say that Jesus is a new Moses, or an Elijah, is to say that in Jesus God was working in the same way as he was working in the saving events in the life of the Old Israel, creating a New Israel, a new people of God.[62] This is the source of what is known as biblical typology, the claim that events in the Old Testament anticipate or prefigure events in the New. The New Testament events are thus said to fulfill or complete their anticipation in the Old.

---

60. For a fuller discussion of Herbert's use of the Book of Common Prayer, see John Booty, "George Herbert: *The Temple* and *The Book of Common Prayer*."

61. In *Mimesis: The Representation of Reality in Western Literature*, trans. Willard R. Trask (Princeton: Princeton University Press, 1953), pp. 3–23.

62. On the dynamics of biblical reading, see Herbert N. Schneidau, *Sacred Discontent: The Bible and Western Tradition* (Berkeley: University of California Press, 1976).

INTRODUCTION

The claim of the New Testament is that in Jesus Christ God acted once for all, to fulfill his promises made to the Old Israel and to open the path to salvation for all mankind. The New Testament in Revelation contains the end of the story started in Genesis; as the world was made by God, so it will end with the full revelation of his glory at the last. Yet that history is incomplete insofar as the present moment of any reader is concerned who comes to it after the close of events recorded in the historical sections of the New Testament. The problem of any reader, such as Herbert or his intended audience, is to find oneself included in the history of God's saving actions recorded in that narrative.

At this point, the importance of the Church becomes clearer; as the context for reading the narrative of God's actions for man in human history, and as the occasion for the celebration of those events in the sacraments, the Church proclaims the openness of God's salvation history to those who constitute its membership. The Church thus becomes the sign of God's continuing activity to incorporate his people into his kingdom, and also the source of his grace, which makes that inclusion possible.

We see Herbert, in *The Temple*, making use of this tradition in a variety of ways. He does so when he uses the Bible as a source for a living language with which to talk about the encounter between God and the reader, or with which to describe his own experiences of God in his own life, as a model for the reader's emulation. In this, the use of typology—the language of the Bible for indicating the significance of the events it describes—is extremely important. When Herbert does this, he is making the claim that the Bible is not a closed narrative, but an account of a story that is still going on. In fact, he is making the claim that the events he relates are part of that narrative, precisely because they can be described in the language that narrative uses.

We see such a use of biblical language in Herbert's poem "Aaron." Here, Herbert begins with a recapitulation of the biblical image of Aaron, the Old Testament type of the true priest:

> Holiness on the head,
> Light and perfections on the breast,
> Harmonious bells below, raising the dead
> To lead them unto life and rest.
> Thus are true Aarons drest.

INTRODUCTION

To this biblical image, Herbert's speaker contrasts his own situation:

> Profaneness in my head,
> Defects and darkness in my breast,
> A noise of passions ringing me for dead
> Unto a place where is no rest.
> Poor priest thus am I drest.

Yet, he remembers, there is another head, heart, and breast, "Another music, making live not dead . . . / In him I am well drest."

> Christ is my only head,
> My alone only heart and breast,
> My only music, striking me ev'n dead;
> That to the old man I may rest,
> And be in him new drest.

As a result, he can proclaim himself, through incorporation in Christ's body, and his priesthood, fit to function as a priest in terms of the biblical type:

> So holy in my head,
> Perfect and light in my dear breast,
> My doctrine tun'd by Christ, (who is not dead,
> But lives in me while I do rest)
> Come people; Aaron's drest.

This poem makes sense only in terms of what A. C. Charity has called "applied typology";[63] the biblical type is a living language with which

---

63. See his important study, *Events and Their Afterlife: The Dialectics of Christian Typology* (Cambridge: Cambridge University Press, 1966). For other discussions of Herbert and typology, see Ira Clark, " 'Lord, in Thee the *Beauty* Lies in the *Discovery*': 'Love Unknown' and Reading Herbert," *ELH* 39 (1972): 560–84; Barbara K. Lewalski, "Typology and Poetry: A Consideration of Herbert, Vaughan, and Marvell," in *Illustrious Evidence: Approaches to English Literature of the Early Seventeenth Century*, ed. Earl Miner (Berkeley: University of California Press, 1975), pp. 41–69; " 'Typological Symbolism' and the 'Progress of the Soul' in Seventeenth Century Literature," in *Literary Uses of Typology from the Late Middle Ages to the Present*, ed. Earl Miner (Princeton: Princeton University Press, 1977), pp. 79–114; and *Protestant Poetics and Seventeenth-Century Literature* (Princeton: Princeton University Press, 1979).

to talk about a present reality because the events described in typological language in the Bible are still open to the speaker of this poem. The Christ-event is not over, a past event, but a living event, still open to the speaker's participation. As a result, the events described in this poem, and others in *The Temple*, take their meaning from that event.

Herbert is thus able to populate his poems with biblical figures and recapitulations of biblical events. In "Christmas (I)" he finds "My dearest Lord" at "the next inn"; in "Redemption" Herbert finds his "rich Lord" among "thieves and murderers: there I him espied, / Who straight, Your suit is granted, said, and died." The point is that for the speaker of this poem, as for us as readers, the past event of the crucifixion is not "past" in our sense of time, but part of the present moment of our experience. If it were not, our "suit" would not be granted; we would be excluded from incorporation into God's salvation history. But, because Herbert, through using the language of "applied typology," can make the saving events of God's history present to us, we gain the sense of the openness of that salvation history to us.

Such a way of applying biblical language to present moments of experience makes two claims. First, it stresses the urgency of the present moment and heightens the importance of the reader's response. Second, it forces the reader into a position of choice. Herbert first uses the rhetoric of demanding choice in the "Perrirhanterium" section of "The Church Porch," where clear options are offered for living out the Christian life and the implications of choice making are made clear. Here, the need to make choices is heightened in importance; to accept the claim that God's salvation history is open to us in the present and to find ourselves within it is one of our options, while the other is to reject the claim those events have over us and to find ourselves excluded, the events merely "past." In this way especially Herbert acts out in his poems the didactic function he outlines for the priest in *The Country Parson*.

Herbert is able to use biblical language in *The Temple* to create a sense of the "presentness" of God's actions because of the way in which he locates the usage in the context of the Church's corporate life. In the daily Offices and the sacramental services of the Book of Common Prayer, the Bible is not merely read as the remembering of God's saving acts, but is used as a living language of the Church's prayer and praise. The Psalter becomes the actual language of address to God; the Song of Mary and the Song of Simeon, to name but two examples, become the actual songs of response to the reading of God's Word. That Word itself, the Bible itself, is not merely read, but expounded in sermons, and thus made applicable to the present moment of its hearers' experience. In this context, it is highly significant that Herbert's dramatization in "The Sacrifice" of Christ's crucifixion is dependent for its form on the Reproaches used in the medieval Mass of the Presanctified on Good Friday.[64]

In addition, such use of biblical language in *The Temple* makes clearer to us Herbert's devotion to the ongoing observation of the Church's liturgical calendar and its services, which proclaim God's saving events through Bible reading and sacramental action.

The poem "Good Friday" begins a series of allusions in *The Temple* of the liturgical calendar of the Church; this is continued in the Easter" poems, the poem "Whitsunday" and the poem "Trinity Sunday," as well as the poems "Christmas" and "Lent" later in the collection. Poems between "Easter" and "Whitsunday," or Pentecost, stress the participation of man in Christ's resurrection through word and sacrament with two poems on the Holy Scriptures, two on Holy Baptism, and one on Holy Communion. Other poems in this section focus on basic aspects of human life—"Nature," "Sin," "Affliction"—and on basic aspects of the Christian life—"Repentance," "Faith," "Prayer," and "Love." Between "Whitsunday," traditionally the birthday of the Church, and "Trinity Sunday" come poems on the activities that take place within the Church—"Praise I," "Matins," and "Evensong"—as well as the poems that reflect the physical features of the Church— "Church-Monuments," "Church-Music," "Church Lock and Key," "The Church-Floor," and "The Windows."

Poems between "Trinity Sunday" and "Christmas" explore various aspects of the Christian life—"Humility," "Frailty," "Constancy," and "Affliction III." "Sunday" treats any of the many Sundays numbered in the Anglican liturgical calendar after Trinity Sunday as a "day most calm, most bright, / The fruit of this, the next world's bud," the "day my Savior rose," since every Sunday is a little Easter. "To all Angels and Saints" may allude to All Saints' Day, while "Employment II" and "Denial" suggest the penitential tone of Advent.

The poems from "Christmas" to "Lent" reflect man's response to

---

64. For a detailed account of this allusion, see Rosemond Tuve, *A Reading of George Herbert* (Chicago: University of Chicago Press, 1952).

God in "Ungratefulness," to the speaker's renewed sense of despair in "Sighs and Groans," and to the entry of sin and death in "The World." The stress on man's pretensions to knowledge in "Vanity I" makes appropriate the opening line of "Lent": "Welcome dear feast of Lent: who loves not thee,/He loves not Temperance, or Authority." With "Lent," Herbert has in a sense gotten back to the beginning of "The Church" by bringing the liturgical year full circle, for after Lent will come Good Friday, Easter, and all the rest.

Poems after "Lent" in "The Church" treat the liturgical year and the physical Church more indirectly. "The Dawning" is another Easter poem, for it asks us to "Arise, arise; / And with his burial linen dry thine eyes." "The British Church" finds the speaker in "joy, dear Mother, when I view / Thy perfect lineaments, and hue / Both sweet and bright," including those aspects of her practice we have already seen. "Love-Joy" notices the details of a stained-glass window. "The Priesthood" and "Aaron" remind us of those who figure forth Christ to his people, while "The Family" proclaims that "the house and family" of the Church are God's. "The Banquet" expands on the Eucharistic elements and the experience of receiving them. What happens, after Herbert establishes the ongoing allusion to the life of the visible Church, is that he feels free to expand on it, to use it as a more remote allusion, to develop and guide more fully the experience of those who participate in that life. As Stanley Fish has put it, "We are dealing here not with a single linear pattern, but with a *rhythm*, and it is a rhythm whose fluctuations are bounded by the two poles between which self-examination moves, repentance and faith."[65] At the same time, that rhythm is constantly seen in the context of the Church, that body which circumscribes all movement in the Christian life.

Other poems in this section, such as "A True Hymn," "The Poesy," and "Praise III," focus on the writing of poetry itself, notably the poems we are reading. Throughout, the stress is on "letting go" to allow God to act:

> if th' heart be moved,
> Although the verse be somewhat scant,
> God doth supply the want.
> As when th' heart says (sighing to be approved)
> *Oh, could I love!* and stops: God writeth, *Loved.*

---

65. Fish, *The Living Temple*, p. 120.

INTRODUCTION

The whole movement in "The Church" points beyond itself; this is
true of the collection as a poetic enterprise as well as a devotional enterprise. If we are constantly drawn toward participation in the life of
the Church, so we are shown that the poetic achievement here makes
sense only when seen in terms of God's ongoing authorship of his salvation history.

Movement in "The Church" section of *The Temple* thus circles
around several points of reference—the circular rhythm of the Christian year, the back-and-forth rhythm of the Christian life marked by
that cycle of remembrance and celebration, the circular repetition of
the weekly round of services. But the movement is also linear, toward
the Last Things, which will usher in the fulfillment of God's loving
acts of redemption. The four last poems in "The Church," but one, are
on the traditional last things, "Death," "Doomsday," "Judgement,"
and "Heaven." Only Hell is missing, but implicit in Herbert's strategies is the argument that if we have read attentively and responsively
this far, that is no concern of ours. If it is, the last poem in "The
Church" reassures us that the final choice is God's and not ours:

> Love bade me welcome: yet my soul drew back,
>   Guilty of dust and sin.
> But quick-ey'd Love, observing me grow slack
>   From my first entrance in,
> Drew nearer to me, sweetly questioning,
>   If I lack'd anything.
>
> A guest, I answer'd, worthy to be here:
>   Love said, You shall be he.
> I the unkind, ungrateful? Ah my dear,
>   I cannot look on thee.
> Love took my hand, and smiling did reply,
>   Why made the eyes but I?
>
> Truth Lord, but I have marr'd them: let my shame
>   Go where it doth deserve,
> And know you not, says Love, who bore the blame?
>   My dear, then I will serve.
> You must sit down, says Love, and taste my meat:
>   So I did sit and eat.

Herbert here recaptitulates the entire movement of *The Temple*, from outside to inside, from individual to corporate participation in the eucharistic banquet, from realization now of God's love to that still to come, from choosing to letting God choose.

What happens in "The Church" is the modeling of a variety of experiences of the Christian life, the judging of our responses, and the moving us toward fuller participation in the life of the Church in anticipation of full participation in God's kingdom. Herbert builds a temple of words, yet it is a temple that is incomplete and unintelligible save in the context of the larger life of the Church to which it constantly alludes.[66] Lest we question that, he constantly reminds us that, even as God concludes poems such as "A True Hymn," so God's Church is his creation, through his cross and resurrection, which he will complete only at the last.

Yet that is not the end of the story, for the specific church built in words, and the specific Church whose life it participates in, must be located in a larger context, the full history of God's salvation history. That is the task of "The Church Militant," a hymn of praise to the "Almighty Lord, who from thy glorious throne / Seest and rules all things ev'n as one." In "The Church Militant," Herbert reviews the history of that institution, from its beginning in the creation of Israel as God's people, through the vicissitudes of its history, to its present position, when "the Church by going west / Still eastward go; because it drew more near / To time and place, where judgement shall appear." Here, the speaker's tone, confident and assertive in "The Church Porch," complex and multifaceted in "The Church," takes on a note of confident supplication, as the speaker praises God and looks toward the fulfillment of his promises.

The concluding section of *The Temple* thus subsumes within itself all that has gone before, as it catches up the life of the individual Christian in his particular time and place and locates it in the context of the ongoing life of the Church in all times and places. The overt directives of "The Church Porch" outline for us the choices open to the Christian

---

66. For other approaches to the unity of *The Temple*, see John David Walker, "The Architectonics of George Herbert's *The Temple*," *ELH* 29 (1962): 289–305; Rickey, *Utmost Art*, pp. 9–15; Sara William Hanley, C.S.J., "Temples in *The Temple*: George Herbert's Study of The Church," *Studies in English Literature* 8 (1968): 121–35; and Valerie Carnes, "The Unity of George Herbert's *The Temple*: A Reconsideration," *ELH* 35 (1968): 505–26.

in his daily life; the thrust of this section leads us inevitably to the Church, where "public [prayer] hath more promises, more love." The many lyrics of "The Church" demonstrate for us the crucial urgency of our choice while they offer us models in light of which we can locate ourselves in the Christian life and find aid and direction for growth. Here again, the constant allusion to the ongoing life of the Church reminds us of that arena in which our growth will take place, if it happens at all. As the context for proclamation of the Word, the Church is seen as the mediator of divine grace and the community in which that grace empowers growth. The movement of "The Church" is from "The Altar," in which the speaker seeks to make an altar of his heart, to "Love (III)" in which the speaker finds he is a guest, by God's choice, at the wedding supper of the Lamb. If we miss the allusion to the Church's corporate worship-life in Herbert's design, the concluding reference at the end of "The Church" to the *Gloria in excelsis,* which ends the Prayer Book's service of Holy Communion, makes his reference unmistakable. In "The Church Militant," the community of the faithful is seen as caught up in God's larger plan, that working out of his salvation which leads the Church onward toward "time and place, where judgement shall appear."

What we have, then, in *The Temple,* is an enormously rich and complex didacticism, Herbert's fullest realization of his attempt to use "all possible art" to move us with him toward the building up of the Church in anticipation of God's actions to fulfill his promises made to that Church. The twin poles of Herbert's devotion, the Bible and the Church as its living context, provide him with both language and purpose. Yet what comes through, finally, are his humility before that purpose and his sense of urgency in acting it out. Herbert's contemporaries saw in him a model of priestly devotion; the inescapable sense of his dedication that comes to us from reading *The Temple* is eloquent testimony to the justness of their vision.

THE TEXT

This volume contains annotated modern-spelling editions of Herbert's prose treatise *A Priest to the Temple, or, The Country Parson* and his poetry collection *The Temple,* along with the texts of two prayers and a few poems not contained in the final version of *The Temple.* In preparing these editions, I have sought to achieve two goals: first, to establish as fully as possible what Herbert actually wrote; and, second, to remove as much as possible, without falsifying the experience of reading Herbert, any impediments the modern reader may experience with the language in which Herbert originally wrote, to "copy fair, what time hath blurr'd." The editor who does more than reprint in facsimile owes his readers an explanation of how the end product of his labors with the text differs from the originals that lie behind it. In the case of this volume, to discharge my obligation means to explain the choice of texts on which my editions are based, as well as to indicate how those texts have been changed in the process of editing and modernization.

Copy-Text

The first task of any editor is to decide which of the texts available to him will serve as the basis, or copy-text, for his edition. For the contents of this volume, I have made the following choices: I. *A Priest to the Temple, or, The Country Parson; Prayers.* Herbert's description of the ideal priest was first published in 1652 as part of a volume entitled *Herbert's Remains. Or, Sundry Pieces of that sweet Singer of The Temple, Mr George Herbert,* which also includes Barnabas Oley's brief Life of Herbert and Herbert's *Jacula Prudentum. Or Outlandish Proverbs, Sentences, And Rule of Holy Life.*[67] The present edition is based on the 1652 text, with corrections from the Errata notes silently incorporated and obvious printing errors silently corrected. The 1652 edition also includes the "Prayer before Sermon" and "Prayer after Sermon," on which the texts included in the present volume are based. *The Country Parson* was also reprinted in 1671 and 1675, without the Prayers, but these editions basically reprint, with minor changes of wording and corrections, the text of 1652; they have no independent textual authority.
II. *The Temple;* Miscellaneous Poems. Herbert's collection of religious poetry was first published in 1633 in a posthumous edition probably seen through the press by his friend Nicholas Ferrar, who wrote the Preface. Initially issued by the Cambridge University Press in a carefully printed volume, *The Temple* was reprinted twelve times before 1709; except as guides to printing errors in the first edition, however,

---

67. See Hutchinson's edition for full bibliographical descriptions of all early editions of Herbert's writings.

these subsequent editions have no textual authority independent of the first edition of 1633. Herbert's religious poetry also exists in two manuscript collections: (1) MS Tanner 307 in the Bodleian Library, Oxford (hereafter referred to as *B*), which contains texts of all the poems printed in the 1633 edition (hereafter referred to as *1633*), and (2) MS Jones B 62, in Dr. Williams's Library, London (hereafter referred to as *W*), which contains texts of sixty-nine of the 164 poems in *B* and *1633*, as well as texts of six poems not found elsewhere. In addition, Walton's *Life* of Herbert (1670) contains texts of three poems not found elsewhere. In this volume, *W*, consulted in the facsimile edition of Amy Charles,[68] provides copy-text for the six poems unique to that text; Walton's *Life* provides copy-text for its unique group of poems. For *The Temple*, the first edition of 1633 serves as copy-text, instead of *B;* although earlier editors have argued for the authority of *B*,[69] I believe that J. Max Patrick has demonstrated convincingly the authority of *1633* and the derivative quality of *B*, which was probably prepared at Little Gidding from the original manuscript by members of Ferrar's community.[70] *W* probably represents an earlier state of the *Temple* collection, prepared some years before Herbert's final version. Occasionally, however, readings from either *W* or *B* illuminate or clarify Herbert's intention or meaning; on the very few occasions when I have incorporated a reading from either *B* or *W* into the text of this edition, I note such departures from copy-text in the annotations. Obvious printing errors in *1633* have also been silently corrected.

I must acknowledge my indebtedness to Canon F. E. Hutchinson, whose magisterial edition of Herbert's *Works* (Oxford: Clarendon, 1941) sets the standard for all modern editors. While I do not agree with Canon Hutchinson on every point, I have found his careful descriptions of the various editions, as well as his meticulous collation of variant readings, of immeasurable aid in working my way through the various problems in Herbert's text.

---

68. *The Williams Manuscript of George Herbert's Poems* (Delmar, N.Y.: Scholars' Facsimiles & Reprints, 1977).

69. Thus, Hutchinson uses *1633* for the actual words of Herbert's text (the substantives) but *B* for punctuation and other accidental features of the text; Barbara K. Lewalski and Andrew J. Sabol use *B* for copy-text throughout, in *Major Poets of the Earlier Seventeenth Century* (New York: Bobbs-Merrill, 1973).

70. See his discussion in "Critical Problems in Editing George Herbert," in *The Editor as Critic and the Critic as Editor*, ed. Murray Krieger (Los Angeles: Clark Memorial Library, 1973), pp. 3–40.

INTRODUCTION

Modernization

Although Herbert's language differs in no essential way from our own, his spellings and sentence structures may appear unusual to the reader who is unfamiliar with early seventeenth-century literature. To remove impediments to the modern reader's apprehension of Herbert caused by changes in the language between his day and ours, I have prepared an edition in modern spelling, within certain strict limits. In the first place, I have modernized the usage of *u* for *v* and *i* for *j*, as well as the alternate form of *s;* I have also expanded abbreviations and added apostrophes to words whose spelling contracts modern forms. In addition, I have made Herbert's spelling conform to American usage where that differs from modern British form (i.e., "favour" → "favor"). Further, those words whose modern-spelling forms do not change either the sound or rhythm of pronunciation have been modernized. I have not, however, modernized those words whose modern equivalents differ in pronunciation from Herbert's original words. I have found this necessary to preserve the rhythms and rhymes of Herbert's verse. Finally, I have let stand those words which lack modern equivalents, or for which the meaning is obscure. In each case, however, I have defined in the annotations all words that would be unclear to the modern reader.

In the case of punctuation and capitalization, I have adhered closely to the various copy-texts. Herbert's use of capital letters provides emphasis for many words, which would be lost if modern conventions were followed. In addition, the structure of Herbert's sentences has an integrity that would be lost if a modern system of punctuation were imposed on them. The punctuation of the copy-texts, whether it is Herbert's or that of the printing shops that produced the early editions, is appropriate to Herbert's style in a way that our own conventions of punctuation are not. Punctuation of Herbert's poems in this edition is essentially that of the copy-texts; punctuation in the prose is also that of the copy-texts except for the occasional addition of parentheses to set off biblical citations. Where Herbert supplies only partial citations for his biblical references, I have expanded them, enclosing my additions in brackets.

Finally, in the *Temple* poems, following the practice of recent editors, I have differentiated poems with similar titles by adding to each title a roman numeral in parentheses indicating whether that particular poem is the first, second, or third one of that title in the text. I have also amended the title of the poem "The 23. Psalm" to read "The 23rd Psalm."

Annotations

In a second approach to making Herbert fully accessible to the modern reader, I have provided a set of annotations to all the texts. Included among the annotations are definitions of obsolete words or those words used in a special or obscure sense, paraphrases of difficult passages, guides to Herbert's biblical allusions, and explanations of technical terms, as well as indications of substantive departures from my copy-texts. The Oxford English Dictionary has been a constant companion in the process of annotation; most of the definitions included here are drawn from that source. I have discovered, however, that no annotator operates in a vacuum. Instead, my work has been made much easier and more pleasurable by former editors of Herbert, especially F. E. Hutchinson, C. A. Patrides, editor of *The English Poems of George Herbert* (London: Dent, 1974), Barbara K. Lewalski and Andrew J. Sabol, editors of *Major Poets of the Earlier Seventeenth Century* (New York: Bobbs-Merrill, 1973), and Mario A. Di Cesare, editor of *George Herbert and the Seventeenth-Century Religious Poets* (New York: Norton, 1978). To work with their editions is to be aware that the annotation of Herbert is a community enterprise, each annotator rising on the shoulders of those who have gone before him. If I have been able to augment their efforts, it is only because they made my labors possible. Specific indebtednesses are recorded in the annotations; I wish here to record a more general gratefulness for their labors.

Herbert's allusions to the Book of Common Prayer are annotated in reference to John Booty's splendid edition of *The Elizabethan Prayer Book* (Charlottesville: University Press of Virginia for The Folger Shakespeare Library, 1976). Herbert's references to the Psalter are consistently to the translation contained in the Great Bible (1539), which was used in public worship in the Anglican Church even after the appearance of other translations; it was finally incorporated into the text of the Book of Common Prayer in 1660. A convenient source for this translation of the Psalms is the 1928 edition of the Prayer Book of the Episcopal Church. Herbert's allusions to other biblical passages may be conveniently located in the Authorized Version of 1611, better known as the King James Bible.

51

A PRIEST TO THE TEMPLE,
OR,
THE COUNTRY PARSON
HIS
CHARACTER,
AND
RULE OF HOLY LIFE.

Title: Amy Charles, argues, with others, that the title *A Priest to the Temple* may be the work of Herbert's literary executors, to link the volume with the title of Herbert's poems (see *A Life*, p. 157). The title *The Country Parson* is clearly Herbert's, and is used to refer to this work throughout the present edition.

The Author to the Reader

BEing desirous (through the Mercy of God) to please Him, for whom I am, and live, and who giveth me my Desires and Performances; and considering with myself, That the way to please him, is to feed my Flock diligently and faithfully, since our Saviour hath made that the argument[1] of a Pastor's love, I have resolved to set down the Form and Character of a true Pastor, that I may have a Mark to aim at:[2] which also I will set as high as I can, since he shoots higher that threatens the Moon, than he that aims at a Tree. Not that I think, if a man do not all which is here expressed, he presently sins, and displeases God, but that it is a good strife to go as far as we can in pleasing of him, who hath done so much for us. The Lord prosper the intention to myself, and others, who may not despise my poor labors, but add to those points, which I have observed, until the Book grow to a complete Pastoral.[3]

1632.

George Herbert.

---

1. *the argument*. See John 21:15–17.
2. *a Mark to aim at.* See Walton's *Life* for a reference to Herbert's setting for himself rules "for the future manage of his life" (pp. 289, 294).
3. *Pastoral.* The OED notes that Samuel Johnson's dictionary defines a pastoral as "A Book relating to the cure of souls." Herbert here brings together in the traditional way images of Christ and his priestly followers as shepherds of their flock, engaged in pastoral activity.

CHAPTER I.

Of a Pastor

A PASTOR is the Deputy of Christ for the reducing[4] of Man to the Obedience of God. This definition is evident, and contains the direct steps of Pastoral Duty and Authority. For first, Man fell from God by disobedience. Secondly, Christ is the glorious instrument of God for the revoking[5] of Man. Thirdly, Christ being not to continue on earth, but after he had fulfilled the work of Reconciliation, to be received up into heaven, he constituted Deputies in his place, and these are Priests. And therefore Saint *Paul* in the beginning of his Epistles, professeth this: and in the first to the *Colossians*[6] plainly avoucheth, that he *fills up that which is behind of the afflictions of Christ in his flesh, for his Body's sake, which is the Church.* Wherein is contained the complete definition of a Minister. Out of this Charter of the Priesthood may be plainly gathered both the Dignity thereof, and the Duty: The Dignity, in that a Priest may do that which Christ did, and by his authority, and as his Vicegerent. The Duty, in that a Priest is to do that which Christ did, and after his manner, both for Doctrine and Life.

CHAPTER II.

Their Diversities

O F Pastors (intending mine own Nation only, and also therein setting aside the Reverend Prelates of the Church, to whom this discourse ariseth not) some live in the Universities, some in Noble Houses, some in Parishes residing on their Cures. Of those that live in the Universities, some live there in office, whose rule is that of the Apostle (*Rom.* 12:6[–8]): *Having gifts differing, according to the grace that is given to us, whether prophecy, let us prophesy according to the proportion of faith; or ministry, let us wait on our minist'ring; or he that teacheth, on teaching,* &c. *he that ruleth, let him do it with diligence,* &c. Some in a preparatory way, whose aim and labor must be not only to get knowl-

---

4. *reducing.* Bringing back from error.
5. *revoking.* Restoring or recalling to correct way of life.
6. *first to the Colossians.* Col. 1:24–25.

edge, but to subdue and mortify all lusts and affections: and not to think, that when they have read the Fathers, or Schoolmen, a Minister is made, and the thing done. The greatest and hardest preparation is within: For, *Unto the ungodly, saith God, Why dost thou preach my Laws, and takest my Covenant in thy mouth?* (*Ps.* 50:16) Those that live in Noble Houses are called Chaplains, whose duty and obligation being the same to the Houses they live in, as a Parson's to his Parish, in describing the one (which is indeed the bent of my Discourse) the other will be manifest. Let not Chaplains think themselves so free, *as many of them do,* and because they have different Names, think their Office different. Doubtless they are Parsons of the families they live in, and are entertained to that end, either by an open, or implicit Covenant. Before they are in Orders, they may be received for Companions, or discoursers; but after a man is once Minister, he cannot agree to come into any house, where he shall not exercise what he is, unless he forsake his plough, and look back. Wherefore they are not to be oversubmissive, and base, but to keep up with the Lord and Lady of the house, and to preserve a boldness with them and all, even so far as reproof to their very face, when occasion calls, but seasonably and discreetly. They who do not thus, while they remember their earthly Lord, do much forget their heavenly; they wrong the Priesthood, neglect their duty, and shall be so far from that which they seek with their oversubmissiveness, and cringings, that they shall ever be despised. They who for the hope of promotion neglect any necessary admonition, or reproof, sell (with *Judas*) their Lord and Master.

CHAPTER III.

The Parson's Life

THE Country Parson is exceeding exact in his Life, being holy, just, prudent, temperate, bold, grave in all his ways. And because the two highest points of Life, wherein a Christian is most seen, are Patience, and Mortification; Patience in regard of afflictions, Mortification in regard of lusts and affections, and the stupifying and deading of all the clamorous powers of the soul, therefore he hath thoroughly studied these, that he may be an absolute Master and commander of himself, for all the purposes which God hath ordained him. Yet in these points he labors most in those things which are most apt to scandalize his Parish. And first, because Country people live hardly,[7] and therefore as feeling their own sweat, and consequently knowing the price of money, are offended much with any, who by hard usage increase their travail, the Country Parson is very circumspect in avoiding all covetousness, neither being greedy to get, nor niggardly to keep, nor troubled to lose any worldly wealth; but in all his words and actions slighting, and disesteeming it, even to a wond'ring, that the world should so much value wealth, which in the day of wrath hath not one dram of comfort for us. Secondly, because Luxury is a very visible sin, the Parson is very careful to avoid all the kinds thereof, but especially that of drinking, because it is the most popular vice; into which if he come, *he prostitutes himself* both to shame, and sin, and by having *fellowship, with the unfruitful works of darkness,*[8] he disableth himself of authority *to reprove them:* For sins make all equal, whom they find together; and then they are worst, who ought to be best. Neither is it for the servant of Christ to haunt Inns, or Taverns, or Ale-houses, *to the dishonor of his person and office.* The Parson doth not so, but orders his Life in such a fashion, that when death takes him, as the Jews and *Judas* did Christ, he may say as He did, *I sat daily with you teaching in the Temple.*[9] Thirdly, because Country people (as indeed all honest men) do much esteem their word, it being the Life of buying, and selling, and dealing in the world; therefore the Parson is very strict in keeping his word, though it be to his own hindrance, as knowing, that if he be not so, he will quickly be discovered, and disregarded: neither will they believe him in the pulpit, whom they cannot trust in his Conversation. As for oaths, and apparel, the disorders thereof are also very manifest. The Parson's yea is yea, and nay nay: and his apparel plain, but reverend, and clean, without spots, or dust, or smell; the purity of his mind breaking out, and dilating itself even to his body, clothes, and habitation.

---

7. *hardly.* Hard and difficult lives.
8. Eph. 5:11.
9. Luke 22:53.

GEORGE HERBERT

Chapter IV.

The Parson's Knowledge

THE Country Parson is full of all knowledge. They say, it is an ill Mason that refuseth any stone: and there is no knowledge, but, in a skillful hand, serves either positively as it is, or else to illustrate some other knowledge. He condescends even to the knowledge of tillage, and pastorage,[10] and makes great use of them in teaching, because people by what they understand, are best led to what they understand not. But the chief and top of his knowledge consists in the book of books, the storehouse and magazine of life and comfort, the holy Scriptures. There he sucks, and lives. In the Scriptures he finds four things; Precepts for life, Doctrines for knowledge, Examples for illustration, and Promises for comfort: These he hath digested severally. But for the understanding of these; the means he useth are first, a holy Life, remembering what his Master saith, that *if any do God's will, he shall know of the Doctrine (John* 7:[17]), and assuring himself, that wicked men, however learned, do not know the Scriptures, because they feel them not, and because they are not understood but with the same Spirit that writ them. The second means is prayer, which if it be necessary even in temporal things, how much more in things of another world, where the well is deep, and we have nothing of ourselves to draw with? Wherefore he ever begins the reading of the Scripture with some short inward ejaculation, as, *Lord, open mine eyes, that I may see the wond'rous things of thy Law.* &c.[11] The third means is a diligent Collation of Scripture with Scripture. For all Truth being consonant to itself, and all being penn'd by one and the self-same Spirit, it cannot be, but that an industrious, and judicious comparing of place with place must be a singular help for the right understanding of the Scriptures. To this may be added the consideration of any text with the coherence thereof, touching what goes before, and what follows after, as also the scope[12] of the Holy Ghost. When the Apostles would have called down fire from Heaven, they were reproved, as ignorant of what spirit they were.[13] For the Law required one thing, and the Gospel another: yet as

---

10. *pastorage.* Pasturage.
11. Ps. 119:18.
12. *scope.* Main design, as opposed to specific words or passages.
13. Luke 9:54–55.

diverse, not as repugnant: therefore the spirit of both is to be considered, and weighed. The fourth means are Commenters and Fathers, who have handled the places controverted, which the Parson by no means refuseth. As he doth not so study others, as to neglect the grace of God in himself, and what the Holy Spirit teacheth him; so doth he assure himself, that God in all ages hath had his servants, to whom he hath revealed his Truth, as well as to him; and that as one Country doth not bear all things, that there may be a Commerce;[14] so neither hath God opened, or will open all to one, that there may be a traffic in knowledge between the servants of God, for the planting both of love, and humility. Wherefore he hath one Comment[15] at least upon every book of Scripture, and ploughing with this, and his own meditations, he enters into the secrets of God treasured in the holy Scripture.

CHAPTER V.

The Parson's Accessory Knowledges

THE Country Parson hath read the Fathers also, and the Schoolmen, and the later Writers, or a good proportion of all, out of all which he hath compiled a book, and body of Divinity, which is the storehouse of his Sermons, and which he preacheth all his Life; but diversely clothed, illustrated, and enlarged. For though the world is full of such composures, yet every man's own is fittest, readiest, and most savory to him. Besides, this being to be done in his younger and preparatory times, it is an honest joy ever after to look upon his well-spent hours. This Body he made by way of expounding the Church Catechism, to which all divinity may easily be reduced. For it being indifferent in itself to choose any Method, that is best to be chosen, of which there is likeliest to be most use. Now Catechizing being a work of singular, and admirable benefit to the Church of God, and a thing required under Canonical obedience,[16] the expounding of our Catechism must needs be the most useful form. Yet hath the Parson, besides this laborious work, a slighter form of Catechizing, fitter

---

14. *a Commerce.* Interaction or dealing.
15. *Comment.* Commentary.
16. *Catechizing . . . required under Canonical obedience.* Hutchinson notes this practice is specified in *Canons Ecclesiastical*, no. 59, of 1604.

for country people; according as his audience is, so he useth one, or other; or sometimes both, if his audience be intermixed. He greatly esteems also of cases of conscience, wherein he is much versed. And indeed, herein is the greatest ability of a Parson to lead his people exactly in the ways of Truth, so that they neither decline to the right hand, nor to the left. Neither let any think this is a slight thing. For every one hath not digested, when it is a sin to take something for money lent, or when not; when it is a fault to discover another's fault, or when not; *when the affections of the soul in desiring and procuring increase of means, or honor, be a sin of covetousness or ambition, and when not; when the appetites of the body in eating, drinking, sleep, and the pleasure that comes with sleep, be sins of gluttony, drunkenness, sloth, lust, and when not,* and so in many circumstances of actions. Now if a shepherd know not which grass will bane,[17] or which not, how is he fit to be a shepherd? Wherefore the Parson hath thoroughly canvassed all the particulars of human actions, at least all those which he observeth are most incident to his Parish.

CHAPTER VI.

The Parson Praying

THE Country Parson, when he is to read divine services, composeth himself to all possible reverence; lifting up his heart and hands, and eyes, and using all other gestures which may express a hearty, and unfeigned devotion. This he doth, first, as being truly touched and amazed[18] with the Majesty of God, before whom he then presents himself; yet not as himself alone, but as presenting with himself the whole Congregation, whose sins he then bears, and brings with his own to the heavenly altar to be bathed, and washed in the sacred Laver[19] of Christ's blood. Secondly, as this is the true reason of his inward fear, so he is content to express this outwardly to the utmost of his power; that being first affected himself, he may affect also his people, knowing that no Sermon moves them so much to a reverence, which they forget again, when they come to pray, as a devout behavior in the very act of praying. Accordingly his voice is humble, his words

---

17. *bane.* Poison.
18. *amazed.* Lost in wonder or astonishment.
19. *Laver.* A vessel or basin for washing.

treatable,[20] and slow; yet not so slow neither, as to let the fervency of the supplicant hang and die between speaking, but with a grave liveliness, between fear and zeal, pausing yet pressing, he performs his duty. Besides his example, he having often instructed his people how to carry themselves in divine service, exacts of them all possible reverence, by no means enduring either talking, or sleeping, or gazing, or leaning, or half-kneeling, or any undutiful behavior in them, but causing them, when they sit, or stand, or kneel, to do all in a straight, and steady posture, as attending to what is done in the Church, and every one, man, and child, answering aloud both Amen, and all other answers, which are on the Clerk's and people's part to answer; which answers also are to be done not in a huddling, or slubbering fashion, gaping, or scratching the head, or spitting even in the midst of their answer, but gently and pausably, thinking what they say; so that while they answer, *As it was in the beginning*, &c.[21] they meditate as they speak, that God hath ever had his people, that have glorified him as well as now, and that he shall have so forever. And the like in other answers. This is that which the Apostle calls a reasonable service (*Rom.* 12:[1]), when we speak not as Parrots, without reason, or offer up such sacrifices as they did of old, which was of beasts devoid of reason; but when we use our reason, and apply our powers to the service of him, that gives them. If there be any of the gentry or nobility of the Parish, who sometimes make it a piece of state[22] not to come at the beginning of service with their poor neighbors, but at mid-prayers, both to their own loss, and of theirs also who gaze upon them when they come in, and neglect the present service of God, he by no means suffers it, but after divers gentle admonitions, if they persevere, he causes them to be presented:[23] or if the poor Churchwardens be affrighted with their greatness, notwithstanding his instruction that they ought not to be so, but even to let the world sink, so they do their duty; he presents them himself, only protesting

---

20. *treatable.* Deliberate, distinct.

21. *As it was in the beginning.* In full, "Glory be to the Father, and to the Son, and to the Holy Ghost. As it was in the beginning, is now, and ever shall be: world without end. Amen." Ending prescribed for Psalms and Canticles used in Morning and Evening Prayer in BCP.

22. *piece of state.* Habit, revealing prestige of rank.

23. *to be presented.* Hutchinson notes, "Canon 111 orders the churchwardens to present the names of any disturbers of divine service at the next visitation of the bishop or archedeacon, but 'because it often cometh to pass that the Churchwardens . . . do forbear to discharge their duties therein, either through fear of their superiors, or through negligence' (Canon 113), the minister may himself present."

to them, that not any ill will draws him to it, but the debt and obligation of his calling, being to obey God rather than men.

CHAPTER VII.

The Parson Preaching

THE Country Parson preacheth constantly, the pulpit is his joy and his throne: if he at any time intermit,[24] it is either for want of health, or against some great Festival, that he may the better celebrate it, or for the variety of the hearers, that he may be heard at his return more attentively. When he intermits, he is ever very well supplied by some able man who treads in his steps, and will not throw down what he hath built; whom also he entreats to press some point, that he himself hath often urged with no great success, that so in the mouth of two or three witnesses the truth may be more established. When he preacheth, he procures attention by all possible art, both by earnestness of speech, it being natural to men to think, that where is much earnestness, there is somewhat[25] worth hearing; and by a diligent, and busy cast of his eye on his auditors, with letting them know, that he observes who marks, and who not; and with particularizing of his speech now to the younger sort, then to the elder, now to the poor, and now to the rich. This is for you, and This is for you; for particulars ever touch, and awake more than generals. Herein also he serves himself of[26] the judgments of God, as of those of ancient times, so especially of the late ones; and those most, which are nearest to his Parish; for people are very attentive at such discourses, and think it behooves them to be so, when God is so near them, and even over their heads. Sometimes he tells them stories, and sayings of others, according as his text invites him; for them also men heed, and remember better than exhortations; which though earnest, yet often die with the Sermon, especially with Country people; which are thick, and heavy, and hard to raise to a point of Zeal, and fervency, and need a mountain of fire to kindle them; but stories and sayings they will well remember. He often tells them, that Sermons are dangerous things, that none goes out of

---

24. *intermit.* Discontinue for a time, suspend practice.
25. *somewhat.* Something.
26. *he serves himself of.* Makes use of, avails himself of.

Church as he came in, but either better, or worse; that none is careless before his Judge, and that the word of God shall judge us. By these and other means the Parson procures attention; but the character of his Sermon is Holiness; he is not witty, or learned, or eloquent, but Holy. A Character, that *Hermogenes*[27] never dream'd of, and therefore he could give no precepts thereof. But it is gained first, by choosing texts of Devotion, not Controversy, moving and ravishing texts, whereof the Scriptures are full. Secondly, by dipping, and seasoning all our words and sentences in our hearts, before they come into our mouths, truly affecting, and cordially expressing all that we say; so that the auditors may plainly perceive that every word is heart-deep. Thirdly, by turning often, and making many Apostrophes to God, as, Oh Lord bless my people, and teach them this point; or, Oh my Master, on whose errand I come, let me hold my peace, and do thou speak thyself; for thou art Love, and when thou teachest, all are Scholars. Some such irradiations scatteringly in the Sermon, carry great holiness in them. The Prophets are admirable in this. So *Isaiah* 64:[1]: *Oh that thou would'st rent the Heavens, that thou would'st come down,* &c. And *Jeremy,*[28] Chapter 10:[23], after he had complained of the desolation of *Israel,* turns to God suddenly, *Oh Lord, I know that the way of man is not in himself,* &c. Fourthly, by frequent wishes of the people's good, and joying therein, though he himself were with Saint *Paul* even sacrificed upon the service of their faith. For there is no greater sign of holiness, than the procuring, and rejoicing in another's good. And herein Saint *Paul* excelled in all his Epistles. How did he put the Romans in all his prayers? (*Rom.* 1:9). And ceased not to give thanks for the *Ephesians* (*Eph.* 1:16). And for the Corinthians ([*1 Corinthians*], chap. 1:4). And for the *Philippians* made request with joy (chap. 1:4). And is in contention for them whether to live, or die; be with them, or Christ, *verse* 23, which, setting aside his care of his Flock, were a madness to doubt of. What an admirable Epistle is the second to the *Corinthians?* how full of affections? he joys, and he is sorry, he grieves, and he glories, never was there such care of a flock expressed, save in the great shepherd of the fold, who first shed tears over *Jerusalem,* and afterwards blood. Therefore this care may be learn'd there, and then woven into Sermons, which will make them appear exceeding reverend, and holy. Lastly, by an often urging of the

---

27. *Hermogenes.* Rhetorician of Tarsus (2nd century AD); author of rhetorical textbook that spells out seven qualities, or characters, of style.

28. *Jeremy.* Jeremiah.

presence, and majesty of God, by these, or such like speeches. Oh, let us all take heed what we do, God sees us, he sees whether I speak as I ought, or you hear as you ought, he sees hearts, as we see faces: he is among us; for if we be here, he must be here, since we are here by him, and without him could not be here. Then turning the discourse to his Majesty, And he is a great God, and terrible, as great in mercy, so great in judgment: There are but two devouring elements, fire, and water, he hath both in him; *His voice is as the sound of many waters* (*Rev.* 1:[15]). And he himself *is a consuming fire* (*Heb.* 12:[29]). Such discourses show very Holy. The Parson's Method in handling of a text consists of two parts; first, a plain and evident declaration of the meaning of the text; and secondly, some choice Observations drawn out of the whole text, as it lies entire, and unbroken in the Scripture itself. This he thinks natural, and sweet, and grave. Whereas the other way of crumbling a text[29] into small parts, as, the Person speaking, or spoken to, the subject, and object, and the like, hath neither in it sweetness, nor gravity, nor variety, since the words apart are not Scripture, but a dictionary, and may be considered alike in all the Scripture. The Parson exceeds not an hour in preaching, because all ages have thought that a competency, and he that profits not in that time, will less afterwards, the same affection which made him not profit before, making him then weary, and so he grows from not relishing, to loathing.

CHAPTER VIII.

The Parson on Sundays

THE Country Parson, as soon as he awakes on Sunday morning, presently falls to work, and seems to himself so as a Marketman is, when the Market day comes, or a shopkeeper, when customers use to come in. His thoughts are full of making the best of the day, and contriving it to his best gains. To this end, besides his ordinary prayers, he makes a peculiar one for a blessing on the exercises of the day, That nothing befall him unworthy of that Majesty before which he is to present himself, but that all may be done with reverence to his glory, and with edification to his flock, humbly beseeching his Master, that how or whenever he punish him, it be not in his Ministry:

---

29. *crumbling a text.* Reference to Puritan style of homiletic exegesis.

then he turns to request for his people, that the Lord would be pleased to sanctify them all, that they may come with holy hearts, and awful[30] minds into the Congregation, and that the good God would pardon all those, who come with less-prepared hearts than they ought. This done, he sets himself to the Consideration of the duties of the day, and if there be any extraordinary addition to the customary exercises, either from the time of the year, or from the State, or from God by a child born, or dead, or any other accident, he contrives how and in what manner to induce[31] it to the best advantage. Afterwards when the hour calls, with his family attending him, he goes to Church, at his first entrance *humbly adoring, and worshipping the invisible majesty, and presence of Almighty God,* and blessing the people either openly, or to himself. Then having read divine Service twice fully, and preached in the morning, and catechized in the afternoon, he thinks he hath in some measure, according to poor, and frail man, discharged the public duties of the Congregation.[32] The rest of the day he spends either in reconciling neighbors that are at variance, or in visiting the sick, or in exhortations to some of his flock by themselves, whom his Sermons cannot, or do not reach. And every one is more awaked, when we come, and say *Thou art the man.*[33] This way he finds exceeding useful, and winning; and these exhortations he calls his privy purse, even as Princes have theirs, besides their public disbursements. At night he thinks it a very fit time, both suitable to the joy of the day, and without hindrance to public duties, either to entertain some of his neighbors, or to be entertained of them, where he takes occasion to discourse *of such things as are both profitable, and pleasant, and to raise up their minds to apprehend God's good blessing to our Church, and State; that order is kept in the one, and peace in the other, without disturbance, or interruption of public divine offices.* As he opened the day with prayer, so he closeth it, humbly beseeching the Almighty to pardon and accept our poor services, and to improve them, that we may grow therein, and that our feet may be like hinds' feet[34] ever climbing up higher, and higher unto him.

---

30. *awful.* Filled with awe.
31. *induce.* Bring in by way of an illustration.
32. For a discussion of Anglican worship, see Booty, *Elizabethan* PB, pp. 372–82.
33. 2 Sam. 12:7.
34. *like hinds' feet.* See Ps. 18:33.

GEORGE HERBERT

CHAPTER IX.

The Parson's State of Life

THE Country Parson considering that virginity is a higher state than Matrimony, and that the Ministry requires the best and highest things, is rather unmarried, than married. But yet as the temper of his body may be, or as the temper of his Parish may be, where he may have occasion to converse with women, and that among suspicious men, *and other like circumstances considered,* he is rather married than unmarried. Let him communicate the thing often by prayer unto God, and as his grace shall direct him, so let him proceed. If he be unmarried, and keep house, he hath not a woman in his house, but finds opportunities of having his meat dress'd and other services done by men-servants at home, and his linen washed abroad. If he be unmarried, and sojourn, he never talks with any woman alone, but in the audience of others, and that seldom, and then also in a serious manner, never jestingly or sportfully. *He is very circumspect in all companies, both of his behavior, speech, and very looks, knowing himself to be both suspected, and envied. If he stand steadfast in his heart, having no necessity, but hath power over his own will, and hath so decreed in his heart, that he will keep himself a virgin, he spends his days in fasting and prayer, and blesseth God for the gift of continency, knowing that it can no way be preserved, but only by those means, by which at first it was obtained. He therefore thinks it not enough for him to observe the fasting days of the Church, and the daily prayers enjoined him by authority, which he observeth out of humble conformity, and obedience; but adds to them, out of choice and devotion, some other days for fasting, and hours for prayers; and by these he keeps his body tame, serviceable, and healthful; and his soul fervent, active, young, and lusty[35] as an eagle. He often readeth the Lives of the Primitive Monks, Hermits, and Virgins, and wond'reth not so much at their patient suffering, and cheerful dying under persecuting Emperors (though that indeed be very admirable) as at their daily temperance, abstinence, watchings, and constant prayers, and mortifications in the times of peace and prosperity. To put on the profound humility, and the exact temperance of our Lord Jesus, with other exemplary virtues of that sort, and to keep them on in the sunshine, and noon of prosperity, he findeth to be as necessary, and as difficult at least, as to be clothed with perfect patience, and Christian fortitude in the cold midnight storms of persecution and adversity.*

---

35. *lusty.* Full of healthy vigor.

THE COUNTRY PARSON

He keepeth his watch and ward, night and day against the proper and peculiar temptations of his state of Life, which are principally these two, Spiritual pride, and Impurity of heart: against these ghostly enemies he girdeth up his loins, keeps the imagination from roving, puts on the whole Armor of God, and by the virtue of the shield of faith,[36] *he is not afraid of the pestilence that walketh in darkness, [carnal impurity,] nor of the sickness that destroyeth at noonday,*[37] *[Ghostly pride and self-conceit]. Other temptations he hath, which like mortal enemies, may sometimes disquiet him likewise; for the human soul being bounded, and kept in in her sensitive faculty, will run out more or less in her intellectual. Original concupiscence is such an active thing, by reason of continual inward, or outward temptations, that it is ever attempting, or doing one mischief or other. Ambition, or untimely desire of promotion to an higher state, or place, under color of accommodation, or necessary provision, is a common temptation to men of any eminency, especially being single men. Curiosity in prying into high speculative and unprofitable questions, is another great stumbling block to the holiness of Scholars. These and many other spiritual wickednesses in high places doth the Parson fear, or experiment,*[38] *or both; and that much more being single, than if he were married; for then commonly the stream of temptations is turned another way, into Covetousness, Love of pleasure, or ease, or the like. If the Parson be unmarried, and means to continue so, he doth at least, as much as hath been said.* If he be married, the choice of his wife was made rather by his ear, than by his eye; his judgment, not his affection found out a fit wife for him, whose humble, and liberal disposition he preferred before beauty, riches, or honor. *He knew that (the good instrument of God to bring women to heaven) a wise and loving husband could out of humility, produce any special grace of faith, patience, meekness, love, obedience, &c. and out of liberality, make her fruitful in all good works.* As he is just in all things, so is he to his wife also, counting nothing so much his own, as that he may be unjust unto it. Therefore he gives her respect both afore[39] her servants, and others, and half at least of the government of the house, reserving so much of the affairs, as serve for a diversion for him; yet never so giving over the reins, but that he sometimes looks how things go, demanding an account, but not by the way of an account. And this must be done the oftener, or the seldomer, according as he is satisfied of his Wife's discretion.

---

36. Eph. 6:11–18.
37. Ps. 91:6.
38. *experiment.* Have experience with.
39. *afore.* Before.

GEORGE HERBERT

CHAPTER X.

The Parson in his House

THE Parson is very exact in the governing of his house, making it a copy and model for his Parish. He knows the temper, and pulse of every person in his house, and accordingly either meets with their vices, or advanceth their virtues. His wife is either religious, or night and day he is winning her to it. Instead of the qualities of the world, he requires only three of her; first, a training up of her children and maids in the fear of God, with prayers, and catechizing, and all religious duties. Secondly, a curing, and healing of all wounds and sores with her own hands; which skill either she brought with her, or he takes care she shall learn it of some religious neighbor. Thirdly, a providing for her family in such sort, as that neither they want a competent sustentation, nor her husband be brought in debt. His children he first makes Christians, and then Commonwealth's men; the one he owes to his heavenly Country, the other to his earthly, having no title to either, except he do good to both. Therefore having seasoned them with all Piety, not only of words in praying, and reading; but in actions, in visiting other sick children, and tending their wounds, and sending his charity by them to the poor, and sometimes giving them a little money to do it of themselves, that they get a delight in it, and enter favor with God, who weighs even children's actions (1 *Kings* 14:12, 13). He afterwards turns his care to fit all their dispositions with some calling, not sparing the eldest, but giving him the prerogative of his Father's profession, which happily[40] for his other children he is not able to do. Yet in binding them prentices (in case he think fit to do so) he takes care not to put them into vain trades, and unbefitting the reverence of their Father's calling, such as are taverns for men, and lace-making for women; because those trades, for the most part, serve but the vices and vanities of the world, which he is to deny, and not augment. However, he resolves with himself never to omit any present good deed of charity, in consideration of providing a stock for his children; but assures himself, that money thus lent to God, is placed surer for his children's advantage, than if it were given to the *Chamber of*

---

40. *happily.* Haply; by chance or accident; perhaps.

London.[41] Good deeds, and good breeding, are his two great stocks for his children; if God give any thing above those, and not spent in them, he blesseth God, and lays it out as he sees cause. His servants are all religious, and were it not his duty to have them so, it were his profit, for none are so well served, as by religious servants, both because they do best, and because what they do, is blessed, and prospers. After religion, he teacheth them, that three things make a complete servant, Truth, and Diligence, and Neatness, or Cleanliness. Those that can read, are allowed times for it, and those that cannot, are taught; for all in his house are either teachers or learners, or both, so that his family is a School of Religion, and they all account, that to teach the ignorant is the greatest alms. Even the walls are not idle,[42] but something is written, or painted there, which may excite the reader to a thought of piety; especially the 101st *Psalm*, which is expressed in a fair table, as being the rule of a family. And when they go abroad, his wife among her neighbors is the beginner of good discourses, his children among children, his servants among other servants; so that as in the house of those that are skill'd in Music, all are Musicians; so in the house of a Preacher, all are preachers. He suffers not a lie or equivocation by any means in his house, but counts it the art, and secret of governing to preserve a directness, and open plainness in all things; so that all his house knows, that there is no help for a fault done, but confession. He *himself*, or his *Wife*, takes account of Sermons, and how everyone profits, comparing this year with the last: and besides the common prayers of the family, he straightly requires of all to pray by themselves before they sleep at night, and stir out in the morning, and knows what prayers they say, and till they have learned them, makes them kneel by him; esteeming that this private praying is a more voluntary act in them, than when they are called to others' prayers, and that, which when they leave the family, they carry with them. He keeps his servants between love, and fear, according as he finds them; but generally he distributes it thus, To his Children he shows more love than terror, to his servants more terror than love; but an old good servant boards a child.[43] The furniture of his house is very plain, but clean, whole, and

---

41. *Chamber of London.* The City Chamberlain's office or treasury; a secure place for money.
42. *Even the walls are not idle.* The walls of the house at Little Gidding were decorated with texts and mottos.
43. *boards a child.* Borders on, approaches the status of a member of the family.

sweet, as sweet as his garden can make; for he hath no money for such things, charity being his only perfume, which deserves cost when he can spare it. His fare is plain, and common, but wholesome, what he hath, is little, but very good; it consisteth most of mutton, beef, and veal, if he adds anything for a great day, or a stranger, his garden or orchard supplies it, or his barn, and back-side:[44] he goes no further for any entertainment, lest he go into the world, esteeming it absurd, that he should exceed, who teacheth others temperance. But those which his home produceth, he refuseth not, as coming cheap, and easy, and arising from the improvement of things, which otherwise would be lost. Wherein he admires and imitates the wonderful providence and thrift of the great householder of the world: for there being two things, which as they are, are unuseful to man, the one for smallness, as crumbs, and scattered corn, and the like; the other for the foulness, as wash, and dirt, and things thereinto fallen; God hath provided Creatures for both; for the first, Poultry; for the second, swine. These save man the labor, and doing that which either he could not do, or was not fit for him to do, by taking both sorts of food into them, do as it were dress and prepare both for man in themselves, by growing themselves fit for his table. The Parson in his house observes fasting days; and particularly, as Sunday is his day of joy, so Friday his day of Humiliation, which he celebrates not only with abstinence of diet, but also of company, recreation, and all outward contentments; and besides, with confession of sins, and all acts of Mortification. Now fasting days contain a treble obligation; first, of eating less that day, than on other days; secondly, of eating no pleasing, or overnourishing things, as the Israelites did eat sour herbs:[45] Thirdly, of eating no flesh, which is but the determination of the second rule by Authority to this particular. The two former obligations are much more essential to a true fast, than the third and last; and fasting days were fully performed by keeping of the two former, had not Authority interposed:[46] so that to eat little, and that unpleasant, is the natural rule of fasting, although it be flesh. For since fasting in Scripture language is an afflicting of our souls, if a piece of dry flesh at my table be more unpleasant to me, than some fish there, certainly to eat the flesh, and not the fish, is to keep the fasting

---

44. *back-side*. Back-garden.
45. Exod. 12:8.
46. Rules for fasting were specified in Acts of Parliament in 1548 and 1552, which were reenacted in the reign of James I.

day naturally. And it is observable, that the prohibiting of flesh came from hot Countries, where both flesh alone, and much more with wine, is apt to nourish more than in cold regions, and where flesh may be much better spared, and with more safety than elsewhere, where both the people and the drink being cold and phlegmatic, the eating of flesh is an antidote to both. For it is certain, that a weak stomach being prepossessed with flesh, shall much better brook and bear a draft of beer, than if it had taken before either fish, or roots, or such things; which will discover itself by spitting, and rheum, or phlegm. To conclude, the Parson, if he be in full health, keeps the three obligations, eating fish, or roots, and that for quantity little, for quality unpleasant. If his body be weak and obstructed, as most Students are, he cannot keep the last obligation, nor suffer others in his house that are so, to keep it; but only the two former, which also in diseases of exinanition[47] (as consumptions) must be broken: For meat was made for man, not man for meat. To all this may be added, not for emboldening the unruly, but for the comfort of the weak, that not only sickness breaks these obligations of fasting, but sickliness also. For it is as unnatural to do anything, that leads me to a sickness, to which I am inclined, as not to get out of that sickness, when I am in it, by any diet. One thing is evident, that an English body, and a Student's body, are two great obstructed vessels, and there is nothing that is food, and not physic, which doth less obstruct, than flesh moderately taken; as being immoderately taken, it is exceeding obstructive. And obstructions are the cause of most diseases.

CHAPTER XI.

The Parson's Courtesy

THE Country Parson owing a debt of Charity to the poor, and of Courtesy to his other parishioners, he so distinguisheth, that he keeps his money for the poor, and his table for those that are above Alms. Not but that the poor are welcome also to his table, whom he sometimes purposely takes home with him, setting them close by him, and carving for them, both for his own humility, and their comfort, who are much cheered with such friendlinesses. But since both is

---

47. *diseases of exinanition*. Afflictions involving emptying out the victim.

to be done, the better sort invited, and meaner relieved, he chooseth rather to give the poor money, which they can better employ to their own advantage, and suitably to their needs, than so much given in meat at dinner. Having then invited some of his Parish, he taketh his times to do the like to the rest; so that in the compass of the year, he hath them all with him, because country people are very observant of such things, and will not be persuaded, but being not invited, they are hated. Which persuasion the Parson by all means avoids, knowing that where there are such conceits, there is no room for his doctrine to enter. Yet doth he oftenest invite those, whom he sees take best courses, that so both they may be encouraged to persevere, and others spurred to do well, that they may enjoy the like courtesy. For though he desire, that all should live well, and virtuously, not for any reward of his, but for virtue's sake; yet that will not be so: and therefore as God, although we should love him only for his own sake, yet out of his infinite pity hath set forth heaven for a reward to draw men to Piety, and is content, if at least so, they will become good. So the Country Parson, who is a diligent observer, and tracker of God's ways, sets up as many encouragements to goodness as he can, both in honor, and profit, and fame; that he may, if not the best way, yet any way, make his Parish good.

Chapter XII.

The Parson's Charity

THE Country Parson is full of Charity; it is his predominant element. For many and wonderful things are spoken of thee, thou great Virtue. To Charity is given the covering of sins (1 *Pet.* 4:8), and the forgiveness of sins (*Matt.* 6:14; *Luke* 7:47), the fulfilling of the Law (*Rom.* 13:10), the life of faith (*James* 2:26), the blessings of this life (*Prov.* 22:9; *Ps.* 41:2), and the reward of the next (*Matt.* 25:35). In brief, it is the body of Religion (*John* 13:35), and the top of Christian virtues (1 *Cor.* 13:[13]). Wherefore all his works relish of Charity. When he riseth in the morning, he bethinketh himself what good deeds he can do that day, and presently doth them; counting that day lost, wherein he hath not exercised his Charity. He first considers his own Parish, and takes care, that there be not a beggar, or idle person in his Parish, but that all be in a competent way of getting their living. This he effects either by bounty, or persuasion, or by authority, making use of that excellent statute,[48] which binds all Parishes to maintain their own. If his Parish be rich, he exacts this of them; if poor, and he able, he easeth them therein. But he gives no set pension to any; for this in time will lose the name and effect of Charity with the poor people, though not with God: for then they will reckon upon it, as on a debt; and if it be taken away, though justly, they will murmur, and repine[49] as much, as he that is disseized[50] of his own inheritance. But the Parson having a double aim, and making a hook of his Charity, causeth them still to depend on him; and so by continual, and fresh bounties, unexpected to them, but resolved to himself, he wins them to praise God more, to live more religiously, and to take more pains in their vocation, as not knowing when they shall be relieved; which otherwise they would reckon upon, and turn to idleness. Besides this general provision, he hath other times of opening his hand; as at great Festivals, and Communions; not suffering any that day that he receives, to want a good meal suiting to the joy of the occasion. But specially, at hard times, and dearths, he even parts his Living, and life among them, giving some corn outright, and selling other at under rates; and when his own stock serves not, working those that are able to the same charity, still pressing it in the pulpit, and out of the pulpit, and never leaving them, till he obtain his desire. Yet in all his Charity, he distinguisheth, giving them most, who live best, and take most pains, and are most charged:[51] So is his charity in effect a Sermon. After the consideration of his Parish, he enlargeth himself, if he be able, to the neighborhood; for that also is some kind of obligation; so doth he also to those at his door, whom God puts in his way, and makes his neighbors. But these he helps not without some testimony, except the evidence of the misery bring testimony with it. For though these testimonies also may be falsified, yet considering that the Law allows these in case they be true, but allows by no means to give without testimony, as he obeys Authority in the one, so that being once satisfied, he allows his Charity some blindness in the other; especially, since of the two commands, we are more enjoined to be charitable, than wise. But evident miseries have a natural privilege, and exemption from all law. Whenever he gives

---

48. *that excellent statute*. The Poor Law Act of 1601, which required churchwardens and elected householders to relieve the poverty of those unable to work.

49. *repine*. Begrudge, be discontented.

50. *disseized*. Deprived.

51. *charged*. Burdened with debts or expenses.

anything, and sees them labor in thanking of him, he exacts of them to let him alone, and say rather, God be praised, God be glorified; that so the thanks may go the right way, and thither only, where they are only due. So doth he also before giving make them say their Prayers first, or the Creed, and ten Commandments, and as he finds them perfect, rewards them the more. For other givings are lay, and secular, but this is to give like a Priest.

Chapter XIII.

The Parson's Church

THE Country Parson hath a special care of his Church, that all things there be decent,[52] and befitting his Name by which it is called. Therefore first he takes order, that all things be in good repair; as walls plastered, windows glazed, floor paved, seats whole, firm, and uniform, especially that the Pulpit, and Desk, and Communion Table, and Font be as they ought, for those great duties that are performed in them. Secondly, that the Church be swept, and kept clean without dust, or Cobwebs, and at great festivals strawed, and stuck with boughs, and perfumed with incense. Thirdly, That there be fit, and proper texts of Scripture everywhere painted, and that all the painting be grave, and reverend, not with light colors, or foolish antics.[53] Fourthly, That all the books appointed by Authority be there, and those not torn, or fouled, but whole and clean, and well bound; and that there be a fitting, and sightly Communion Cloth *of fine linen, with an handsome, and seemly Carpet of good and costly Stuff, or Cloth, and all kept sweet and clean, in a strong and decent chest, with a Chalice, and Cover, and a Stoop, or Flagon; and a Basin for Alms and offerings; besides which, he hath a Poor-man's Box conveniently seated, to receive the charity of well-minded people, and to lay up treasure for the sick and needy.* And all this he doth, not as out of necessity, or as putting a holiness in the things, but as desiring to keep the middle way between superstition, and slovenliness, and as following the Apostle's two great and admirable Rules in

---

52. *all things there be decent.* Hutchinson notes that most of the details Herbert prescribes for furnishing a Church are drawn from the Book of Common Prayer, the Canons of 1604, or the Visitation Articles of contemporary bishops.

53. *foolish antics.* Grotesque representations of animals or flowers.

things of this nature: The first whereof is, *Let all things be done decently, and in order:* The second, *Let all things be done to edification* (1 *Cor.* 14:[26, 40]). For these two rules comprise and include the double object of our duty, God, and our neighbor; the first being for the honor of God; the second for the benefit of our neighbor. So that they excellently score out the way, and fully, and exactly contain, even in external and indifferent things, what course is to be taken; and put them to great shame, who deny the Scripture to be perfect.

CHAPTER XIV.

The Parson in Circuit

THE Country Parson upon the afternoons in the weekdays, takes occasion sometimes to visit in person, now one quarter of his Parish, now another. For there he shall find his flock most naturally as they are, wallowing[54] in the midst of their affairs: whereas on Sundays it is easy for them to compose themselves to order, which they put on as their holy-day clothes, and come to Church in frame,[55] but commonly the next day put off both. When he comes to any house, first he blesseth it, and then as he finds the persons of the house employed, so he forms his discourse. Those that he finds religiously employed, he both commends them much, and furthers them when he is gone, in their employment; as if he finds them reading, he furnisheth them with good books; if curing poor people, he supplies them with Receipts, and instructs them further in that skill, showing them how acceptable such works are to God, and wishing them ever to do the Cures with their own hands, and not to put them over to servants. Those that he finds busy in the works of their calling, he commendeth them also: for it is a good and just thing for everyone to do their own business. But then he admonisheth them of two things; first, that they dive not too deep into worldly affairs, plunging themselves over head and ears into carking,[56] and caring; but that they so labor, as neither to labor anxiously, nor distrustfully, nor profanely. Then they labor anxiously, when they overdo it, to the loss of their quiet, and health: then distrustfully, when they doubt God's providence, thinking that their

---

54. *wallowing.* Engaged in, without the present negative connotations.
55. *in frame.* In appropriate dress and demeanor.
56. *carking.* Being full of anxious thoughts, burdened with care.

own labor is the cause of their thriving, as if it were in their own hands to thrive, or not to thrive. *Then they labor profanely, when they set themselves to work like brute beasts, never raising their thoughts to God, nor sanctifying their labor with daily prayer; when on the Lord's day they do unnecessary servile work, or in time of divine service on other holy days, except in the cases of extreme poverty, and in the seasons of Seed-time, and Harvest.* Secondly, he adviseth them so to labor for wealth and maintenance, as that they make not that the end of their labor, but that they may have wherewithal to serve God the better, and to do good deeds. After these discourses, if they be poor and needy, whom he thus finds laboring, he gives them somewhat; and opens not only his mouth, but his purse to their relief, that so they go on more cheerfully in their vocation, and himself be ever the more welcome to them. Those that the Parson finds idle, or ill-employed, he chides not at first, for that were neither civil, nor profitable; but always in the close, before he departs from them: yet in this he distinguisheth; for if he be a plain countryman, he reproves him plainly; for they are not sensible of fineness: if they be of higher quality, they commonly are quick, and sensible, and very tender of reproof: and therefore he lays his discourse so, that he comes to the point very leisurely, and oftentimes, as *Nathan* did,[57] in the person of another, making them to reprove themselves. However, one way or other, he ever reproves them, that he may keep himself pure, and not be entangled in others' sins. Neither in this doth he forbear, though there be company by: for as when the offense is particular, and against me, I am to follow our Savior's rule, and to take my brother aside, and reprove him;[58] so when the offense is public, and against God, I am then to follow the Apostle's rule (1 *Tim.* 5:20), and to *rebuke openly* that which is done openly. Besides these occasional discourses, the Parson questions what order is kept in the house, as about prayers morning, and evening on their knees, reading of Scripture, catechizing, singing of Psalms at their work, and on holy days; who can read, who not; and sometimes he hears the children read himself, and blesseth them, encouraging also the servants to learn to read, and offering to have them taught on holy days by his servants. If the Parson were ashamed of particularizing in these things, he were not fit to be a Parson: but he holds the Rule, that Nothing is little in God's service: If it once have the honor of that Name, it grows great instantly. Wherefore neither

---

57. *Nathan.* See 2 Sam. 12:1–16 for an account of his technique for pointing out indirectly David's wrongdoing.

disdaineth he to enter into the poorest Cottage, though he even creep into it, and though it smell never so loathsomely. For both God is there also, and those for whom God died: and so much the rather doth he so, as his access to the poor is more comfortable,[59] than to the rich; and in regard of himself, it is more humiliation. These are the Parson's general aims in his Circuit; but with these he mingles other discourses for conversation sake, and to make his higher purposes slip the more easily.

CHAPTER XV.

The Parson Comforting

THE Country Parson, when any of his cure is sick, or afflicted with loss of friend, or estate, or any ways distressed, fails not to afford his best comforts, and rather goes to them, than sends for the afflicted, though they can, and otherwise ought to come to him. To this end he hath thoroughly digested all the points of consolation, as having continual use of them, such as are from God's general providence extended even to lilies;[60] from his particular, to his Church;[61] from his promises, from the examples of all Saints, that ever were; from Christ himself, perfecting our Redemption no other way, than by sorrow; from the Benefit of affliction, which softens, and works the stubborn heart of man; from the certainty both of deliverance, and reward, if we faint not; from the miserable comparison of the moment of griefs here with the weight of joys hereafter. *Besides this, in his visiting the sick, or otherwise afflicted, he followeth the Church's counsel,[62] namely, in persuading them to particular confession, laboring to make them understand the great good use of this ancient and pious ordinance, and how necessary it is in some cases: he also urgeth them to do some pious charitable works, as a necessary evidence and fruit of their faith, at that time especially: the participation of the holy Sacrament, how comfortable, and Sovereign a Medicine it is to all sin-sick souls; what strength, and joy, and peace it administers against all temptations, even to death itself, he plainly, and generally intimateth to the*

---

58. Allusion to Luke 17:3.
59. *comfortable.* Providing comfort.
60. Luke 12:27–28.
61. Matt. 28:20.
62. See The Order for the Visitation of the Sick in BCP; Booty, pp. 300–08.

disaffected,[63] *or sick person, that so the hunger and thirst after it may come rather from themselves, than from his persuasion.*

CHAPTER XVI.

The Parser a Father

THE Country Parson is not only a father to his flock, but also professeth himself thoroughly of the opinion, carrying it about with him as fully, as if he had begot his whole Parish. And of this he makes great use. For by this means, when any sins, he hateth him not as an officer, but pities him as a Father: and even in those wrongs which either in tithing, or otherwise are done to his own person, he considers the offender as a child, and forgives, so he may have any sign of amendment; so also when after many admonitions, any continue to be refractory, yet he gives him not over, but is long before he proceed to disinheriting, or perhaps never goes so far; knowing, that some are called at the eleventh hour, and therefore he still expects, and waits, lest he should determine God's hour of coming;[64] which as he cannot, touching the last day, so neither touching the intermediate days of Conversion.

CHAPTER XVII.

The Parson in Journey

THE Country Parson, when a just occasion calleth him out of his Parish (which he diligently, and strictly weigheth, his Parish being all his joy, and thought) leaveth not his Ministry behind him; but is himself wherever he is. Therefore those he meets on the way he blesseth audibly, and with those he overtakes or that overtake him, he begins good discourses, such as may edify, interposing sometimes some short, and honest refreshments, which may make his other discourses more welcome, and less tedious. And when he comes to his Inn, he refuseth not to join,[65] that he may enlarge the glory of

---

63. *disaffected.* Afflicted with disease.
64. Matt. 24:36.
65. *join.* I.e., join in.

God to the company he is in, by a due blessing of God for their safe arrival, and saying grace at meat, and at going to bed by giving the Host notice, that he will have prayers in the hall, wishing him to inform his guests thereof, that if any be willing to partake, they may resort thither. The like he doth in the morning, using pleasantly the outlandish proverb,[66] that *Prayers and Provender never hinder journey*. When he comes to any other house, where *his kindred, or other relations give him any authority over the Family*, if he be to stay for a time, he considers diligently the state thereof to Godward, and that in two points: First, what disorders there are either in Apparel, or Diet, or too open a Buttery,[67] or reading vain books, or swearing, or breeding up children to no Calling, but in idleness, or the like. Secondly, what means of Piety, whether daily prayers be used, Grace, reading of Scriptures, and other good books, how *Sundays, holy days, and fasting days* are kept. And accordingly, as he finds any defect in these, he first considers with himself, what kind of remedy fits the temper of the house best, and then he faithfully, and boldly applieth it; yet seasonably, and discreetly, by taking aside the Lord, or Lady; or *Master* and *Mistress* of the house, and showing them clearly, that they respect them most, who wish them best, and that not a desire to meddle with others' affairs, but the earnestness to do all the good he can, moves him to say thus and thus.

CHAPTER XVIII.

The Parson in Sentinel

THE Country Parson, wherever he is, keeps God's watch; that is, there is nothing spoken, or done in the Company where he is, but comes under his Test and censure:[68] If it be well spoken, or done, he takes occasion to commend, and enlarge it; if ill, he presently lays hold of it, lest the poison steal into some young and unwary spirits, and possess them even before they themselves heed it. But

---

66. *outlandish*. Unusual, curious, foreign. Herbert's fondness for proverbs is exhibited frequently in his various works and letters; he is credited by many scholars with compiling a collection of over 1,000 *Outlandish Proverbs*, first published in 1640, of which this is no. 277. See Hutchinson, *Works*, pp. 321–35.

67. *Buttery*. Room for storing strong drink and other provisions.

68. *censure*. Evaluation, without present negative connotation.

this he doth discreetly, with mollifying, and suppling[69] words; This was not so well said, as it might have been forborne;[70] We cannot allow this: or else if the thing will admit interpretation; Your meaning is not thus, but thus; or, So far indeed what you say is true, and well said; but this will not stand. This is called keeping God's watch, when the baits which the enemy lays in company, are discovered and avoided: This is to be on God's side, and be true to his party. Besides, if he perceive in company any discourse tending to ill, either by the wickedness or quarrelsomeness thereof, he either prevents it judiciously, or breaks it off seasonably by some diversion. Wherein a pleasantness of disposition is of great use, men being willing to sell the interest, and engagement of their discourses for no price sooner, than that of mirth; whether the nature of man, loving refreshment, gladly betakes itself, even to the loss of honor.

CHAPTER XIX.

The Parson in Reference

THE Country Parson is sincere and upright in all his relations. And first, he is just to his Country; as when he is set at[71] an armor, or horse, he borrows them not to serve the turn, nor provides slight, and unuseful, but such as are every way fitting to do his Country true and laudable service, when occasion requires. To do otherwise, is deceit; and therefore not for him, who is hearty, and true in all his ways, as being the servant of him, in whom there was no guile. Likewise in any other Country duty, he considers what is the end of any Command, and then he suits things faithfully according to that end. Secondly, he carries himself very respectively,[72] as to all the Fathers of the Church, so especially to his Diocesan, honoring him both in word, and behavior, and resorting unto him in any difficulty, either in his studies or in his Parish. He observes Visitations, and being there, makes due use of them, as of Clergy councils, for the benefit of the Diocese. And therefore before he comes, having observed some defects in

---

69. *suppling.* Making supple, intended figuratively, i.e., causing to become flexible, changeable.
70. *forborne.* Avoided.
71. *set at.* Assessed for military service.
72. *respectively.* Respectfully.

the Ministry, he then either in Sermon, if he preach, or at some other time of the day, propounds among his Brethren what were fitting to be done. Thirdly, he keeps good Correspondence with all the neighboring Pastors round about him, performing for them any Ministerial office, which is not to the prejudice of his own Parish. Likewise he welcomes to his house any Minister, how poor or mean soever, with as joyful a countenance, as if he were to entertain some great Lord. Fourthly, he fulfills the duty, and debt of neighborhood to all the Parishes which are near him. For the Apostle's rule (*Phil.* 4:[8]) being admirable, and large, that *we should do whatsoever things are honest, or just, or pure, or love-ly, or of good report, if there be any virtue, or any praise.* And Neighbor-hood[73] being ever reputed, even among the Heathen, as an obligation to do good, rather than to those that are further, where things are oth-erwise equal, therefore he satisfies this duty also. Especially, if God have sent any calamity either by fire, or famine, to any neighboring Parish, then he expects no Brief;[74] but taking his Parish together *the next Sunday*, or *holy day*, and exposing to them the uncertainty of hu-man affairs, none knowing whose turn may be next, and then when he hath affrighted them with this, exposing the obligation of Charity, and Neighborhood, he first gives himself liberally, and then incites them to give; making together a sum either to be sent, or, which were more comfortable, all together choosing some fit day to carry it themselves, and cheer the Afflicted. So, if any neighboring village be overburdened with poor, and his own less charged, he finds some way of relieving it, and reducing the Manna, and bread of Charity to some equality, repre-senting to his people, that the Blessing of God to them ought to make them the more charitable, and not the less, lest he cast their neighbors' poverty on them also.

---

73. *Neighborhood.* Neighborly feeling; condition of being neighbors.
74. *expects no Brief.* Does not wait for authorization to take up a collection, but acts quickly, out of charity.

81

Chapter XX.

The Parson in God's Stead

THE Country Parson is in God's stead to his Parish, and dischargeth God what he can of his promises. Wherefore there is nothing done either well or ill, whereof he is not the rewarder, or punisher. If he chance to find any reading in another's Bible, he provides him one of his own. If he find another giving a poor man a penny, he gives him a tester[75] for it, if the giver be fit to receive it; or if he be of a condition above such gifts, he sends him a good book, or easeth him in his Tithes, telling him when he hath forgotten it, This I do, because at such, and such a time you were charitable. This is in some sort a discharging of God; as concerning this life, who hath promised, that Godliness shall be gainful: but in the other God is his own immediate paymaster, rewarding all good deeds to their full proportion. *The Parson's punishing of sin and vice, is rather by withdrawing his bounty and courtesy from the parties offending, or by private, or public reproof, as the case requires, than by causing them to be presented, or otherwise complained of. And yet as the malice of the person, or heinousness of the crime may be, he is careful to see condign*[76] *punishment inflicted, and with truly godly zeal, without hatred to the person, hungereth and thirsteth after righteous punishment of unrighteousness. Thus both in rewarding virtue, and in punishing vice, the Parson endeavoreth to be in God's stead, knowing that Country people are drawn, or led by sense, more than by faith, by present rewards, or punishments, more than by future.*

Chapter XXI.

The Parson Catechizing

THE Country Parson values Catechizing highly: for there being three points of his duty, the one, to infuse a competent knowledge of salvation in every one of his Flock; the other, to multiply, and build up this knowledge, to a spiritual Temple; the third, to inflame this knowledge, to press, and drive it to practice, turning it to

---

75. *tester.* A half-shilling.
76. *condign.* Fitting, appropriate.

reformation of life, by pithy and lively exhortations; Catechizing is the first point, and but by Catechizing, the other cannot be attained. Besides, whereas in Sermons there is a kind of state, in Catechizing there is an humbleness very suitable to Christian regeneration, which exceedingly delights him as by way of exercise upon himself, and by way of preaching to himself, for the advancing of his own mortification. For in preaching to others, he forgets not himself, but is first a Sermon to himself, and then to others; growing with the growth of his Parish. He useth, and preferreth the ordinary Church Catechism, partly for obedience to Authority,[77] partly for uniformity sake, that the same common truths may be everywhere professed, especially since many remove from Parish to Parish, who like Christian Soldiers are to give the word,[78] and to satisfy the Congregation by their Catholic answers. He exacts of all the Doctrine of the Catechism; of the younger sort, the very words; of the elder, the substance. Those he Catechizeth publicly, these privately, giving age honor, according to the Apostle's rule (1 Tim. 5:1). He requires all to be present at Catechizing: First, for the authority of the work; Secondly, that Parents, and Masters, as they hear the answers prove, may when they come home, either commend or reprove, either reward or punish. Thirdly, that those of the elder sort, who are not well grounded, may then by an honorable way take occasion to be better instructed. Fourthly, that those who are well grown in the knowledge of Religion, may examine their grounds, renew their vows, and by occasion of both, enlarge their meditations. When once all have learned the words of the Catechism, he thinks it the most useful way that a Pastor can take, to go over the same, but in other words: for many say the Catechism by rote, as parrots, without ever piercing into the sense of it. In this course the order of the Catechism would be kept, but the rest varied: as thus, in the Creed: How came this world to be as it is? Was it made, or came it by chance? Who made it? Did you see God make it? Then are there some things to be believed that are not seen? Is this the nature of belief? Is not Christianity full of such things, as are not to be seen, but believed? You said, God made the world; Who is God? And so forward, requiring answers to all these, and helping and cherishing the Answerer, by making the Question very plain with comparisons, and making much even of a word of truth from him. This

---

77. *Authority.* Hutchinson notes Herbert's practice here as prescribed by directions in BCP, Canons 59 and 79, and special instructions from Archbishop Abbot in 1622.

78. *the word.* The password.

order being used to one, would be a little varied to another. And this is an admirable way of teaching, wherein the Catechized will at length find delight, and by which the Catechizer, if he once get the skill of it, will draw out of ignorant and silly[79] souls, even the dark and deep points of Religion. *Socrates* did thus in Philosophy, who held that the seeds of all truths lay in everybody, and accordingly by questions well-ordered he found Philosophy in silly Tradesmen. That position will not hold in Christianity, because it contains things above nature: but after that the Catechism is once learn'd, that which nature is towards Philosophy, the Catechism is towards Divinity. To this purpose, some dialogues in *Plato* were worth the reading, where the singular dexterity of *Socrates* in this kind may be observed, and imitated. Yet the skill consists but in these three points: First, an aim and mark of the whole discourse, whither to drive the Answerer, which the Questionist must have in his mind before any question be propounded, upon which and to which the questions are to be chained. Secondly, a most plain and easy framing the question, even containing in virtue[80] the answer also, especially to the more ignorant. Thirdly, when the answerer sticks, an illustrating the thing by something else, which he knows, making what he knows to serve him in that which he knows not: As, when the Parson once demanded after other questions about man's misery; since man is so miserable, what is to be done? And the answerer could not tell; He asked him again, what he would do, if he were in a ditch? This familiar illustration made the answer so plain, that he was even ashamed of his ignorance; for he could not but say, he would haste out of it as fast he could. Then he proceeded to ask, whether he could get out of the ditch alone, or whether he needed a helper, and who was that helper. This is the skill, and doubtless the Holy Scripture intends thus much, when it condescends to the naming of a plow, a hatchet, a bushel, leaven, boys piping and dancing; showing that things of ordinary use are not only to serve in the way of drudgery, but to be washed, and cleansed, and serve for lights even of Heavenly Truths. This is the Practice which the Parson so much commends to all his fellow laborers; the secret of whose good consists in this, that at Sermons, and Prayers, men may sleep or wander; but when one is asked a question, he must discover what he is. This practice exceeds even Sermons in teaching: but there being two things in Sermons, the one Informing,

---

79. *silly.* Innocent, rustic, unlearned.
80. *in virtue.* Virtually.

the other Inflaming; as Sermons come short of questions in the one, so they far exceed them in the other. For questions cannot inflame or ravish, that must be done by a set, and labored, and continued speech.

CHAPTER XXII.

The Parson in Sacraments

THE Country Parson being to administer the Sacraments, is at a stand with himself, how or what behavior to assume for so holy things. Especially at Communion times he is in a great confusion, as being not only to receive God, but to break, and administer him. Neither finds he any issue in this, but to throw himself down at the throne of grace, saying, Lord, thou knowest what thou didst, when thou appointedst it to be done thus; therefore do thou fulfill what thou didst appoint; for thou art not only the feast, but the way to it. At Baptism, being himself in white, he requires the presence of all, and Baptizeth not willingly, but on Sundays, or great days. He admits no vain or idle names, but such as are usual and accustomed. He says that prayer with great devotion, where God is thanked for calling us to the knowledge of his grace,[81] Baptism being a blessing, that the world hath not the like. He willingly and cheerfully crosseth the child, and thinketh the Ceremony not only innocent, but reverend. He instructeth the Godfathers, and Godmothers, that it is no complemental[82] or light thing to sustain that place, but a great honor, and no less burden, as being done both in the presence of God, and his Saints, and by way of undertaking for a Christian soul. He adviseth all to call to mind their Baptism often; for if wise men have thought it the best way of preserving a state to reduce it to its principles by which it grew great; certainly, it is the safest course for Christians also to meditate on their Baptism often (being the first step into their great and glorious calling) and upon what terms, and with what vows they were Baptized. At the times of the Holy Communion, he first takes order with the Church Wardens, that the elements be of the best, not cheap, or coarse, much less ill-tasted, or unwholesome. Secondly, he considers and looks into

---

81. See the prayer after the Gospel reading in the service for Public Baptism, BCP: Booty, p. 272.
82. *complemental.* Accessory, purely formal or ceremonial.

the ignorance, or carelessness of his flock, and accordingly applies himself with Catechizings, and lively exhortations, not on the Sunday of the Communion only (for then it is too late) but the Sunday, or Sundays before the Communion, or on the Eves of all those days. If there be any, who having not received yet, is to enter into this great work, he takes the more pains with them, that he may lay the foundation of future Blessings. The time of everyone's first receiving is not so much by years, as by understanding: particularly, the rule may be this: When anyone can distinguish the Sacramental from common bread, knowing the Institution, and the difference, he ought to receive, of what age soever. Children and youths are usually deferred too long, under pretense of devotion to the Sacrament, but it is for want of Instruction; their understandings being ripe enough for ill things, and why not then for better? But Parents, and Masters should make haste in this, as to a great purchase for their children, and servants; which while they defer, both sides suffer; the one, in wanting many excitings of grace; the other, in being worse served and obeyed. The saying of the Catechism is necessary, but not enough; because to answer in form may still admit ignorance: but the Questions must be propounded loosely and wildly,[83] and then the Answerer will discover what he is. Thirdly, For the manner of receiving, as the Parson useth all reverence himself, so he administers to none but to the reverent. The Feast indeed requires sitting, because it is a Feast; but man's unpreparedness asks kneeling. He that comes to the Sacrament, hath the confidence of a Guest, and he that kneels, confesseth himself an unworthy one, and therefore differs from other Feasters: but he that sits, or lies, puts up to an Apostle:[84] Contentiousness in a feast of Charity is more scandal than any posture. Fourthly, touching the frequency of the Communion, the Parson celebrates it, if not duly once a month, yet at least five or six times in the year; as, at Easter, Christmas, Whitsuntide, afore and after Harvest, and the beginning of Lent. And this he doth, not only for the benefit of the work, but also for the discharge of the Church Wardens, who being to present all that receive not[85] thrice a year; if there be but three Communions, neither can all the people so order their affairs as

---

83. *loosely and wildly.* In no set form or sequence.
84. *puts up to an Apostle.* Refutes the authority of Church tradition.
85. *present all that receive not.* Hutchinson notes that Canon 112 required ministers and wardens to present to the bishop or his chancellor names of those who did not make their Easter communion within forty days of Easter.

to receive just at those times, nor the Church Wardens so well take notice who receive thrice, and who not.

CHAPTER XXIII.

The Parson's Completeness

THE Country Parson desires to be all to his Parish, and not only
a Pastor, but a Lawyer also, and a Physician. Therefore he en-
dures not that any of his Flock should go to Law; but in any
Controversy, that they should resort to him as their Judge. To this end,
he hath gotten to himself some insight in things ordinarily incident[86]
and controverted, by experience, and by reading some initiatory trea-
tises in the Law, with *Dalton's* Justice[87] of Peace, and the Abridge-
ments of the Statutes, as also by discourse with men of that profession,
whom he hath ever some cases to ask, when he meets with them; hold-
ing that rule, that to put men to discourse of that, wherein they are
most eminent, is the most gainful way of Conversation. Yet whenever
any controversy is brought to him, he never decides it alone, but sends
for three or four of the ablest of the Parish to hear the cause with him,
whom he makes to deliver their opinion first; out of which he gathers,
in case he be ignorant himself, what to hold; and so the thing passeth
with more authority, and less envy. In Judging, he follows that, which
is altogether right; so that if the poorest man of the Parish detain but a
pin unjustly from the richest, he absolutely restores it as a Judge; but
when he hath so done, then he assumes the Parson, and exhorts to
Charity. Nevertheless, there may happen sometimes some cases,
wherein he chooseth to permit his Parishioners rather to make use of
the Law, than himself: As in cases of an obscure and dark nature, not
easily determinable by Lawyers themselves; or in cases of high consequence, as establishing of inheritances: or Lastly, when the persons in
difference are of a contentious disposition, and cannot be gained,[88] but
that they still fall from all compromises that have been made. But then
he shows them how to go to Law, even as Brethren, and not as enemies, neither avoiding therefore one another's company, much less de-

---

86. *incident.* Likely to happen.
87. *Dalton's Justice.* Michael Dalton's *The Country Justice*, pub. 1618.
88. *gained.* Won over to one's point of view.

faming one another. Now as the Parson is in Law, so is he in sickness also: if there be any of his flock sick, he is their Physician, or at least his Wife, of whom instead of the qualities of the world, he asks no other, but to have the skill of healing a wound, or helping the sick. But if neither himself, nor his wife have the skill, and his means serve, he keeps some young practitioner in his house for the benefit of his Parish, whom yet he ever exhorts not to exceed his bounds, but in tickle cases[89] to call in help. If all fail, then he keeps good correspondence with some neighbor Physician, and entertains him for the Cure of his Parish. Yet is it easy for any Scholar to attain to such a measure of Physic, as may be of much use to him both for himself, and others. This is done by seeing one Anatomy,[90] reading one Book of Physic, having one Herbal by him. And let *Fernelius*[91] be the Physic Author, for he writes briefly, neatly, and judiciously; especially let his Method of Physic be diligently perused, as being the practical part, and of most use. Now both the reading of him, and the knowing of herbs may be done at such times, as they may be an help, and a recreation to more divine studies, Nature serving Grace both in comfort of diversion, and the benefit of application when need requires; as also by way of illustration, even as our Savior made plants and seeds to teach the people: for he was the true householder, who bringeth out of his treasure things new and old; the old things of Philosophy, and the new of Grace; and maketh the one serve the other. And I conceive, our Savior did this for three reasons: first, that by familiar things he might make his Doctrine slip the more easily into the hearts even of the meanest. Secondly, that laboring people (whom he chiefly considered) might have everywhere monuments of his Doctrine, rememb'ring in gardens, his mustard-seed, and lilies; in the field, his seed-corn, and tares; and so not be drowned altogether in the works of their vocation, but sometimes lift up their minds to better things, even in the midst of their pains. Thirdly, that he might set a Copy for Parsons. In the knowledge of simples,[92] wherein the manifold wisdom of God is wonderfully to be seen, one thing would be carefully observed; which is, to know what herbs may be used instead of drugs of the same nature, and to make the garden the shop: For home-bred medicines are both more

---

89. *in tickle cases.* Those requiring special and cautious handling.

90. *one Anatomy.* Either a dissected body or a model of one.

91. *Fernelius.* Jean Francois Fernel, author of *Universa Medicina* (1586), was a standard medical authority.

92. *simples.* Medicines made of a single ingredient.

easy for the Parson's purse, and more familiar for all men's bodies. So, where the Apothecary useth either for loosing, Rhubarb, or for binding, Bolearmena,[93] the Parson useth damask of white Roses for the one, and plantain,[94] shepherd's purse, knot-grass for the other, and that with better success. As for spices, he doth not only prefer home-bred things before them, but condemns them for vanities, and so shuts them out of his family, esteeming that there is no spice comparable, for herbs, to rosemary, thyme, savory, mints; and for seeds, to Fennel, and Carroway seeds. Accordingly, for salves, his wife seeks not the city, but prefers her garden and fields before all outlandish[95] gums. And surely hyssop, valerian, mercury, adder's tongue, yarrow, melilot, and Saint *John's* wort made into a salve; And Elder, camomile, mallows, comphrey and smallage made into a Poultice, have done great and rare cures.[96] In curing of any, the Parson and his Family use to premise[97] prayers, for this is to cure like a Parson, and this raiseth the action from the Shop, to the Church. But though the Parson sets forward all Charitable deeds, yet he looks not in this point of Curing beyond his own Parish, except the person be so poor, that he is not able to reward the Physician: for as he is Charitable, so he is just also. Now it is a justice and debt to the Commonwealth he lives in, not to encroach on others' Professions, but to live on his own. And justice is the ground of Charity.

CHAPTER XXIV.

The Parson Arguing

THE Country Parson, if there be any of his parish that hold strange Doctrines, useth all possible diligence to reduce them to the common Faith. The first means he useth is Prayer, beseeching the Father of lights to open their eyes, and to give him power so to fit his discourse to them, that it may effectually pierce their

---

93. *Bolearmena.* An astringent earth from Armenia.
94. *plantain.* A low flowering herb with broad, flat leaves, used for healing surface wounds.
95. *outlandish.* Foreign.
96. See Jane O'Hara-May, *The Elizabethan Dyetary of Health* (Lawrence, Kansas: Coronado Press, 1977), and Eleanor Sinclair Rohde, *The Old English Herbal* (London: Longmans Green, 1922), for discussions of Renaissance medicine and herb lore.
97. *premise.* Perform, use beforehand.

hearts, and convert them. The second means is a very loving, and sweet usage of them, both in going to, and sending for them often, and in finding out Courtesies to place on them; as in their tithes, or otherwise. The third means is the observation what is the main foundation, and pillar of their cause, wherein they rely; as if he be a Papist, the Church is the hinge he turns on; if a Schismatic, scandal.[98] Wherefore the Parson hath diligently examined these two with himself, as what the Church is, how it began, how it proceeded, whether it be a rule to itself, whether it hath a rule, whether having a rule, it ought not to be guided by it; whether any rule in the world be obscure, and how then should the best be so, at least in fundamental things, the obscurity in some points being the exercise of the Church, the light in the foundations being the guide; The Church needing both an evidence, and an exercise. So for Scandal: what scandal is, when given or taken; whether, there being two precepts, one of obeying Authority, the other of not giving scandal, that ought not to be preferred, especially since in disobeying there is scandal also: whether things once indifferent, being made by the precept of Authority more than indifferent, it be in our power to omit or refuse them. These and the like points he hath accurately digested, having ever besides two great helps and powerful persuaders on his side; the one, a strict religious life; the other an humble, and ingenuous search of truth; being unmoved in arguing, and void of all contentiousness: which are two great lights able to dazzle the eyes of the misled, while they consider, that God cannot be wanting to them in Doctrine, to whom he is so gracious in Life.

---

98. *scandal.* In the New Testament sense, a stumbling block, or cause of offense.

CHAPTER XXV.

The Parson Punishing

WHENSOEVER the Country Parson proceeds so far as to call in Authority, and to do such things of legal opposition either in the presenting, or punishing of any, as the vulgar ever consters[99] for signs of ill will; he forbears not in any wise to use the delinquent as before, in his behavior and carriage towards him, not avoiding his company, or doing anything of averseness, save in the very act of punishment: neither doth he esteem him for an enemy, but as a brother still, except some small and temporary estranging may corroborate the punishment to a better subduing, and humbling of the delinquent: which if it happily take effect, he then comes on the faster, and makes so much the more of him, as before he alienated himself; doubling his regards, and showing by all means, that the delinquent's return is to his advantage.

CHAPTER XXVI.

The Parson's Eye

THE Country Parson at spare times from action, standing on a hill, and considering his Flock, discovers two sorts of vices, and two sorts of vicious persons. There are some vices, whose natures are always clear, and evident, as Adultery, Murder, Hatred, Lying, &c. There are other vices, whose natures, at least in the beginning, are dark and obscure: as Covetousness, and Gluttony. So likewise there are some persons, who abstain not even from known sins; there are others, who when they know a sin evidently, they commit it not. It is true indeed, they are long aknowing it, being partial to themselves, and witty[100] to others who shall reprove them from it. A man may be both Covetous, and Intemperate, and yet hear Sermons against both, and himself condemn both in good earnest: and the reason hereof is, because the natures of these vices being not evidently discussed, or

---

99. *consters*. Construes.
100. *witty*. Here, impudent, saucy.

known commonly, the beginnings of them are not easily observable: and the beginnings of them are not observed, because of the sudden passing from that which was just now lawful, to that which is presently unlawful, even in one continued action. So a man dining, eats at first lawfully; but proceeding on, comes to do unlawfully, even before he is aware; not knowing the bounds of the action, nor when his eating begins to be unlawful. So a man storing up money for his necessary provisions, both in present for his family, and in future for his children, hardly perceives when his storing becomes unlawful: yet is there a period for his storing, and a point, or center, when his storing, which was even now good, passeth from good to bad. Wherefore the Parson being true to his business, hath exactly sifted the definitions of all virtues, and vices; especially canvassing those, whose natures are most stealing, and beginnings uncertain. Particularly, concerning these two vices, not because they are all that are of this dark, and creeping disposition, but for example sake, and because they are most common, he thus thinks: first, for covetousness, he lays this ground: Whosoever when a just occasion calls, either spends not at all, or not in some proportion to God's blessing upon him, is covetous. The reason of the ground is manifest, because wealth is given to that end to supply our occasions. Now, if I do not give everything its end, I abuse the Creature, I am false to my reason which should guide me, I offend the supreme Judge, in perverting that order which he hath set both to things, and to reason. The application of the ground would be infinite; but in brief, a poor man is an occasion, my country is an occasion, my friend is an occasion, my Table is an occasion, my apparel is an occasion: if in all these, and those more which concern me, I either do nothing, or pinch, and scrape, and squeeze blood undecently to the station wherein God hath placed me, I am Covetous. More particularly, and to give one instance for all, if God have given me servants, and I either provide too little for them, or that which is unwholesome, being sometimes baned[101] meat, sometimes too salt, and so not competent nourishment, I am Covetous. I bring this example, because men usually think, that servants for their money are as other things that they buy, even as a piece of wood, which they may cut, or hack, or throw into the fire, and so they pay them their wages, all is well. Nay, to descend yet more particularly, if a man hath wherewithal to buy a spade, and yet he chooseth rather to use his neighbor's, and wear out that, he is covetous. Nevertheless, few bring covetous-

---

101. *baned.* Ruined.

ness thus low, or consider it so narrowly, which yet ought to be done, since there is a Justice in the least things, and for the least there shall be a judgment. Country people are full of these petty injustices, being cunning to make use of another, and spare themselves: And Scholars ought to be diligent in the observation of these, and driving of their general School rules ever to the smallest actions of Life; which while they dwell in their books, they will never find; but being seated in the Country, and doing their duty faithfully, they will soon discover: especially if they carry their eyes ever open, and fix them on their charge, and not on their preferment. Secondly, for Gluttony, The Parson lays this ground, He that either for quantity eats more than his health or employments will bear, or for quality is licorous after dainties, is a glutton; as he that eats more than his estate will bear, is a Prodigal; and he that eats offensively to the Company, either in his order, or length of eating, is scandalous and uncharitable. These three rules generally comprehend the faults of eating, and the truth of them needs no proof: so that men must eat neither to the disturbance of their health, nor of their affairs, (which being overburdened, or studying dainties too much, they cannot well dispatch) nor of their estate, nor of their brethren. One act in these things is bad, but it is the custom and habit that names a glutton. Many think they are at more liberty than they are, as if they were Masters of their health, and so they will stand to the pain, all is well. But to eat to one's hurt, comprehends, besides the hurt, an act against reason, because it is unnatural to hurt oneself; and this they are not masters of. Yet of hurtful things, I am more bound to abstain from those, which by mine own experience I have found hurtful, than from those which by a Common tradition, and vulgar knowledge are reputed to be so. That which is said of hurtful meats, extends to hurtful drinks also. As for the quantity, touching our employments, none must eat so as to disable themselves from a fit discharging either of Divine duties, or duties of their calling. So that if after dinner they are not fit (or unwieldly) either to pray, or work, they are gluttons. Not that all must presently work after dinner; (For they rather must not work, especially Students, and those that are weakly) but that they must rise so, as that it is not meat or drink that hinders them from working. To guide them in this, there are three rules: first, the custom, and knowledge of their own body, and what it can well disgest:[102] The second, the feeling of themselves in time of eating, which because it is

---

102. *disgest*. Digest.

deceitful; (for one thinks in eating, that he can eat more, than afterwards he finds true:) The third is the observation with what appetite they sit down. This last rule joined with the first, never fails. For knowing what one usually can well disgest, and feeling when I go to meat in what disposition I am, either hungry or not, according as I feel myself, either I take my wonted proportion, or diminish of it. Yet Physicians bid those that would live in health, not keep an uniform diet, but to feed variously, now more, now less: And *Gerson*,[103] a spiritual man, wisheth all to incline rather to too much, than to too little; his reason is, because diseases of exinanition are more dangerous, than diseases of repletion.[104] But the Parson distinguisheth according to his double aim, either of Abstinence a moral virtue, or Mortification a divine. When he deals with any that is heavy, and carnal; he gives him those freer rules: but when he meets with a refined, and heavenly disposition, he carries them higher, even sometimes to a forgetting of themselves, knowing that there is one, who when they forget, remembers for them; As when the people hung'red and thirsted after our Savior's Doctrine, and tarried so long at it, that they would have fainted, had they returned empty, He suffered it not; but rather made food miraculously, than suffered so good desires to miscarry.

CHAPTER XXVII.

The Parson in Mirth

THE Country Parson is generally sad, because he knows nothing but the Cross of Christ, his mind being defixed on it[105] with those nails wherewith his Master was: or if he have any leisure to look off from thence, he meets continually with two most sad spectacles, Sin, and Misery; God dishonored every day, and man afflicted. Nevertheless, he sometimes refresheth himself, as knowing that nature will not bear everlasting droopings, and that pleasantness of disposition is a great key to do good; not only because all men shun the company of perpetual severity, but also for that when they are in com-

---

103. *Gerson.* Jean Charlier de Gerson (1363–1429), mystic, reformer, and Chancellor of the University of Paris.

104. *repletion.* Eating and drinking to excess.

105. *defixed.* Fixed. The reading here is from the edition of 1675; 1652 and 1671 read "defixed on, and with."

pany, instructions seasoned with pleasantness, both enter sooner, and root deeper. Wherefore he condescends to human frailties both in himself and others; and intermingles some mirth in his discourses occasionally, according to the pulse of the hearer.

CHAPTER XXVIII.

The Parson in Contempt

THE Country Parson knows well, that both for the general ignominy which is cast upon the profession, and much more for those rules, which out of his choicest judgment he hath resolved to observe, and which are described in this Book, he must be despised; because this hath been the portion of God his Master, and of God's Saints his Brethren, and this is foretold, that it shall be so still, until things be no more. Nevertheless, according to the Apostle's rule,[106] he endeavors that none shall despise him; especially in his own Parish he suffers it not to his utmost power; for that, where contempt is, there is no room for instruction. This he procures, first by his holy and unblameable life; which carries a reverence with it, even above contempt. Secondly, by a courteous carriage, and winning behavior: he that will be respected, must respect; doing kindnesses, but receiving none; at least of those, who are apt to despise: for this argues a height and eminency of mind, which is not easily despised, except it degenerate to pride. Thirdly, by a bold and impartial reproof, even of the best in the Parish, when occasion requires: for this may produce hatred in those that are reproved, but never contempt either in them, or others. Lastly, if the contempt shall proceed so far as to do anything punishable by law, as contempt is apt to do, if it be not thwarted, *the Parson having a due respect both to the person, and to the cause, referreth the whole matter to the examination, and punishment of those which are in Authority;* that so the sentence lighting upon one, the example may reach to all. But if the Contempt be not punishable by Law, or being so, the Parson think it in his discretion either unfit, or bootless to contend, then when any despises him, he takes it either in an humble way, saying nothing at all; or else in a slighting way, showing that reproaches touch him no more, than a stone thrown against heaven, where he is, and lives; or in

---

106. *the Apostle's rule.* See 1 Tim. 4:12.

a sad way, grieved at his own, and others' sins, which continually break God's Laws, and dishonor him with those mouths, which he continually fills, and feeds: or else in a doctrinal way, saying to the condemner, Alas, why do you thus? you hurt yourself, not me; he that throws a stone at another, hits himself; and so between gentle reasoning, and pitying, he overcomes the evil: or lastly, in a Triumphant way, being glad, and joyful, that he is made conformable to his Master; and being in the world as he was, hath this undoubted pledge of his salvation. These are the five shields, wherewith the Godly receive the darts of the wicked; leaving anger, and retorting, and revenge to the children of the world, whom another's ill mastereth, and leadeth captive without any resistance, even in resistance, to the same destruction. For while they resist the person that reviles, they resist not the evil which takes hold of them, and is far the worse enemy.

CHAPTER XXIX.

The Parson with his Church Wardens

THE Country Parson doth often, both publicly, and privately instruct his Church Wardens, what a great Charge lies upon them, and that indeed the whole order and discipline of the Parish is put into their hands. If himself reform anything, it is out of the overflowing of his Conscience, whereas they are to do it by Command, and by Oath. Neither hath the place its dignity from the Ecclesiastical Laws only, since even by the Common Statute-Law they are taken for a kind of Corporation, as being persons enabled[107] by that Name to take moveable goods, or chattels, and to sue, and to be sued at the Law concerning such goods for the use and profit of their Parish: and by the same Law they are to levy penalties for negligence in resorting to church, or for disorderly carriage in time of divine service. Wherefore the Parson suffers not the place to be vilified or debased, by being cast on the lower rank of people; but invites and urges the best unto it, showing that they do not lose, or go less, but gain by it; it being the greatest honor of this world, to do God and his chosen service; or as *David* says, to be even a doorkeeper in the house of God.[108] Now the

---

107. *enabled.* Legally empowered.
108. *David says.* Ps. 84:10.

Canons being the Church Wardens' rule, the Parson adviseth them to read, or hear them read often, as also the visitation Articles,[109] which are grounded upon the Canons, that so they may know their duty, and keep their oath the better; in which regard, considering the great Consequence of their place, and more of their oath, he wisheth them by no means to spare any, though never so great; but if after gentle, and neighborly admonitions they still persist in ill, to present them;[110] yea though they be tenants, or otherwise engaged to the delinquent: for their obligation to God, and their own soul, is above any temporal tie. Do well, and right, and let the world sink.

CHAPTER XXX.

The Parson's Consideration of Providence

THE Country Parson considering the great aptness Country people have to think that all things come by a kind of natural course; and that if they sow and soil[111] their grounds, they must have corn; if they keep and fodder well their cattle, they must have milk, and Calves; labors to reduce them to see God's hand in all things, and to believe, that things are not set in such an inevitable order, but that God often changeth it according as he sees fit, either for reward or punishment. To this end he represents to his flock, that God hath and exerciseth a threefold power in everything which concerns man. The first is a sustaining power; the second a governing power; the third a spiritual power. By his sustaining power he preserves and actuates everything in his being; so that corn doth not grow by any other virtue,[112] than by that which he continually supplies, as the corn needs it; without which supply the corn would instantly dry up, as a river would if the fountain were stopped. And it is observable, that if

---

109. *visitation Articles.* Instructions for conduct of parish life, church furnishings, and the like, put forth by either national or diocesan church authority to promote uniformity of practice among the local churches.

110. Churchwardens were bound by oath to present to higher ecclesiastical authority the names of those members of their parish who did not follow various disciplines of parish life, including frequency of communion, proper behavior in church, and proper conduct of daily life.

111. *soil.* Manure.

112. *virtue.* Means.

anything could presume of an inevitable course, and constancy in their operations, certainly it should be either the sun in heaven, or the fire on earth, by reason of their fierce, strong, and violent natures: yet when God pleased, the sun stood still, the fire burned not. By God's governing power he preserves and orders the references of things one to the other, so that though the corn do grow, and be preserved in that act by his sustaining power, yet if he suit not other things to the growth, as seasons, and weather, and other accidents by his governing power, the fairest harvests come to nothing. And it is observable, that God delights to have men feel, and acknowledge, and reverence his power, and therefore he often overturns things, when they are thought past danger; that is his time of interposing: As when a Merchant hath a ship come home after many a storm, which it hath escaped, he destroys it sometimes in the very Haven; or if the goods be housed, a fire hath broken forth, and suddenly consumed them. Now this he doth, that men should perpetuate, and not break off their acts of dependence, how fair soever the opportunities present themselves. So that if a farmer should depend upon God all the year, and being ready to put hand to sickle, shall then secure himself, and think all cock-sure; then God sends such weather, as lays the corn, and destroys it: or if he depend on God further, even till he embarn his corn, and then think all sure; God sends a fire, and consumes all that he hath: for that he ought not to break off, but to continue his dependence on God, not only before the corn is inned, but after also; and indeed, to depend, and fear continually. The third power is spiritual, by which God turns all outward blessings to inward advantages. So that if a Farmer hath both a fair harvest, and that also well inned, and embarned, and continuing safe there; yet if God give him not the Grace to use, and utter[113] this well, all his advantages are to his loss. Better were his corn burnt, than not spiritually improved. And it is observable in this, how God's goodness strives with man's refractoriness; Man would sit down at this world, God bids him sell it, and purchase a better: Just as a Father, who hath in his hand an apple, and a piece of Gold under it; the Child comes, and with pulling, gets the apple out of his Father's hand: his Father bids him throw it away, and he will give him the gold for it, which the Child utterly refusing, eats it, and is troubled with worms: So is the carnal and willful man with the worm of the grave in this world, and the worm of Conscience in the next.

---

113. *utter.* Offer for sale.

CHAPTER XXXI.

The Parson in Liberty

THE Country Parson observing the manifold wiles of Satan (who plays his part sometimes in drawing God's Servants from him, sometimes in perplexing them in the service of God) stands fast in the Liberty wherewith Christ hath made us free. This Liberty he compasseth by one distinction, and that is, of what is Necessary, and what is Additionary. As for example: It is necessary, that all Christians should pray twice a day, every day of the week, and four times on Sunday, if they be well.[114] This is so necessary, and essential to a Christian, that he cannot without this maintain himself in a Christian state. Besides this, the Godly have ever added some hours of prayer, as at nine, or at three, or at midnight, or as they think fit, and see cause, or rather as God's spirit leads them. But these prayers are not necessary, but additionary. Now it so happens, that the godly petitioner upon some emergent interruption in the day, or by oversleeping himself at night, omits his additionary prayer. Upon this his mind begins to be perplexed, and troubled, and Satan, who knows the exigent,[115] blows the fire, endeavoring to disorder the Christian, and put him out of his station, and to enlarge the perplexity, until it spread, and taint his other duties of piety, which none can perform so well in trouble, as in calmness. Here the Parson interposeth with his distinction, and shows the perplexed Christian, that this prayer being additionary, not necessary; taken in, not commanded, the omission thereof upon just occasion ought by no means trouble him. God knows the occasion as well as he, and He is as a gracious Father, who more accepts a common course of devotion, than dislikes an occasional interruption. And of this he is so to assure himself, as to admit no scruple, but to go on as cheerfully, as if he had not been interrupted. By this it is evident, that the distinction is of singular use and comfort, especially to pious minds, which are ever tender, and delicate. But here there are two Cautions to be added. First, that this interruption proceed not out of slackness, or coldness, which will appear if the Pious soul foresee and prevent such interruptions, what he may, before they come, and when

---

114. See Walton's *Life* for a description of Herbert's adherence to this principle in the life of his parish at Bemerton (p. 302ff.).

115. *the exigent.* The emergency.

for all that they do come, he be a little affected therewith, but not afflicted, or troubled; if he resent it to a mislike,[116] but not a grief. Secondly, that this interruption proceed not out of shame. As for example: A godly man, not out of superstition, but of reverence to God's house, resolves whenever he enters into a Church, to kneel down, and pray, either blessing God, that he will be pleased to dwell among men; or beseeching him, that whenever he repairs to his house, he may behave himself so as befits so great a presence; and this briefly. But it happens, that near the place where he is to pray, he spies some scoffing ruffian, who is likely to deride him for his pains: if he now, shall either for fear or shame, break his custom, he shall do passing ill: so much the rather ought he to proceed, as that by this he may take into his Prayer humiliation also. On the other side, if I am to visit the sick in haste, and my nearest way lie through the Church, I will not doubt to go without staying to pray there (but only, as I pass, in my heart) because this kind of Prayer is additionary, not necessary, and the other duty overweighs it: So that if any scruple arise, I will throw it away, and be most confident, that God is not displeased. This distinction may run through all Christian duties, and it is a great stay and settling to religious souls.

Chapter XXXII.

The Parson's Surveys

THE Country Parson hath not only taken a particular Survey of the faults of his own Parish, but a general also of the diseases of the time, that so when his occasions carry him abroad, or bring strangers to him, he may be the better armed to encounter them. The great and national sin of this Land he esteems to be Idleness; great in itself, and great in Consequence: For when men have nothing to do, then they fall to drink, to steal, to whore, to scoff, to revile, to all sorts of gamings. Come, say they, we have nothing to do, let's go to the Tavern, or to the stews, or what not. Wherefore the Parson strongly opposeth this sin, wheresoever he goes. And because Idleness is twofold, the one in having no calling, the other in walking carelessly in our calling,

---

116. *mislike*. Disliking. The parson should be concerned if a person habitually misses additionary prayers and only dislike his behavior instead of grieve for it.

he first represents to everybody the necessity of a vocation. The reason of this assertion is taken from the nature of man, wherein God hath placed two great Instruments, Reason in the soul, and a hand in the Body, as engagements of working: So that even in Paradise man had a calling, and how much more out of Paradise, when the evils which he is now subject unto, may be prevented, or diverted by reasonable employment. Besides, every gift or ability is a talent to be accounted for,[117] and to be improved to our Master's Advantage. Yet is it also a debt to our Country to have a Calling, and it concerns the Commonwealth, that none should be idle, but all busied. Lastly, riches are the blessing of God, and the great Instrument of doing admirable good; therefore all are to procure them honestly, and seasonably, when they are not better employed. Now this reason crosseth not our Savior's precept of selling what we have,[118] because when we have sold all, and given it to the poor, we must not be idle, but labor to get more, that we may give more, according to St. *Paul's* rule (*Eph.* 4:28; 1 *Thess.* 4:11–12). So that our Savior's selling is so far from crossing Saint *Paul's* working, that it rather establisheth it, since they that have nothing, are fittest to work. Now because the only opposer to this Doctrine is the Gallant, who is witty enough to abuse both others, and himself, and who is ready to ask, if he shall mend shoes, or what he shall do? Therefore the Parson unmoved, showeth, that *ingenuous and fit* employment is never wanting to those that seek it. But if it should be, the Assertion stands thus: All are either to have a Calling, or prepare for it: He that hath or can have yet no employment, if he truly, and seriously prepare for it, he is safe and within bounds. Wherefore all are either presently to enter into a Calling, if they be fit for it, and it for them; or else to examine with care, and advice, what they are fittest for, and to prepare for that with all diligence. But it will not be amiss in this exceeding useful point to descend to particulars: for exactness lies in particulars. Men are either single, or married: The married and housekeeper hath his hands full, if he do what he ought to do. For there are two branches of his affairs; first, the improvement of his family, by bringing them up in the fear and nurture of the Lord; and secondly, the improvement of his grounds, by drowning,[119] or draining, stocking, or fencing, and ordering his land to the best advantage both of himself, and his neighbors.

---

117. See Matt. 25:14–30.
118. See Matt. 19:21.
119. *drowning.* Intentional flooding.

The *Italian* says, None fouls his hands in his own business:[120] and it is an honest, and just care, so it exceed not bounds, for everyone to employ himself to the advancement of his affairs, that he may have wherewithal to do good. But his family is his best care, to labor Christian souls, and raise them to their height, even to heaven; to dress and prune them, and take as much joy in a straight-growing child, or servant, as a Gardener doth in a choice tree. Could men find out this delight, they would seldom be from home; whereas now, of any place, they are least there. But if after all this care well dispatched, the housekeeper's Family be so small, and his dexterity so great, that he have leisure to look out, the Village or Parish which either he lives in, or is near unto it, is his employment. He considers everyone there, and either helps them in particular, or hath general Propositions to the whole Town or Hamlet, of advancing the public Stock, and managing Commons, or Woods, according as the place suggests. But if he may be of the Commission of Peace, there is nothing to that:[121] No Commonwealth in the world hath a braver Institution than that of Justices of the Peace: For it is both a security to the King, who hath so many dispersed Officers at his beck throughout the Kingdom, accountable for the public good; and also an honorable Employment of a Gentle, or Nobleman in the Country he lives in, enabling him with power to do good, and to restrain all those, who might both trouble him and the whole State. Wherefore it behooves all, who are come to the gravity, and ripeness of judgment for so excellent a Place, not to refuse, but rather to procure it. And whereas there are usually three Objections made against the Place; the one, the abuse of it, by taking petty Country bribes; the other, the casting of it on mean persons, especially in some Shires: and lastly, the trouble of it: These are so far from deterring any good man from the place, that they kindle them rather to redeem the Dignity either from true faults, or unjust aspersions. Now, for single men, they are either Heirs, or younger Brothers: The Heirs are to prepare in all the forementioned points against the time of their practice. Therefore they are to mark their Father's discretion in ordering his House and Affairs; and also elsewhere, when they see any remarkable point of Education or good husbandry, and to transplant it in time to his own home, with the same care as others, when they meet with good fruit, get a graft of the tree, enriching their Orchard, and ne-

---

120. Another example of Herbert's interest in foreign proverbs.
121. *nothing to that.* Nothing to compare with that.

glecting their House. Besides, they are to read Books of Law, and Justice; especially, the Statutes at large. As for better Books of Divinity, they are not in this Consideration, because we are about a Calling, and a preparation thereunto. But chiefly, and above all things, they are to frequent Sessions and Sizes;[122] for it is both an honor which they owe to the Reverend Judges and Magistrates, to attend them, at least in their Shire; and it is a great advantage to know the practice of the Land; for our Law is Practice. Sometimes he may go to Court, as the eminent place both of good and ill. At other times he is to travel over the King's Dominions, cutting out the Kingdom into Portions, which every year he surveys piecemeal. When there is a Parliament, he is to endeavor by all means to be a Knight or Burgess[123] there; for there is no School to a Parliament. And when he is there, he must not only be a morning man, but at Committees also; for there the particulars are exactly discussed, which are brought from thence to the House but in general.[124] When none of these occasions call him abroad, every morning that he is at home he must either ride the Great Horse,[125] or exercise some of his Military gestures. For all Gentlemen, that are not weakened, and disarmed with sedentary lives, are to know the use of their Arms: and as the Husbandman labors for them, so must they fight for, and defend them, when occasion calls. This is the duty of each to other, which they ought to fulfill: And the Parson is a lover and exciter to justice in all things, even as *John the Baptist* squared out to[126] every one (even to Soldiers) what to do.[127] As for younger Brothers, those whom the Parson finds loose, and not engaged into some Profession by their Parents, whose neglect in this point is intolerable, and a shameful wrong both to the Commonwealth, and their own House: To them, after he hath showed the unlawfulness of spending the day in dressing, Complementing, visiting, and sporting, he first commends the study of the Civil Law, as a brave, and wise knowledge, the Professors whereof were much employed by Queen *Elizabeth*, because it is the key of Commerce, and discovers the Rules of foreign Nations. Secondly, he commends the Mathematics, as the only wonder-working knowledge, and therefore requiring the best spirits. After the several

---

122. *Sizes.* Assizes, session of court.
123. *a Knight or Burgess.* A country or borough Member of Parliament.
124. Herbert served in the session of Parliament held in 1624.
125. *Great Horse.* A charger built heavily so as to carry a rider in full armor.
126. *squared out to.* Gave appropriate advice to.
127. See Luke 3:14.

knowledge of these, he adviseth to insist and dwell chiefly on the two noble branches thereof, of Fortification, and Navigation; The one being useful to all Countries, and the other especially to Islands. But if the young Gallant think these Courses dull, and phlegmatic, where can he busy himself better, than in those new Plantations, and discoveries,[128] which are not only a noble, but also as they may be handled, a religious employment? Or let him travel into *Germany*, and *France*, and observing the Artifices and Manufactures there, transplant them hither, as divers have done lately, to our Country's advantage.

CHAPTER XXXIII.

The Parson's Library

THE Country Parson's Library is a holy Life: for besides the blessing that that brings upon it, there being a promise, that if the Kingdom of God be first sought, all other things shall be added, even itself is a Sermon. For the temptations with which a good man is beset, and the ways which he used to overcome them, being told to another, whether in private conference, or in the Church, are a Sermon. He that hath considered how to carry himself at table about his appetite, if he tell this to another, preacheth; and much more feelingly, and judiciously, than he writes his rules of temperance out of books. So that the Parson having studied, and mastered all his lusts and affections within, and the whole Army of Temptations without, hath ever so many sermons ready penn'd, as he hath victories. And it fares in this as it doth in Physic: He that hath been sick of a Consumption, and knows what recovered him, is a Physician so far as he meets with the same disease, and temper; and can much better, and particularly do it, than he that is generally learned, and was never sick. And if the same person had been sick of all diseases, and were recovered of all by things that he knew; there were no such Physician as he, both for skill and tenderness. Just so it is in Divinity, and that not without manifest reason: for though the temptations may be diverse in divers Christians, yet the victory is alike in all, being by the selfsame Spirit. Neither is this true only in the military state of a Christian life, but even in the peaceable also; when the servant of God, freed for a while from temptation, in a

---

128. *those new Plantations, and discoveries.* The American colonies.

quiet sweetness seeks how to please his God. Thus the Parson considering that repentance is the great virtue of the Gospel, and one of the first steps of pleasing God, having for his own use examined the nature of it, is able to explain it after to others. And particularly, having doubted sometimes, whether his repentance were true, or at least in that degree it ought to be, since he found himself sometimes to weep more for the loss of some temporal things, than for offending God, he came at length to this resolution, that repentance is an act of the mind, not of the Body, even as the Original signifies; and that the chief thing, which God in Scriptures requires, is the heart, and the spirit, and to worship him in truth, and spirit.[129] Wherefore in case a Christian endeavor to weep, and cannot, since we are not Masters of our bodies, this sufficeth. And consequently he found, that the essence of repentance, that it may be alike in all God's children (which as concerning weeping it cannot be, some being of a more melting temper than others) consisteth in a true detestation of the soul, abhorring, and renouncing sin, and turning unto God in truth of heart, and newness of life: Which acts of repentance are and must be found in all God's servants: Not that weeping is not useful, where it can be, that so the body may join in the grief, as it did in the sin; but that, so the other acts be, that is not necessary: so that he as truly repents, who performs the other acts of repentance, when he cannot more, as he that weeps a flood of tears. This Instruction and comfort the Parson getting for himself, when he tells it to others, becomes a Sermon. The like he doth in other Christian virtues, as of Faith, and Love, and the Cases of Conscience belonging thereto, wherein (as Saint *Paul* implies that he ought, *Rom.* 2:[21]) he first preacheth to himself, and then to others.

CHAPTER XXXIV.

The Parson's Dexterity in Applying of Remedies

THE Country Parson knows, that there is a double state of a Christian even in this Life, the one military, the other peaceable. The military is, when we are assaulted with temptations either from within or from without. The Peaceable is, when the Devil for a time leaves us, as he did our Savior, and the Angels minister to us

---

129. John 4:24.

their own food, even joy, and peace; and comfort in the holy Ghost. These two states were in our Savior, not only in the beginning of his preaching, but afterwards also, as *Matthew* 22:35. He was tempted: And *Luke* 10:21. He rejoiced in Spirit: And they must be likewise in all that are his. Now the Parson having a Spiritual Judgment, according as he discovers any of his Flock to be in one or the other state, so he applies himself to them. Those that he finds in the peaceable state, he adviseth to be very vigilant, and not to let go the reins as soon as the horse goes easy. Particularly, he counseleth them to two things: First, to take heed, lest their quiet betray them (as it is apt to do) to a coldness, and carelessness in their devotions, but to labor still to be as fervent in Christian Duties, as they remember themselves were, when affliction did blow the Coals. Secondly, not to take the full compass, and liberty of their Peace: not to eat of all those dishes at table, which even their present health otherwise admits; nor to store their house with all those furnitures which even their present plenty of wealth otherwise admits; nor when they are among them that are merry, to extend themselves to all that mirth, which the present occasion of wit, and company other-wise admits; but to put bounds, and hoops to their joys: so will they last the longer, and when they depart, return the sooner. If we would judge ourselves, we should not be judged; and if we would bound our-selves, we should not be bounded. But if they shall fear, that at such, or such a time their peace and mirth have carried them further than this moderation, then to take *Job's* admirable Course,[130] who sacrificed lest his Children should have transgressed in their mirth: So let them go, and find some poor afflicted soul, and there be bountiful, and liberal; for with such sacrifices God is well pleased. Those that the Parson finds in the military state, he fortifies, and strengthens with his utmost skill. Now in those that are tempted, whatsoever is unruly, falls upon two heads; either they think, that there is none that can or will look after things, but all goes by chance, or wit: Or else, though there be a great Governor of all things, yet to them he is lost, as if they said, God doth forsake and persecute them, and there is none to deliver them. If the Parson suspect the first, and find sparks of such thoughts now and then to break forth, then without opposing directly (for disputation is no Cure for Atheism) he scatters in his discourse three sorts of argu-ments; the first taken from Nature, the second from the Law, the third from Grace.

---

130. See Job 1:4–5.

For Nature, he sees not how a house could be either built without a builder, or kept in repair without a housekeeper. He conceives not possibly, how the winds should blow so much as they can, and the sea rage as much as it can, and all things do what they can, and all, not only without dissolution of the whole, but also of any part, by taking away so much as the usual seasons of summer and winter, earing[131] and harvest. Let the weather be what it will, still we have bread, though sometimes more, sometimes less; wherewith also a careful *Joseph* might meet.[132] He conceives not possibly, how he that would believe a Divinity, if he had been at the Creation of all things, should less believe it, seeing the Preservation of all things; For Preservation is a Creation; and more, it is a continued Creation, and a creation every moment.

Secondly, for the Law, there may be so evident, though unused a proof of Divinity taken from thence, that the Atheist, or Epicurean can have nothing to contradict. The Jews yet live, and are known: they have their Law and Language bearing witness to them, and they to it: they are Circumcised to this day, and expect the promises of the Scripture; their Country also is known, the places, and rivers traveled unto, and frequented by others, but to them an unpenetrable rock, an unaccessible desert. Wherefore if the Jews live, all the great wonders of old live in them, and then who can deny the stretched-out arm of a mighty God? Especially since it may be a just doubt, whether, considering the stubbornness of the Nation, their living then in their Country under so many miracles were a stranger thing, than their present exile, and disability to live in their Country. And it is observable, that this very thing was intended by God, that the Jews should be his proof, and witnesses, as he calls them (*Isa.* 43:12). And their very dispersion in all Lands, was intended not only for a punishment to them; but for an exciting of others by their sight, to the acknowledging of God, and his power (*Ps.* 59:11). And therefore this kind of Punishment was chosen rather than any other.

Thirdly, for Grace. Besides the continual succession (since the Gospel) of holy men, who have borne witness to the truth (there being no reason, why any should distrust Saint *Luke,* or *Tertullian,* or *Chrysostom,* more than *Tully,*[133] *Virgil,* or *Livy*); There are two Prophecies in

---

131. *earing.* Ploughing.
132. *a careful Joseph might meet.* I.e., might be prepared for.
133. *Tully.* Cicero, the Roman orator.

the Gospel, which evidently argue Christ's Divinity by their success: the one concerning the woman that spent the ointment on our Savior, for which he told, that it should never be forgotten, but with the Gospel itself be preached to all ages (*Matt.* 26:13). The other concerning the destruction of *Jerusalem;* of which our Savior said, that that generation should not pass, till all were fulfilled (*Luke* 21:32). Which *Josephus* his story[134] confirmeth, and the continuance of which verdict is yet evident. To these might be added the Preaching of the Gospel in all Nations (*Matt.* 24:14), which we see even miraculously effected in these new discoveries, God turning men's Covetousness, and Ambitions to the effecting of his Word. Now a prophecy is a wonder sent to Posterity, lest they complain of want of wonders. It is a letter sealed, and sent, which to the bearer is but paper, but to the receiver, and opener, is full of power. He that saw Christ open a blind man's eyes, saw not more Divinity, than he that reads the woman's ointment in the Gospel, or sees *Jerusalem* destroyed. With some of these heads enlarged, and woven into his discourse, at several times and occasions, the Parson settleth wavering minds. But if he sees them nearer desperation, than Atheism; not so much doubting a God, as that he is theirs; then he dives unto the boundless Ocean of God's Love, and the unspeakable riches of his loving kindness. He hath one argument unanswerable. If God hate them, either he doth it as they are Creatures, dust and ashes; or as they are sinful. As Creatures, he must needs love them; for no perfect Artist ever yet hated his own work. As sinful, he must much more love them; because notwithstanding his infinite hate of sin, his Love overcame that hate; and with an exceeding great victory, which in the Creation needed not,[135] gave them love for love, even the son of his love out of his bosom of love. So that man, which way soever he turns, hath two pledges of God's Love, that in the mouth of two or three witnesses every word may be established; the one in his being, the other in his sinful being: and this as the more faulty in him, so the more glorious in God. And all may certainly conclude, that God loves them, till either they despise that Love, or despair of his Mercy: not any sin else, but is within his Love; but the despising of Love must needs be without it. The thrusting away of his arm makes us only not embraced.[136]

---

134. *Josephus his story.* Joseph ben Matthias, Jewish historian (AD 37–100), author of *Antiquities of the Jews.*

135. *needed not.* Was not needed.

136. *only not embraced.* Hutchinson paraphrases, "It is only our rejection of his arm which can prevent our being embraced."

Chapter XXXV.

The Parson's Condescending

THE Country Parson is a Lover of old Customs, if they be good, and harmless; and the rather, because Country people are much addicted to them, so that to favor them therein is to win their hearts, and to oppose them therein is to deject them. If there be any ill in the custom, that may be severed from the good, he pares the apple, and gives them the clean to feed on. Particularly, he loves Procession,[137] and maintains it, because there are contained therein four manifest advantages. First, a blessing of God for the fruits of the field: Secondly, justice in the Preservation of bounds: Thirdly, Charity in loving walking, and neighborly accompanying one another, with reconciling of differences at that time, if there be any: Fourthly, Mercy in relieving the poor by a liberal distribution and largesse, which at that time is, or ought to be used. Wherefore he exacts of all to be present at the perambulation, and those that withdraw, and sever themselves from it, he mislikes, and reproves as uncharitable, and unneighborly; and if they will not reform, presents them. Nay, he is so far from condemning such assemblies, that he rather procures them to be often, as knowing that absence breeds strangeness, but presence love. Now Love is his business, and aim; wherefore he likes well, that his Parish at good times invite one another to their houses, and he urgeth them to it: and sometimes, where he knows there hath been or is a little difference, he takes one of the parties, and goes with him to the other, and all dine or sup together. There is much preaching in this friendliness. Another old Custom there is of saying, when light is brought in, God send us the light of heaven;[138] and the Parson likes this very well; neither is he afraid of praising, or praying to God at all times, but is rather glad of catching opportunities to do them. Light is a great Blessing, and as great as food, for which we give thanks: and those that think this superstitious, neither know superstition, nor themselves. As for those that are ashamed to use this form, as being old, and obsolete, and not the fashion, he reforms, and teaches them, that at Baptism they professed

---

137. *Procession.* Reference to custom of "beating the bounds" on Rogation Days, of processing around the geographical boundaries of the parish, with Litany and Psalms, to invoke God's blessings on the growing crops.

138. Survival from traditional vesper service.

not to be ashamed of Christ's Cross,[139] or for any shame to leave that which is good. He that is ashamed in small things, will extend his pusillanimity to greater. Rather should a Christian Soldier take such occasions to harden himself, and to further his exercises of Mortification.

CHAPTER XXXVI.

The Parson Blessing

THE Country Parson wonders, that Blessing the people is in so little use with his brethren: whereas he thinks it not only a grave, and reverend thing, but a beneficial also. Those who use it not, do so either out of niceness, because they like the salutations, and complements, and forms of worldly language better; which conformity and fashionableness is so exceeding unbefitting a Minister, that it deserves reproof, not refutation: Or else, because they think it empty and superfluous. But that which the Apostles used so diligently in their writings, nay, which our Savior himself used (*Mark* 10:16), cannot be vain and superfluous. But this was not proper to Christ, or the Apostles only, no more than to be a spiritual Father was appropriated to them. And if temporal Fathers bless their children, how much more may, and ought Spiritual Fathers? Besides, the Priests of the Old Testament were commanded to Bless the people, and the form thereof is prescribed (*Num.* 6:[23–26]). Now as the Apostle argues in another case; if the Ministration of condemnation did bless, how shall not the ministration of the spirit exceed in blessing?[140] The fruit of this blessing good *Hannah* found, and received with great joy (1 *Sam.* 1:18), though it came from a man disallowed by God: for it was not the person, but Priesthood, that blessed; so that even ill Priests may bless.[141] Neither have the Ministers power of Blessing only, but also of cursing. So in the Old Testament *Elisha* cursed the children (2 *Kings* 2:24), which though our Savior reproved as unfitting for his particular, who was to show all humility before his Passion, yet he allows in his Apostles.[142]

---

139. Reference to controversy with Puritans over use of the sign of the cross in Baptism.
140. See 2 Cor. 3:8–11.
141. *ill Priests.* See No. 26 of the Articles of Religion, "Of the Unworthiness of the Ministers, which hinders not the effect of the Sacrament."
142. Reference to Luke 18:15–17 and Matt. 18:18?

And therefore St. *Peter* used that fearful imprecation to *Simon Magus* (*Acts* 8:[20–23]), *Thy money perish with thee:* and the event confirmed it. So did St. *Paul* (2 *Tim.* 4:14, and 1 *Tim.* 1:20). Speaking of *Alexander* the Coppersmith, who had withstood his preaching, *The Lord* (saith he) *reward him according to his works.* And again, of *Hymeneus* and *Alexander,* he saith, he had *delivered them to Satan, that they might learn not to Blaspheme.* The forms both of Blessing, and cursing are expounded in the Common Prayer book: the one in, The Grace of our Lord Jesus Christ, &c. and: The Peace of God, &c. The other in general, in the Commination.[143] Now blessing differs from prayer, in assurance, because it is not performed by way of request, but of confidence, and power, effectually applying God's favor to the blessed, by the interesting[144] of that dignity wherewith God hath invested the Priest, and engaging of God's own power and institution for a blessing. The neglect of this duty in Ministers themselves, hath made the people also neglect it; so that they are so far from craving this benefit from their ghostly Father, that they oftentimes go out of church, before he hath blessed them. In the time of Popery, the Priest's *Benedicite,*[145] and his holy water were overhighly valued; and now we are fallen to the clean contrary, even from superstition to coldness, and Atheism. But the Parson first values the gift in himself, and then teacheth his parish to value it. And it is observable, that if a Minister talk with a great man in the ordinary course of complementing language, he shall be esteemed as ordinary complementers; but if he often interpose a Blessing, when the other gives him just opportunity, by speaking any good, this unusual form begets a reverence, and makes him esteemed according to his Profession. The same is to be observed in writing Letters also. To conclude, if all men are to bless upon occasion, as appears (*Rom.* 12:14), how much more those, who are spiritual Fathers?

---

143. *Commination.* Special service in BCP, to be used after Morning Prayer, together with the Litany, on Ash Wednesday and other occasions.

144. *interesting.* Investing with a share in.

145. *Benedicite.* Blessing; literally, "bless you."

GEORGE HERBERT

Chapter XXXVII.

Concerning Detraction

THE Country Parson perceiving, that most, when they are at leisure, make others' faults their entertainment and discourse, and that even some good men think, so they speak truth, they may disclose another's fault, finds it somewhat difficult how to proceed in this point. For if he absolutely shut up men's mouths, and forbid all disclosing of faults, many an evil may not only be, but also spread in his Parish, without any remedy (which cannot be applied without notice) to the dishonor of God, and the infection of his flock, and the discomfort, discredit, and hindrance of the Pastor. On the other side, if it be unlawful to open faults, no benefit or advantage can make it lawful: for we must not do evil, that good may come of it. Now the Parson taking this point to task, which is so exceeding useful, and hath taken so deep root, that it seems the very life and substance of Conversation, hath proceeded thus far in the discussing of it. Faults are either notorious, or private. Again notorious faults are either such as are made known by common fame (and of these, those that know them, may talk, so they do it not with sport, but commiseration); or else such as have passed judgment, and been corrected either by whipping, or imprisoning, or the like. Of these also men may talk, and more, they may discover them to those that know them not: because infamy is a part of the sentence against malefactors, which the Law intends, as is evident by those, which are branded for rogues, that they may be known; or put into the stocks, that they may be looked upon. But some may say, though the Law allow this, the Gospel doth not, which hath so much advanced Charity, and ranked backbiters among the generation of the wicked (*Rom.* 1:30). But this is easily answered: As the executioner is not uncharitable, that takes away the life of the condemned, except besides his office, he add a tincture of private malice in the joy, and haste of acting his part; so neither is he that defames him, whom the Law would have defamed, except he also do it out of rancor. For in infamy, all are executioners, and the Law gives a malefactor to all to be defamed. And as malefactors may lose and forfeit their goods, or life; so may they their good name, and the possession thereof, which before their offense, and Judgment they had in all men's breasts: for all are honest, till the contrary be proved. Besides, it concerns the Commonwealth, that Rogues should be known, and Charity to the public hath the precedence of private charity. So that it is so far from being a fault to discover such offenders, that it is a duty rather, which may do much good, and save much harm. Nevertheless, if the punished delinquent shall be much troubled for his sins, and turn quite another man, doubtless then also men's affections and words must turn, and forbear to speak of that, which even God himself hath forgotten.

* * *

The Author's PRAYER before SERMON

Oh Almighty and everliving Lord God! Majesty, and Power, and Brightness, and Glory! How shall we dare to appear before thy face, who are contrary to thee, in all we call thee? for we are darkness, and weakness, and filthiness, and shame. Misery and sin fill our days: yet art thou our Creator, and we thy work: Thy hands both made us, and also made us Lords of all thy creatures; giving us one world in ourselves, and another to serve us: then didst thou place us in Paradise, and wert proceeding still on in thy Favors, until we interrupted thy Counsels, disappointed thy Purposes, and sold our God, our glorious, our gracious God for an apple. Oh write it! Oh brand it in our foreheads forever: for an apple once we lost our God, and still lose him for no more; for money, for meat, for diet: But thou Lord, art patience and pity, and sweetness, and love; therefore we sons of men are not consumed. Thou hast exalted thy mercy above all things; and hast made our salvation, not our punishment, thy glory: so that then where sin abounded, not death, but grace superabounded; accordingly, when we had sinned beyond any help in heaven or earth, then thou saidest, Lo, I come! then did the Lord of life, unable of himself to die, contrive to do it. He took flesh, he wept, he died; for his enemies he died; even for those that derided him then, and still despise him. Blessed Savior! many waters could not quench thy love! nor no pit overwhelm it. But though the streams of thy blood were current[1] through darkness, grave, and hell; yet by these thy conflicts, and seemingly hazards, didst thou arise triumphant, and therein mad'st us victorious.

---

1. *current.* flowing.

Neither doth thy love yet stay here! for, this word of thy rich peace, and reconciliation, thou hast committed, not to Thunder, or Angels, but to silly and sinful men: even to me, pardoning my sins, and bidding me go feed the people of thy love.

Blessed be the God of Heaven and Earth! who only doth wond'rous things. Awake therefore, my Lute, and my Viol! awake all my powers to glorify thee! We praise thee! we bless thee! we magnify thee forever![2] And now, Oh Lord! in the power of thy Victories, and in the ways of thy Ordinances, and in the truth of thy Love, Lo, we stand here, beseeching thee to bless thy word, wherever spoken this day throughout the universal Church. Oh, make it a word of power and peace, to convert those who are not yet thine, and to confirm those that are: particularly, bless it in this thy own Kingdom, which thou hast made a Land of light, a storehouse of thy treasures and mercies: Oh, let not our foolish and unworthy hearts rob us of the continuance of this thy sweet love: but pardon our sins, and perfect what thou hast begun. Ride on Lord, because of the word of truth, and meekness, and righteousness; and thy right hand shall teach thee terrible things. Especially, bless this portion here assembled together, with thy unworthy Servant speaking unto them: Lord Jesu! teach thou me, that I may teach them: Sanctify, and enable all my powers; that in their full strength they may deliver thy message reverently, readily, faithfully, and fruitfully. Oh, make thy word a swift word, passing from the ear to the heart, from the heart to the life and conversation: that as the rain returns not empty, so neither may thy word, but accomplish that for which it is given. Oh Lord hear, Oh Lord forgive! Oh Lord, hearken, and do so for thy blessed Son's sake, in whose sweet and pleasing words, we say, *Our Father,* &c.

A PRAYER after SERMON

Blessed be God! and the Father of all mercy! who continueth to pour his benefits upon us. Thou hast elected us, thou hast called us, thou hast justified us, sanctified, and glorified us; Thou wast born for us, and thou livedst and diedst for us: Thou hast given us the blessings of this life, and of a better. Oh Lord! thy blessings hang in clusters,

---

2. Allusion to the *Gloria in excelsis,* used in BCP at the end of the Service of Holy Communion; see BCP, p. 265.

they come trooping upon us! they break forth like mighty waters on every side. And now Lord, thou hast fed us with the bread of life: so man did eat Angel's food: Oh Lord, bless it: Oh Lord, make it health and strength unto us; still striving and prospering so long within us, until our obedience reach the measure of thy love, who hast done for us as much as may be. Grant this dear Father, for thy Son's sake, our only Savior: To whom with thee, and the Holy Ghost, three Persons, but one most glorious, incomprehensible God, be ascribed all Honor, and Glory, and Praise, ever. Amen.

THE
TEMPLE.
SACRED POEMS
AND
PRIVATE EJACULATIONS.

Psalm 29[:9]
In his Temple doth every
man speak of his honor.

1633

THE DEDICATION

Lord, my first fruits present themselves to thee;
Yet not mine neither: for from thee they came,
And must return. Accept of them and me,
And make us strive, who shall sing best thy name.
    Turn their eyes hither, who shall make a gain:
    Theirs, who shall hurt themselves or me, refrain.

THE DEDICATION

The Printers to the Reader[1]

The dedication of this work having been made by the Author to the *Divine Majesty* only, how should we now presume to interest any mortal man in the patronage of it? Much less think we it meet to seek the recommendation of the Muses, for that which himself was confident to have been inspired by a diviner breath than flows from *Helicon*.[2] The world therefore shall receive it in that naked simplicity, with which he left it, without any addition either of support or ornament, more than is included in itself. We leave it free and unforestalled to every man's judgment, and to the benefit that he shall find by perusal. Only for the clearing of some passages, we have thought it not unfit to make the common Reader privy to some few particularities of the condition and disposition of the Person.

Being nobly born, and as eminently endued with gifts of the mind, and having by industry and happy education perfected them to that great height of excellency, whereof his fellowship of Trinity College in Cambridge, and his Oratorship in the University, together with that knowledge which the King's Court had taken of him, could make relation far above ordinary. Quitting both his deserts and all the opportunities that he had for worldly preferment, he betook himself to the Sanctuary and Temple of God, choosing rather to serve at God's Altar, than to seek the honor of State employments. As for those inward enforcements to this course (for outward there was none) which many of these ensuing verses bear witness of, they detract not from the freedom, but add to the honor of this resolution in him. As God had enabled him, so he accounted him meet not only to be called, but to be compelled to this service: Wherein his faithful discharge was such, as may make him justly a companion to the primitive Saints, and a pattern or more for the age he lived in.

To testify his independency upon all others, and to quicken his diligence in this kind, he used in his ordinary speech, when he made

---

1. *The Printers to the Reader.* Preface to *The Temple* by Nicholas Ferrar (1592–1637), Anglican deacon and spiritual leader of the religious community at Little Gidding known to its Puritan opponents as his "Arminian nunnery." A friend of Herbert, Ferrar served as his first literary executor; see textual introduction.

2. *Helicon.* A mountain in southwest Boeotia, Greece, traditionally considered the home of the Muses in Greek mythology.

119

mention of the blessed name of our Lord and Savior Jesus Christ, to add, *My Master.*

Next God, he loved that which God himself hath magnified above all things, that is, his Word: so as he hath been heard to make solemn protestation, that he would not part with one leaf thereof for the whole world, if it were offered him in exchange.

His obedience and conformity to the Church and the discipline thereof was singularly remarkable. Though he abounded in private devotions, yet went he every morning and evening with his family to the Church; and by his example, exhortations, and encouragements drew the greater part of his parishioners to accompany him daily in the public celebration of Divine Service.

As for worldly matters, his love and esteem to them was so little, as no man can more ambitiously seek, than he did earnestly endeavor the resignation of an Ecclesiastical dignity,[3] which he was possessor of. But God permitted not the accomplishment of this desire, having ordained him his instrument for reedifying of the Church belonging thereunto, that had lain ruinated almost twenty years. The reparation whereof, having been uneffectually attempted by public collections, was in the end by his own and some few others' private freewill offerings successfully effected. With the remembrance whereof, as of an especial good work, when a friend[4] went about to comfort him on his deathbed, he made answer, *It is a good work, if it be sprinkled with the blood of Christ:* otherwise than in this respect he could find nothing to glory or comfort himself with, neither in this, nor in any other thing.

And these are but a few of many that might be said, which we have chosen to premise as a glance to some parts of the ensuing book, and for an example to the Reader. We conclude all with his own Motto, with which he used to conclude all things that might seem to tend any way to his own honor:

Less than the least of God's mercies.[5]

---

3. *an Ecclesiastical dignity.* Herbert, holder of the prebend of Leighton Ecclesia, with its attendant property at Leighton Bromswold, five miles from Little Gidding, sought to have this benefice transferred to Nicholas Ferrar. He was, instead, persuaded to undertake improvement of the ruined church at that place.

4. *a friend.* Arthur Woodnoth (1590?–1650?), cousin of Nicholas Ferrar, who was with Herbert at his death, according to Walton; see his *Life,* pp. 315–19.

5. *Less than the least.* Refrain of "The Poesy," see p. 309, also adopted as a motto at Little Gidding. See the words of Jacob at Gen. 32:10, after his return to Edom from his

THE CHURCH PORCH

PERIRRHANTERIUM[1]

Thou, whose sweet youth and early hopes enhance
Thy rate and price, and mark thee for a treasure;
Harken unto a Verser, who may chance
Rhyme thee to good, and make a bait of pleasure.
    A verse may find him, who a sermon flies,   *5*
    And turn delight into a sacrifice.[2]

Beware of lust: it doth pollute and foul
Whom God in Baptism washt with his own blood.
It blots thy lesson written in thy soul;
The holy lines cannot be understood.   *10*
    How dare those eyes upon a Bible look,
    Much less towards God, whose lust is all their book?

Abstain wholly, or wed. Thy bounteous Lord
Allows thee choice of paths: take no byways;
But gladly welcome what he doth afford;   *15*
Not grudging, that thy lust hath bounds and stays.
    Continence hath his joy: weigh both; and so
    If rottenness have more, let Heaven go.[3]

---

sojourn with Laban, as part of his concern for what will happen when he meets Esau again: "I am not worthy of the least of all the mercies, and of all the truth, which thou hast shewed unto thy servant; for with my staff I passed over this Jordan; and now I am become two bands."

    1. *Perirrhanterium*. Greek term for instrument used for sprinkling holy water (Latin *aspergillum*). Here it suggests that the poem that follows is a preparatory ritual of cleansing or "setting-apart" before entering the "Church" section of *The Temple*, another of many uses of the analogy of *The Temple* poems with an actual church building.

    2. There may be echoes here of Sir Philip Sidney's definition of the poet: "For these indeed to merely make to imitate, and imitate both to delight and teach; and delight, to move men to take that goodness in hand, which without delight they would fly as from a stranger; and teach, to make them know that goodness whereunto they are moved" (*A Defence of Poetry*, in *Miscellaneous Prose*, ed. K. Duncan-Jones and J. Van Dorsten [Oxford; Clarendon, 1973], p. 81).

    3. See Prov. 12:4.

If God had laid all common, certainly
Man would have been th'encloser: but since now   *20*
God hath impal'd us,[4] on the contrary
Man breaks the fence, and every ground will plough.
  Oh what were man, might he himself misplace!
  Sure to be cross[5] he would shift feet and face.

Drink not the third glass,[6] which thou canst not tame,   *25*
When once it is within thee; but before
Mayst rule it, as thou list; and pour the shame,
Which it would pour on thee, upon the floor.
  It is most just to throw that on the ground,
  Which would throw me there, if I keep the round.[7]   *30*

He that is drunken, may his mother kill
Big with his sister: he hath lost the reins,
Is outlaw'd by himself: all kind of ill
Did with his liquor slide into his veins.
  The drunkard forfeits Man,[8] and doth divest[9]   *35*
  All worldly right, save what he hath by beast.

Shall I, to please another's wine-sprung mind,
Lose all mine own? God hath giv'n me a measure
Short of his canne,[10] and body; must I find
A pain in that, wherein he finds a pleasure?   *40*
  Stay at the third glass: if thou lose thy hold,
  Then thou art modest,[11] and the wine grows bold.

If reason move not Gallants,[12] quit the room,
(All in a shipwreck shift their several way)

---

4. *impal'd us.* Fenced us in.
5. *cross.* Perverse, contrarious.
6. *the third glass.* Traditionally, the point of inebriation.
7. *keep the round.* Accept a refill each time the bottle is passed.
8. *forfeits Man.* Gives up his claim to human status in the hierarchy of nature.
9. *divest.* Give up claim to.
10. *canne.* A drinking-vessel.
11. *modest.* Retiring, unassuming; here, suggesting incapacity to control oneself when inebriated.
12. *Gallants.* Men of fashion.

Let not a common ruin thee entomb: *45*
Be not a beast in courtesy; but stay,
   Stay at the third cup, or forego the place.
   Wine above all things doth God's stamp deface.

Yet, if thou sin in wine or wantonness,
Boast not thereof; nor make thy shame thy glory.[13]   *50*
Frailty gets pardon by submissiveness;
But he that boasts, shuts that out of his story.
   He makes flat war with God, and doth defy
   With his poor clod of earth the spacious sky.

Take not his name, who made thy mouth, in vain: *55*
It gets thee nothing, and hath no excuse.
Lust and wine plead a pleasure, avarice gain:
But the cheap swearer through his open sluice
   Lets his soul run for nought, as little fearing.
   Were I an *Epicure*,[14] I could bate[15] swearing.   *60*

When thou dost tell another's jest, therein
Omit the oaths, which true wit cannot need:
Pick out of tales the mirth, but not the sin.
He pares his apple, that will cleanly feed.[16]
   Play not away the virtue of that name,   *65*
   Which is thy best stake,[17] when griefs make thee tame.

The cheapest sins most dearly punisht are;
Because to shun them also is so cheap:
For we have wit to mark them, and to spare.
Oh crumble not away thy soul's fair heap.   *70*
   If thou wilt die, the gates of hell are broad:
   Pride and full sins have made the way a road.

---

13. See Phil. 3:19.

14. *Were I an Epicure.* Even if I were one who recognized no religious motives for conduct.

15. *bate.* Put an end to; leave off.

16. Repeated in *The Country Parson;* see p. 109.

17. *stake.* That which is placed at hazard, i.e., as in a game of chance.

Lie not; but let thy heart be true to God,
Thy mouth to it, thy actions to them both:
Cowards tell lies, and those that fear the rod;   75
The stormy working soul spits lies and froth.
    Dare to be true. Nothing can need a lie:
    A fault, which needs it most, grows two thereby.

Fly idleness, which yet thou canst not fly
By dressing, mistressing,[18] and compliment.   80
If those take up thy day, the sun will cry
Against thee: for his light was only lent.
    God gave thy soul brave wings; put not those feathers
    Into a bed, to sleep out all ill weathers.

Art thou a Magistrate? then be severe: 85
If studious, copy fair, what time hath blurr'd;
Redeem truth from his jaws: if soldier,
Chase brave employments with a naked sword
    Throughout the world. Fool not: for all may have,
    If they dare try, a glorious life, or grave.   90

Oh England! full of sin, but most of sloth;[19]
Spit out thy phlegm,[20] and fill thy breast with glory:
Thy Gentry bleats, as if thy native cloth
Transfus'd a sheepishness into thy story:
    Not that they all are so; but that the most   95
    Are gone to grass, and in the pasture lost.

This loss springs chiefly from our education.
Some till their ground, but let weeds choke their son:
Some mark a partridge, never their child's fashion:
Some ship them over,[21] and the thing is done.   100
    Study this art, make it thy great design;
    And if God's image move thee not, let thine.

---

18. *mistressing.* Courting.
19. *sloth.* See *The Country Parson,* p. 100.
20. *thy phlegm.* In "humour" psychology, which held the body to contain four fluids—blood, choler, phlegm, and bile—an excess of phlegm caused indolence.
21. *ship them over.* Send abroad, with sense of "get rid of."

Some great estates provide, but do not breed
A mast'ring mind; so both are lost thereby:
Or else they breed them tender, make them need   *105*
All that they leave: this is flat poverty.
 For he, that needs five thousand pound to live,
 Is full as poor as he, that needs but five.

The way to make thy son rich, is to fill
His mind with rest, before his trunk with riches: *110*
For wealth without contentment, climbs a hill
To feel those tempests, which fly over ditches.
 But if thy son can make ten pound his measure,
 Then all thou addest may be call'd his treasure.

When thou dost purpose[22] ought, (within thy power)   *115*
Be sure to do it, though it be but small:
Constancy knits the bones, and makes us stowre,[23]
When wanton pleasures beckon us to thrall.[24]
 Who breaks his own bond, forfeiteth himself:
 What nature made a ship, he makes a shelf.[25]   *120*

Do all things like a man, not sneakingly:
Think the king sees thee still; for his King does.
Simp'ring is but a lay-hypocrisy:
Give it a corner, and the clue[26] undoes.
 Who fears to do ill, sets himself to task: *125*
 Who fears to do well, sure should wear a mask.

Look to thy mouth; diseases enter there.
Thou hast two sconses,[27] if thy stomach call;
Carve, or discourse; do not a famine fear.
Who carves, is kind to two; who talks, to all.   *130*

---

22. *purpose.* Intend.
.23. *stowre.* Sturdy, stalwart.
24. *thrall.* I.e., thraldom, bondage.
25. *shelf.* Reef, submerged ledge of rock, likely to cause shipwreck.
26. *clue.* Ball of thread; i.e., a ball of thread will unwind if hidden in a corner.
27. *sconses.* Protective screens or shelters; also, small forts built for protection of a ford, pass, castle gate.

Look on meat, think it dirt, then eat a bit;[28]
And say withall, Earth to earth I commit.[29]

Slight those who say amidst their sickly healths,
Thou liv'st by rule. What doth not so, but man?
Houses are built by rule, and commonwealths.   *135*
Entice the trusty sun, if that you can,
   From his Ecliptic[30] line: beckon the sky.
   Who lives by rule then, keeps good company.

Who keeps no guard upon himself, is slack,
And rots to nothing at the next great thaw.   *140*
Man is a shop of rules, a well truss'd pack,
Whose every parcel underwrites[31] a law.
   Lose not thy self, nor give thy humors[32] way:
   God gave them to thee under lock and key.

By all means use sometimes to be alone.   *145*
Salute thyself: see what thy soul doth wear.
Dare to look in thy chest; for 'tis thine own:
And tumble up and down what thou find'st there.
   Who cannot rest till he good fellows[33] find,
   He breaks up house, turns out of doors his mind.   *150*

Be thrifty, but not covetous: therefore give
Thy need, thine honor, and thy friend his due.
Never was scraper[34] brave man. Get to live;
Then live, and use it: else it is not true
   That thou hast gotten. Surely use alone   *155*
   Makes money not a contemptible stone.

---

28. See Job 28:5.
29. See BCP Burial Office, Booty, pp. 309–13.
30. *Ecliptic.* Apparent path of the sun through the sky.
31. *underwrites.* Confirms allegiance to by signature.
32. *humors.* In "humour" psychology, the role of reason is to keep the humors in balance, to prevent emotions from dominating the personality.
33. *good fellows.* Boon companions.
34. *scraper.* A money-grubber.

Never exceed thy income. Youth may make
Ev'n with the year: but age, if it will hit,
Shoots a bow short, and lessens still his stake,
As the day lessens, and his life with it.   *160*
    Thy children, kindred, friends upon thee call;
    Before thy journey fairly part with all.

Yet in thy thriving still misdoubt[35] some evil;
Lest gaining gain on thee, and make thee dim
To all things else. Wealth is the conjurer's devil;   *165*
Whom when he thinks he hath, the devil hath him.
    Gold thou mayst safely touch; but if it stick
    Unto thy hands, it woundeth to the quick.

What skills it,[36] if a bag of stones or gold
About thy neck do drown thee? raise thy head;   *170*
Take stars for money;[37] stars not to be told
By any art, yet to be purchased.
    None is so wasteful as the scraping dame.
    She loseth three for one; her soul, rest, fame.

By no means run in debt: take thine own measure.   *175*
Who cannot live on twenty pound a year,
Cannot on forty: He's a man of pleasure,
A kind of thing that's for itself too dear.
    The curious unthrift makes his cloth too wide,
    And spares himself, but would his tailor chide.   *180*

Spend not on hopes. They that by pleading clothes
Do fortunes seek, when worth and service fail,
Would have their tale believed for their oaths,
And are like empty vessels under sail.
    Old courtiers know this; therefore set out so,   *185*
    As all the day thou mayst hold out to go.

---

35. *misdoubt.* Suspect the existence of.
36. *What skills it?* "What difference does it make?"
37. See Luke 12:33.

In clothes, cheap handsomeness doth bear the bell.[38]
Wisdom's a trimmer thing, than shop e're gave.
Say not then, This with that lace will do well;
But, This with my discretion will be brave.[39]   *190*
   Much curiousness is a perpetual wooing
   Nothing with labor; folly long adoing.

Play not for gain, but sport. Who plays for more
Than he can lose with pleasure, stakes his heart;
Perhaps his wife's too, and whom she hath bore: *195*
Servants and churches also play their part.
   Only a herald, who that way doth pass,
   Finds his crackt[40] name at length in the church glass.

If yet thou love game at so dear a rate,
Learn this, that hath old gamesters dearly cost: *200*
Dost lose? rise up: dost win? rise in that state.
Who strive to sit out losing hands, are lost.
   Game is a civil gunpowder, in peace
   Blowing up houses with their whole increase.

In conversation boldness now bears sway.
But know, that nothing can so foolish be,
As empty boldness: therefore first assay
To stuff thy mind with solid bravery;
   Then march on gallant:[41] get substantial worth.
   Boldness gilds finely, and will set it forth.   *210*

Be sweet to all. Is thy complexion sour?
Then keep such company; make them thy allay:[42]
Get a sharp[43] wife, a servant that will lour.[44]
A stumbler stumbles least in rugged way.

---

38. *doth bear the bell.* Take first place.
39. *brave.* Handsome, finely dressed.
40. *crackt.* Damaged, i.e., because church window is damaged with age and thus provides no surcease from the ravages a damaged reputation can work on one's name.
41. *gallant.* Grandly, splendidly.
42. *allay.* Alloy, combination of humors.
43. *sharp.* Harsh, sharp-tongued.
44. *lour.* Frown, scowl.

Command thyself in chief. He life's war knows,   *215*
Whom all his passions follow, as he goes.

Catch not at quarrels. He that dares not speak
Plainly and home,[45] is coward of the two.
Think not thy fame at ev'ry twitch will break:
By great deeds show, that thou canst little do;   *220*
   And do them not: that shall thy wisdom be;
   And change thy temperance into bravery.

If that thy fame with ev'ry toy be pos'd,[46]
'Tis a thin web, which poisonous fancies make:
But the great soldier's honor was compos'd   *225*
Of thicker stuff, which would endure a shake.
   Wisdom picks friends; civility plays[47] the rest.
   A toy shunn'd cleanly passeth with the best.

Laugh not too much: the witty man laughs least:
For wit is news only to ignorance.   *230*
Less at thine own things laugh; lest in the jest
Thy person share, and the conceit advance.
   Make not thy sport, abuses: for the fly
   That feeds on dung, is colored thereby.

Pick out of mirth, like stones out of thy ground,   *235*
Profaneness, filthiness, abusiveness.
These are the scum, with which coarse wits abound:
The fine may spare these well, yet not go less.
   All things are big with jest: nothing that's plain,
   But may be witty, if thou hast the vein.   *240*

Wit's an unruly engine, wildly striking
Sometimes a friend, sometimes the engineer.
Hast thou the knack? pamper it not with liking:
But if thou want[48] it, buy it not too dear.

---

45. *home.* Adverb, "directly to the heart of the matter."
46. *pos'd.* Called into question.
47. *plays.* Manages, deals with.
48. *want.* Lack.

Many affecting wit beyond their power,   *245*
Have got to be a dear fool for an hour.

A sad[49] wise valor is the brave complexion,
That leads the van, and swallows up the cities.
The gig'ler is a milk-maid, whom infection,
Or a fir'd beacon frighteth from his ditties.   *250*
    Then he's the sport: the mirth then in him rests,
    And the sad man is cock of all his jests.

Towards great persons use respective[50] boldness:
That temper gives them theirs, and yet doth take
Nothing from thine: in service, care, or coldness   *255*
Doth ratably[51] thy fortunes mar or make.
    Feed no man in his sins: for adulation
    Doth make thee parcel-devil[52] in damnation.

Envy not greatness: for thou mak'st thereby
Thyself the worse, and so the distance greater.   *260*
Be not thine own worm: yet such jealousy
As hurts not others, but may make thee better,
    Is a good spur. Correct thy passion's spite;
    Then may the beasts[53] draw thee to happy light.

When baseness is exalted, do not bate[54]   *265*
The place its honor, for the person's sake.
The shrine is that which thou dost venerate;
And not the beast, that bears it on his back.[55]
    I care not though the cloth of state should be
    Not of rich arras, but mean tapestry.   *270*

---

    49. *sad.* Settled, steadfast, firm, constant.
    50. *respective.* Respectful (which is the reading of *W* at this point).
    51. *ratably.* Proportionately.
    52. *parcel-devil.* Partially responsible for damnation.
    53. *beasts.* The passions.
    54. *bate.* Deprive.
    55. Cf. a fable by Aesop, in which an ass carrying an image assumes the veneration
paid the image by bystanders is for him and not the image.

Thy friend put in thy bosom: wear his eyes
Still in thy heart, that he may see what's there.
If cause require, thou art his sacrifice;
Thy drops of blood must pay down all his fear:
 But love is lost; the way of friendship's gone,   *275*
 Though *David* had his *Jonathan, Christ* his *John.*

Yet be not surety,[56] if thou be a father.
Love is a personal debt. I cannot give
My children's right, nor ought he take it: rather
Both friends should die, than hinder them to live.   *280*
 Fathers first enter bonds to nature's ends;
 And are her sureties, ere they are a friend's.

If thou be single, all thy goods and ground
Submit to love; but yet not more than all.
Give one estate, as one life. None is bound   *285*
To work for two, who brought himself to thrall.
 God made me one man; love makes me no more,
 Till labor come, and make my weakness score.[57]

In thy discourse, if thou desire to please:
All such is courteous, useful, new, or witty.   *290*
Usefulness comes by labor, wit by ease;
Courtesy grows in court; news in the city.
 Get a good stock of these, then draw the card;[58]
 That suits him best, of whom thy speech is heard.

Entice all neatly to what they know best;   *295*
For so thou dost thyself and him a pleasure:
(But a proud ignorance will lose his rest,[59]
Rather than show his cards) steal from his treasure

---

 56. *surety*. One who takes on a specific responsibility for another who remains liable.
 57. *score*. Twenty; i.e., labor added to love multiplies the effectiveness even of human weakness.
 58. *then draw the card*. Then participate in game of conversation.
 59. *rest*. Stakes kept in reserve in the card game Primero.

What to ask further. Doubts well rais'd do lock
The speaker to thee, and preserve thy stock.   *300*

If thou be Master-gunner,[60] spend not all
That thou canst speak, at once; but husband it,
And give men turns of speech: do not forestall
By lavishness thine own, and others' wit,
   As if thou mad'st thy will.[61] A civil guest   *305*
   Will no more talk all, than eat all the feast.

Be calm in arguing: for fierceness makes
Error a fault, and truth discourtesy.
Why should I feel another man's mistakes
More, than his sicknesses or poverty?   *310*
   In love I should: but anger is not love,
   Nor wisdom neither: therefore gently move.

Calmness is great advantage: he that lets
Another chafe, may warm him at his fires,
Mark all his wand'rings, and enjoy his frets;   *315*
As cunning fencers suffer heat to tire.
   Truth dwells not in the clouds: the bow[62] that's there,
   Doth often aim at, never hit the sphere.

Mark what another says: for many are
Full of themselves, and answer their own notion.   *320*
Take all into thee; then with equal care
Balance each dram of reason, like a potion.
   If truth be with thy friend, be with them both:
   Share in the conquest, and confess a troth.[63]

Be useful where thou livest, that they may   *325*
Both want and wish thy pleasing presence still.
Kindness, good parts, great places[64] are the way

---

60. *master-gunner.* Fig., leader of conversation.
61. *mad'st thy will.* Fig., have discussion go all one's own way.
62. *bow.* Rainbow.
63. *troth.* Faithfulness.
64. *great places.* Positions of social or political importance.

To compass[65] this. Find out men's wants and will,
   And meet them there. All worldly joys go less
   To the one joy of doing kindnesses.   *330*

Pitch thy behavior low, thy projects high;
So shalt thou humble and magnanimous be:
Sink not in spirit: who aimeth at the sky,
Shoots higher much than he that means[66] a tree.
   A grain of glory mixt with humbleness   *335*
   Cures both a fever and lethargicness.

Let thy mind still be bent, still plotting where,
And when, and how the business may be done.
Slackness breeds worms; but the sure traveller,
Though he alight sometimes, still goeth on.   *340*
   Active and stirring spirits live alone.
   Write on the others, Here lies such a one.

Slight not the smallest loss, whether it be
In love or honor: take account of all;
Shine like the sun in every corner: see   *345*
Whether thy stock of credit swell, or fall.
   Who say, I care not, those I give for lost;
   And to instruct them, 'twill not quit[67] the cost.

Scorn no man's love, though of a mean degree;
(Love is a present for a mighty king)   *350*
Much less make any one thine enemy.
As guns destroy, so may a little sling.[68]
   The cunning workman never doth refuse
   The meanest tool, that he may chance to use.

All foreign wisdom doth amount to this,   *355*
To take all that is given; whether wealth,

---

65. *compass.* Encompass, achieve.
66. *means.* Aims at.
67. *quit.* Be equivalent to.
68. *a little sling.* As David did Goliath, see 1 Sam. 17:50.

Or love, or language; nothing comes amiss:
A good digestion turneth all to health:
    And then as far as fair behavior may,
    Strike off all scores;[69] none are so clear as they.   *360*

Keep all thy native good, and naturalize
All foreign of that name; but scorn their ill:
Embrace their activeness, not vanities.
Who follows all things, forfeiteth his will.
    If thou observest strangers in each fit,[70]   *365*
    In time they'll run thee out of all thy wit.

Affect in things about thee cleanliness,
That all may gladly board[71] thee, as a flower.
Slovens[72] take up their stock of noisomeness
Beforehand, and anticipate their last hour.   *370*
    Let thy mind's sweetness have his operation
    Upon thy body, clothes, and habitation.

In Alms regard thy means, and others' merit.
Think heav'n a better bargain, than to give
Only thy single market-money[73] for it.   *375*
Join hands with God to make a man to live.
    Give to all something; to a good poor man,
    Till thou change names, and be where he began.[74]

Man is God's image; but a poor man is
Christ's stamp to boot: both images regard.   *380*
God reckons for him, counts the favor his:
Write, So much giv'n to God; thou shalt be heard.
    Let thy alms go before,[75] and keep heav'n's gate
    Open for thee; or both may come too late.

---

69. *strike off all scores*. Repay all indebtedness.
70. *observest . . . . in each fit*. Follow in every particular.
71. *board*. Approach.
72. *Slovens*. Persons of low character.
73. *market-money*. Lowest price.
74. See Mark 10:31.
75. See Acts 10:4.

Restore to God his due in tithe and time: *385*
A tithe purloin'd cankers the whole estate.
Sundays observe: think when the bells do chime,
'Tis angels' music; therefore come not late.
    God then deals blessings: If a king did so,
    Who would not haste, nay give, to see the show?   *390*

Twice on the day[76] his due is understood;
For all the week thy food so oft he gave thee.
Thy cheer is mended; bate not of the food,
Because 'tis better, and perhaps may save thee.
    Thwart not th' Almighty God: Oh be not cross.   *395*
    Fast when thou wilt; but then 'tis gain, not loss.

Though private prayer be a brave design,
Yet public hath more promises, more love:
And love's a weight[77] to hearts, to eyes a sign.
We all are but cold suitors; let us move   *400*
    Where it is warmest. Leave thy six and seven;[78]
    Pray with the most: for where most pray, is heaven.

When once thy foot enters the church, be bare.[79]
God is more there, than thou: for thou art there
Only by his permission. Then beware,   *405*
And make thyself all reverence and fear.
    Kneeling ne'er spoil'd silk stocking: quit thy state.
    All equal are within the church's gate.

Resort to sermons, but to prayers most:
Praying's the end of preaching. Oh be drest;   *410*
Stay not for th' other pin: why thou hast lost

---

76. *Twice on the day*. According to Walton, Herbert kept to a daily routine of reading the offices of Morning and Evening Prayer according to the Book of Common Prayer, in addition to his observance of them on Sunday; see his *Life*, p. 302.

77. *weight*. Impetus, claim to consideration.

78. *six and seven*. From usage in dice, here suggesting risky behavior, carelessness to the consequence of one's actions. L and S suggest a reference to small groups, or families, at prayer.

79. *bare*. Bareheaded.

A joy for it worth worlds. Thus hell doth jest
  Away thy blessings, and extremely flout thee,
  Thy clothes being fast, but thy soul loose about thee.

In time of service seal[80] up both thine eyes,   *415*
And send them to thine heart; that spying sin,
They may weep out the stains by them did rise:
Those doors being shut, all by the ear comes in.
  Who marks in church-time others' symmetry,
  Makes all their beauty his deformity.   *420*

Let vain or busy thoughts have there no part:
Bring not thy plough, thy plots,[81] thy pleasures thither.
Christ purg'd his temple;[82] so must thou thy heart.
All worldly thoughts are but thieves met together
  To cozen[83] thee. Look to thy actions well: *425*
  For churches are either our heav'n or hell.

Judge not the preacher; for he is thy Judge:
If thou mislike him, thou conceiv'st him not.
God calleth preaching folly.[84] Do not grudge
To pick out treasures from an earthen pot.[85]   *430*
  The worst speak something good: if all want sense,
  God takes a text, and preacheth patience.

He that gets patience, and the blessing which
Preachers conclude with, hath not lost his pains.
He that by being at church escapes the ditch,   *435*
Which he might fall in by companions, gains.
  He that loves God's abode, and to combine
  With saints on earth, shall one day with them shine.

Jest not at preacher's language, or expression:
How know'st thou, but thy sins made him miscarry?   *440*

---

80. *seal.* In special sense of marking for a special destination.
81. *plots.* Projects, not of necessity secret or devious.
82. *purg'd his temple.* See Mark 11:15ff.
83. *cozen.* Deceive.
84. See 1 Cor. 1:21.
85. See 2 Cor. 4:7.

Then turn thy faults and his into confession:
God sent him, whatsoe'er he be: Oh, tarry,
   And love him for his Master: his condition,
   Though it be ill, makes him no ill Physician.

None shall in hell such bitter pangs endure,   *445*
As those, who mock at God's way of salvation.
Whom oil and balsams kill, what salve can cure?
They drink with greediness a full damnation.
   The Jews refused thunder;[86] and we, folly.
   Though God do hedge us in, yet who is holy?   *450*

Sum up at night, what thou hast done by day;
And in the morning, what thou hast to do.
Dress and undress thy soul: mark the decay
And growth of it: if with thy watch, that too
   Be down, then wind up both; since we shall be   *455*
   Most surely judg'd, make thy accounts agree.

In brief, acquit thee bravely; play the man.
Look not on pleasures as they come, but go.
Defer not the least virtue: life's poor span
Make not an ell,[87] by trifling in thy woe.   *460*
   If thou do ill; the joy fades, not the pains:
   If well; the pain doth fade, the joy remains.

SUPERLIMINARY[88]

Thou, whom the former precepts have
Sprinkled[89] and taught, how to behave

---

86. *thunder.* See Exod. 19:16 and 1 Cor. 1:18.

87. *ell.* A unit of measurement amounting to 45 inches.

88. *Superliminary.* Title: Literally, above the threshhold, suggesting the lintel over the passageway between the church porch and the church proper; here, figuratively, the poem that is the passage from "The Church Porch" to "The Church."

89. *Sprinkled.* See note to "Perirrhanterium" above.

Thyself in church; approach, and taste
The church's mystical repast.[90]

Avoid profaneness; come not here: 5
Nothing but holy, pure, and clear,
Or that which groaneth to be so,
May at his peril further go.

---

90. *mystical repast.* Link between the functioning of the poems that follow and the Eucharist, the Church's sharing in Christ's body and blood "and all other benefits of his passion" (BCP, p. 264).

THE CHURCH

THE ALTAR

A broken A L T A R, Lord, thy servant rears,
Made of a heart, and cemented with tears:[1]
    Whose parts are as thy hand did frame;
    No workman's tool hath touch'd the same.
        A H E A R T alone   5
        Is   such   a   stone,[2]
        As   nothing   but
        Thy pow'r doth cut.[3]
        Wherefore each part
        Of my hard heart   10
        Meets in this frame,
        To praise thy name.
    That if I chance to hold my peace,
    These stones to praise thee may not cease.[4]
Oh let thy blessed S A C R I F I C E be mine,[5]   15
And   sanctify   this   A L T A R   to   be   thine.

THE SACRIFICE

Oh, all ye, who pass by,[6] whose eyes and mind
To worldly things are sharp, but to me blind;
To me, who took eyes that I might you find:
    Was ever grief like mine?

The Princes of my people make a head[7]   5
Against their Maker: they do wish me dead,

---

1. See Ps. 51:17.
2. See Deut. 27:2–6 and 2 Cor. 3:2–3.
3. See Ezek. 36:25–27 and Zech. 7:12.
4. See Luke 19:40.
5. See prayer after reception in BCP Communion, Booty, p. 264.
6. See Lam. 1:12.
7. *made a head.* Move in opposition.

Who cannot wish, except I give them bread:
    Was ever grief like mine?

Without me each one, who doth now me brave,[8]
Had to this day been an Egyptian slave.   *10*
They use that power against me, which I gave:
    Was ever grief like mine?

Mine own Apostle, who the bag did bear,[9]
Though he had all I had, did not forbear
To sell me also, and to put me there: *15*
    Was ever grief like mine?

For thirty pence he did my death devise,
Who at three hundred did the ointment prize,[10]
Not half so sweet as my sweet sacrifice:
    Was ever grief like mine?   *20*

Therefore my soul melts, and my heart's dear treasure
Drops blood (the only beads) my words to measure:
Oh let this cup pass, if it be thy pleasure:[11]
    Was ever grief like mine?

These drops being temper'd with a sinner's tears,   *25*
A Balsam are for both the Hemispheres:
Curing all wounds, but mine; all, but my fears:
    Was ever grief like mine?

Yet my Disciples sleep: I cannot gain
One hour of watching; but their drowsy brain   *30*
Comforts not me, and doth my doctrine stain:
    Was ever grief like mine?

Arise, arise, they come. Look how they run.
Alas! what haste they make to be undone!

---

8. *brave.* Defy, menace, perhaps boastfully.
9. Judas; see John 12:6.
10. *three hundred.* See John 12:1–8.
11. See Luke 22:42.

How with their lanterns do they seek the sun!   *35*
    Was ever grief like mine?

With clubs and staves they seek me, as a thief,
Who am the way of truth, the true relief;[12]
Most true to those, who are my greatest grief: *40*
    Was ever grief like mine?

Judas, dost thou betray me with a kiss?
Canst thou find hell about my lips? and miss
Of life, just at the gates of life and bliss?
    Was ever grief like mine?

See, they lay hold on me, not with the hands   *45*
Of faith, but fury:[13] yet at their commands
I suffer binding, who have loos'd their bands:[14]
    Was ever grief like mine?

All my Disciples fly; fear puts a bar
Betwixt my friends and me. They leave the star,   *50*
That brought the wise men of the East from far.
    Was ever grief like mine?

Then from one ruler to another bound
They lead me; urging, that it was not sound
What I taught: Comments would the text confound.   *55*
    Was ever grief like mine?

The Priest and rulers all false witness seek
'Gainst him, who seeks not life, but is the meek
And ready Paschal Lamb of this great week:
    Was ever grief like mine?   *60*

Then they accuse me of great blasphemy,
That I did thrust into the Deity,

---

12. See John 14:6.
13. An inversion of Paul's counsel, "Fight the good fight of faith, lay hold on eternal life" (1 Tim. 6:12).
14. A combination of Ezek. 34:27 and Ps. 116:16.

Who never thought that any robbery:[15]
  Was ever grief like mine?

Some said, that I the Temple to the floor   *65*
In three days raz'd, and raised as before.
Why, he that built the world can do much more:
  Was ever grief like mine?

Then they condemn me all with that same breath,
Which I do give them daily, unto death.   *70*
Thus *Adam* my first breathing rendereth:
  Was ever grief like mine?

They bind, and lead me unto *Herod:* he
Sends me to *Pilate*. This makes them agree;
But yet their friendship is my enmity: *75*
  Was ever grief like mine?

Herod and all his bands do set me light,[16]
Who teach all hands to war, fingers to fight,
And only am the Lord of hosts and might:
  Was ever grief like mine?   *80*

Herod in judgment sits, while I do stand;
Examines me with a censorious hand:
I him obey, who all things else command:
  Was ever grief like mine?

The *Jews* accuse me with despitefulness;[17]   *85*
And vying malice with my gentleness,
Pick quarrels with their only happiness:
  Was ever grief like mine?

I answer nothing, but with patience prove[18]
If stony hearts will melt with gentle love.   *90*

---

15. *any robbery.* See Phil. 2:6.
16. *set me light.* Despise, take lightly.
17. *despitefulness.* Contemptuousness, cruelty.
18. *prove.* Try to discover. See Ezek. 11:19 and 36:26. See also notes 1–5.

But who does hawk at eagles with a dove?
　　Was ever grief like mine?

My silence rather doth augment their cry;
My dove doth back into my bosom fly,[19]
Because the raging waters still are high: *95*
　　Was ever grief like mine?

Hark how they cry aloud still, *Crucify:*
It is not fit he live a day, they cry,
Who cannot live less than eternally:
　　Was ever grief like mine?   *100*

Pilate a stranger holdeth off; but they,
Mine own dear people, cry, *Away, away,*
With noises confused frighting the day:
　　Was ever grief like mine?

Yet still they shout, and cry, and stop their ears,   *105*
Putting my life among their sins and fears,
And therefore wish *my blood on them and theirs:*
　　Was ever grief like mine?

See how spite cankers things. These words aright
Used, and wished, are the whole world's light: *110*
But honey is their gall, brightness their night:
　　Was ever grief like mine?

They choose a murderer, and all agree
In him to do themselves a courtesy:
For it was their own cause who killed me: *115*
　　Was ever grief like mine?

And a seditious murderer he was:
But I the Prince of peace; peace that doth pass
All understanding, more than heav'n doth glass:[20]
　　Was ever grief like mine?   *120*

---

19. See Gen. 8:9.
20. *glass.* See 1 Cor. 13:12.

Why, Caesar is their only King, not I:
He clave the stony rock, when they were dry;[21]
But surely not their hearts, as I well try:
    Was ever grief like mine?

Ah! how they scourge me! yet my tenderness   *125*
Doubles each lash: and yet their bitterness
Winds up my grief to a mysteriousness:
    Was ever grief like mine?

They buffet me, and box me as they list,
Who grasp the earth and heaven with my fist,   *130*
And never yet, whom I would punish, miss'd:
    Was ever grief like mine?

Behold, they spit on me in scornful wise,
Who by my spittle gave the blind man eyes,[22]
Leaving his blindness to mine enemies: *135*
    Was ever grief like mine?

My face they cover, though it be divine.
As *Moses'* face was veiled,[23] so is mine,
Lest on their double-dark souls either shine:
    Was ever grief like mine?   *140*

Servants and abjects[24] flout me; they are witty:
Now prophesy who strikes thee, is their ditty.
So they in me deny themselves all pity:
    Was ever grief like mine?

And now I am deliver'd unto death,   *145*
Which each one calls for so with utmost breath,
That he before me well nigh suffereth:
    Was ever grief like mine?

---

21. Ironic allusion to Moses' striking the rock with his rod (Num. 20:8).
22. See Mark 8:22–25.
23. *veiled.* See Exod. 34:30ff.
24. *abjects.* Degraded persons.

Weep not, dear friends, since I for both have wept
When all my tears were blood, the while you slept: *150*
Your tears for your own fortunes should be kept:
     Was ever grief like mine?

The soldiers lead me to the common hall;
There they deride me, they abuse me all:
Yet for twelve heav'nly legions I could call: *155*
     Was ever grief like mine?

Then with a scarlet robe they me array:
Which shows my blood to be the only way,
And cordial left to repair man's decay:
     Was ever grief like mine?   *160*

Then on my head a crown of thorns I wear:
For these are all the grapes *Sion* doth bear,
Though I my vine planted[25] and wat'red there:
     Was ever grief like mine?

So sits the earth's great curse in *Adam's* fall   *165*
Upon my head: so I remove it all
From th' earth unto my brows, and bear the thrall:[26]
     Was ever grief like mine?

Then with the reed they gave to me before,
They strike my head, the rock[27] from whence all store   *170*
Of heav'nly blessings issue evermore:
     Was ever grief like mine?

They bow their knees to me, and cry, *Hail king:*
Whatever scoffs or scornfulness can bring,
I am the floor, the sink,[28] where they it fling: *175*
     Was ever grief like mine?

---

25. *vine planted.* See Isa. 5:1–7 for imagery of the vineyard as the House of Israel.
26. *thrall.* Misery, condition of servitude or bondage.
27. *rock.* See 1 Cor. 10:4.
28. *sink.* Receptacle for waste; cesspool.

Yet since man's scepters are as frail as reeds,
And thorny all their crowns, bloody their weeds;[29]
I, who am Truth, turn into truth their deeds:
      Was ever grief like mine?   *180*

The soldiers also spit upon that face,
Which Angels did desire to have the grace,[30]
And Prophets once to see,[31] but found no place:
      Was ever grief like mine?

Thus trimmed forth they bring me to the rout,   *185*
Who *Crucify him,* cry with one strong shout.
God holds his peace at man, and man cries out:
      Was ever grief like mine?

They lead me in once more, and putting then
Mine own clothes on, they lead me out again.   *190*
Whom devils fly, thus is he toss'd of men:
      Was ever grief like mine?

And now weary of sport, glad to engross[32]
All spite in one, counting my life their loss,
They carry me to my most bitter cross: *195*
      Was ever grief like mine?

My cross I bear myself, until I faint:
Then Simon bears it for me by constraint,
The decreed burden of each mortal Saint:
      Was ever grief like mine?   *200*

Oh all ye who pass by, behold and see;
Man stole the fruit, but I must climb the tree;[33]

---

29. *weeds.* Clothing.
30. See 1 Pet. 1:12.
31. See Luke 10:24.
32. *engross.* Concentrate, collect.
33. Tuve sketches the typological tradition that Christ on the Cross is the fruit reversing the fall caused by the taking of the fruit by Adam and Eve in the Garden of Eden (see *A Reading of George Herbert,* pp. 3–93).

The tree of life to all, but only me:
    Was ever grief like mine?

Lo, here I hang, charg'd with a world of sin,   *205*
The greater world o' th' two; for that came in
By words, but this by sorrow I must win:[34]
    Was ever grief like mine?

Such sorrow, as if sinful man could feel,
Or feel his part, he would not cease to kneel   *210*
Till all were melted, though he were all steel:
    Was ever grief like mine?

But, *Oh, my God, my God!* why leav'st thou me,
The son, in whom thou dost delight to be?
*My God, my God*_____
    Never was grief like mine.

Shame tears my soul, my body many a wound;
Sharp nails pierce this, but sharper that confound;
Reproaches, which are free, while I am bound,
    Was ever grief like mine?   *220*

Now heal thyself, Physician; now come down.[35]
Alas! I did so, when I left my crown
And father's smile for you, to feel his frown:
    Was ever grief like mine?

In healing not myself, there doth consist   *225*
All that salvation, which ye now resist;
Your safety in my sickness doth subsist:
    Was ever grief like mine:

Betwixt two thieves I spend my utmost breath,
As he that for some robbery suffereth.   *230*

---

34. In Genesis 1, the world was created by divine speech; the second world, that dominated by sin must be won by the Word becoming flesh (John 1).
35. A conflation of Luke 4:23 with Matt. 27:40.

Alas! what have I stolen from you? death:
    Was ever grief like mine?

A king my title is, prefixt on high;
Yet by my subjects am condemn'd to die
A servile death in servile company: 235
    Was ever grief like mine?

They gave me vinegar mingled with gall,
But more with malice: yet, when they did call,
With Manna, Angel's food, I fed them all:[36]
    Was ever grief like mine?   240

They part my garments, and by lot dispose
My coat,[37] the type of love, which once cur'd those
Who sought for help, never malicious foes:
    Was ever grief like mine?

Nay, after death their spite shall further go;   245
For they will pierce my side, I full well know;
That as sin came, so Sacraments might flow:[38]
    Was ever grief like mine?

But now I die; now all is finished.
My woe, man's weal: and now I bow my head.   250
Only let others say, when I am dead,
    Never was grief like mine.

THE THANKSGIVING

Oh King of grief! (a title strange, yet true,
  To thee of all kings only due)
Oh King of wounds! how shall I grieve for thee,

---

36. See Ps. 78:25.
37. *My coat.* See Matt. 14:36.
38. As Eve was taken from Adam's side, so from Christ's wounded side came "blood and water" (John 19:34), the sacraments of the Church through which the consequences of Eve's sin are reversed.

Who in all grief preventest[39] me?
Shall I weep blood? why thou hast wept such store[40]   *5*
That all thy body was one door.[41]
Shall I be scourged, flouted, boxed, sold?
  'Tis but to tell the tale is told.
My God, my God, why dost thou part from me?[42]
  Was such a grief as cannot be.   *10*
Shall I then sing, skipping thy doleful story,[43]
  And side with thy triumphant glory?
Shall thy strokes be my stroking? thorns, my flower?
  Thy rod, my poesy? cross, my bower?
But how then shall I imitate thee, and   *15*
  Copy thy fair, though bloody hand?
Surely I will revenge me on thy love,
  And try who shall victorious prove.
If thou dost give me wealth, I will restore
  All back unto thee by the poor.[44]   *20*
If thou dost give me honor, men shall see,
  The honor doth belong to thee.
I will not marry; or, if she be mine,
  She and her children shall be thine.
My bosom friend, if he blaspheme thy name,   *25*
  I will tear thence his love and fame.
One half of me being gone, the rest I give
  Unto some Chapel, die or live.
As for thy passion—But of that anon,
  When with the other I have done.   *30*
For thy predestination I'll contrive,
  That three years hence, if I survive,
I'll build a spittle,[45] or mend common ways,
  But mend mine own without delays.
Then I will use the works of thy creation,   *35*
  As if I us'd them but for fashion.

---

39. *preventest.* Surpasses, anticipates.
40. *store.* Abundance.
41. *door.* See John 10:9.
42. See Matt. 27:46.
43. *W* clarifies the meaning here with its reading "neglecting thy sad story."
44. *by the poor.* By means of; see Prov. 19:17.
45. *spittle.* Hospital, or alms-house.

The world and I will quarrel; and the year
  Shall not perceive, that I am here.[46]
My music shall find thee, and ev'ry string
  Shall have his attribute to sing;   *40*
That all together may accord in thee,
  And prove one God, one harmony.
If thou shalt give me wit, it shall appear,
  If thou hast giv'n it me, 'tis here.
Nay, I will read thy book, and never move   *45*
  Till I have found therein thy love;
Thy art of love,[47] which I'll turn back on thee,
  Oh my dear Savior, Victory!
Then for thy passion—I will do for that—
  Alas, my God, I know not what.   *50*

THE REPRISAL[48]

    I have consider'd it, and find
There is no dealing with thy mighty passion:
For though I die for thee, I am behind;
    My sins deserve the condemnation.

    Oh make me innocent, that I   *5*
May give a disentangled state and free:
And yet thy wounds still my attempts defy,
    For by thy death I die for thee.

    Ah! was it not enough that thou
By thy eternal glory didst outgo me?   *10*
Couldst thou not grief's sad conquests me allow,
    But in all vict'ries overthrow me?

---

46. *here*. In this collection of poems.
47. *art of love*. Divine love, as opposed to Ovid's *Ars Amatoria*.
48. *The Reprisal*. Title: In *W*, the title is "The Second Thanks-giving," which links the poem to its predecessor. "Reprisal" is used in the musical sense as a return to an earlier theme. The shape of the stanzas suggests a roughly cruciform pattern.

THE CHURCH

Yet by confession will I come
Into the conquest.⁴⁹ Though I can do nought
Against thee, in thee I will overcome   *15*
   The man, who once against thee fought.⁵⁰

THE AGONY⁵¹

Philosophers have measur'd mountains,
Fathom'd the depths of seas, of states, and kings,
Walk'd with a staff⁵² to heav'n, and traced fountains:
   But there are two vast, spacious things,
The which to measure it doth more behove: *5*
Yet few there are that sound them; Sin and Love.

Who would know Sin, let him repair
Unto Mount Olivet; there shall he see
A man so wrung with pains, that all his hair,
   His skin, his garments bloody be.   *10*
Sin is that press and vice, which forceth pain
To hunt his cruel food through ev'ry vein.

Who knows not Love, let him assay
And taste that juice, which on the cross a pike
Did set again abroach;⁵³ then let him say   *15*
   If ever he did taste the like.
Love is that liquour sweet and most divine,
Which my God feels as blood; but I, as wine.

---

49. Both mss. read "Into thy conquest."
50. Alluded to here are both Jacob's wrestling with God (Gen. 32:22–31) and Paul's concept of the "new man" (as in Col. 3:10).
51. Patrick suggests that the visual shape of this poem's stanza-form implies the "press" of line 11, in the same way that the shapes of "Easter-wings" and "The Altar" reflect their subjects. Hutchinson points out that the central metaphor of the poem derives from Isa. 63:1–3, which is part of the reading for the Epistle appointed for the Monday before Easter in the BCP calendar: "What is he this that cometh from God. . . . . Wherefore then is thy clothing red, and thy raiment like his that treadeth in the wine press? I have trodden the press myself alone, and of all people there is not one with me."
52. *with a staff.* A rod for measuring distances and heights.
53. *Did set again abroach.* Pierced and left running.

GEORGE HERBERT

THE SINNER

Lord, how I am all ague,[54] when I seek
  What I have treasur'd in my memory!
  Since, if my soul make even with the week,
Each seventh note by right is due to thee
I find there quarries of pil'd vanities,   *5*
  But shreds of holiness, that dare not venture
  To show their face, since cross to thy decrees:
There the circumference earth is, heav'n the center.
In so much dregs the quintessence is small:
  The spirit and good extract of my heart   *10*
  Comes to about the many hundredth part.
Yet Lord restore thine image, hear my call:
  And though my hard heart scarce to thee can groan,
  Remember that thou once didst write in stone.[55]

GOOD FRIDAY[56]

        Oh my chief good,
   How shall I measure out thy blood?
   How shall I count what thee befell,
       And each grief tell?

        Shall I thy woes   *5*
  Number according to thy foes?
  Or, since one star show'd thy first breath,
       Shall all thy death?

        Or shall each leaf,
  Which falls in Autumn, score[57] a grief?   *10*
  Or cannot leaves, but fruit, be sign
       Of the true vine?

---

54. *ague.* In a fit of shaking, as in one stage of a violent fever.
55. See Exod. 31:18 and 2 Cor. 3:3, along with Ezek. 36:25–27.
56. Patrick points out the roughly cruciform shape of this poem's stanza-form.
57. *score.* Mark, as in counting.

THE CHURCH

Then let each hour
Of my whole life one grief devour;
That thy distress through all may run,   *15*
And be my sun.

Or rather let
My several sins their sorrows get;
That as each beast his cure doth know,
Each sin may so.   *20*

[THE PASSION][58]

Since blood is fittest, Lord, to write
Thy sorrows in, and bloody fight;
My heart hath store, write there, where in
One box doth lie both ink and sin:

That when sin spies so many foes,   *5*
Thy whips, thy nails, thy wounds, thy woes,
All come to lodge there, sin may say,
No room for me, and fly away.

Sin being gone, oh fill the place,
And keep possession with thy grace;   *10*
Lest sin take courage and return,
And all the writings blot or burn.

---

58. Title: Taken from *W*; in *B*, these lines appear at the beginning of a page, but with no title, while in *1633* these lines follow directly the ending of "Good Friday." Thus, in all subsequent editions, these lines appear as lines 21–32 of "Good Friday," although since *1638*, the initial "Since" has been printed with a large capital letter, suggesting the beginning of a new poem, or a new section of the poem. On internal evidence, I believe these lines are a poem distinct from "Good Friday"—hence the difference in stanza form and the difference in content—thus I have restored their original title from *W* and given them their due as a separate poem.

GEORGE HERBERT

REDEMPTION

Having been tenant long to a rich Lord,
  Not thriving, I resolved to be bold,
  And make a suit unto him, to afford
A new small-rented lease, and cancel th' old.[59]

In heaven at his manor I him sought: *5*
  They told me there, that he was lately gone
  About some land, which he had dearly bought
Long since on earth, to take possession.

I straight return'd, and knowing his great birth,
  Sought him accordingly in great resorts;   *10*
  In cities, theaters, gardens, parks, and courts:
At length I heard a ragged noise and mirth

  Of thieves and murderers: there I him espied,
  Who straight, *Your suit is granted*, said, and died.

SEPULCHER

Oh blessed body! Whither art thou thrown?
No lodging for thee, but a cold hard stone?
So many hearts on earth, and yet not one
              Receive thee?

Sure there is room within our hearts' good store;   *5*
For they can lodge transgressions by the score:
Thousands of toys[60] dwell there, yet out of door
             They leave thee.

But that which shows them large, shows them unfit.
Whatever sin did this pure rock commit,   *10*

---

59. *th'old.* The Old Covenant, as opposed to the New Covenant of Grace.
60. *toys.* Trifling things.

Which holds thee now? Who hath indicted it
        Of murder?

Where our hard hearts have took up stones[61] to brain thee,
And missing this, most falsely did arraign thee;
Only these stones in quiet entertain thee,
        And order.

And as of old, the law by heav'nly art
Was writ in stone; so thou, which also art
The letter of the word,[62] find'st no fit heart
        To hold thee.

Yet do we still persist as we began,   *20*
And so should perish, but that nothing can,
Though it be cold, hard, foul, from loving man
        Withhold thee.

EASTER [(I)][63]

Rise heart; thy Lord is risen. Sing his praise
        Without delays,
Who takes thee by the hand, that thou likewise
        With him mayst rise:
That, as his death calcined[64] thee to dust,   *5*
His life may make thee gold, and much more just.

Awake, my lute, and struggle for thy part
        With all thy art.
The cross taught all wood to resound his name,
        Who bore the same.   *10*

---

61. *took up stones.* See John 10:31.
62. *The letter of the word.* See Heb. 8:10 and Prov. 3:3, 7:3.
63. Title: In *1633*, what appears here as "Easter [I]" and "[Easter II]" is printed as one poem; the title "Easter II" is from *W*. Since critics agree that "Easter II" is the speaker's response to his call in "Easter [I]" for his lute to "awake" (1.7), I believe that restoring the division found in *W* is appropriate.
64. *calcined.* Burnt to ashes.

His stretched sinews taught all strings, what key
Is best to celebrate that most high day.

Consort both heart and lute, and twist[65] a song
  Pleasant and long:
Or since all music is but three parts vied[66]   *15*
  And multiplied;
Oh let thy blessed Spirit bear a part,
And make up our defects with his sweet art.

[EASTER (II)][67]

I got me flowers to straw thy way;
I got me boughs off many a tree:
But thou wast up by break of day,
And brought'st thy sweets along with thee.

The Sun arising in the East,   *5*
Though he give light, and th' East perfume;
If they should offer to contest
With thy arising, they presume.

Can there be any day but this,
Though many suns to shine endeavor?   *10*
We count three hundred, but we miss:
there is but one, and that one ever.

---

65. *twist*. Weave together, as in polyphonic music.
66. *vied*. Increased in number by addition or repetition.
67. Title: From *W*.

THE CHURCH

EASTER WINGS

Lord, who createdst man in wealth and store,
    Though foolishly he lost the same,
        Decaying more and more,
           Till he became
             Most poor: *5*
             With thee
          Oh let me rise[68]
        As larks, harmoniously,
     And sing this day thy victories:
Then shall the fall further the flight in me.   *10*

    My tender age in sorrow did begin:
    And still with sicknesses and shame
        Thou didst so punish sin,
           That I became
             Most thin.   *15*
             With thee
          Let me combine,
        And feel this day thy victory:
    For, if I imp[69] my wing on thine,
Affliction shall advance the flight in me.   *20*

HOLY BAPTISM (I)

As he that sees a dark and shady grove,
    Stays not, but looks beyond it on the sky;
    So when I view my sins, mine eyes remove
More backward still, and to that water fly,

Which is above the heav'ns, whose spring and rent   *5*
    Is in my dear Redeemer's pierced side.

---

68. *Oh let me rise.* See Isa. 40:31 and Mal. 4:2.
69. *imp.* To imp, in falconry, is to engraft feathers in a damaged wing, so as to improve or restore damaged powers of flight.

Oh blessed streams! either ye to prevent
And stop our sins from growing thick and wide,

Or else give tears to drown them, as they grow.
  In you Redemption measures all my time,   *10*
  And spreads the plaister[70] equal to the crime:
You taught the Book of Life my name, that so

  Whatever future sins should me miscall,
  Your first acquaintance might discredit all.

HOLY BAPTISM (II)

      Since, Lord, to thee
    A narrow way and little gate
Is all the passage,[71] on my infancy
    Thou didst lay hold, and antedate
      My faith in me.   *5*

      Oh let me still
    Write thee great God, and me a child:
Let me be soft and supple to thy will,
    Small to myself, to others mild,
      Behither[72] ill.   *10*

      Although by stealth
    My flesh get on; yet let her sister
My soul bid nothing, but preserve her wealth:
    The growth of flesh is but a blister;
      Childhood is health.   *15*

---

70. *plaister*. A curative substance applied over an injury.
71. See Matt. 7:13–14.
72. *Behither*. Short of, barring, on this side of.

THE CHURCH

NATURE

Full of rebellion, I would die,
Or fight, or travel, or deny
That thou hast ought to do with me.
      Oh tame my heart;
    It is thy highest art   5
To captivate strong holds[73] to thee.

If thou shalt let this venom lurk,
And in suggestions fume and work,
My soul will turn to bubbles straight,
      And thence by kind[74]   10
    Vanish into a wind,
Making thy workmanship deceit.

Oh smooth my rugged heart, and there
Engrave thy rev'rend law and fear;
Or make a new one, since the old   15
      Is sapless grown,
    And a much fitter stone
To hide my dust, than thee to hold.[75]

SIN (I)

Lord, with what care hast thou begirt us round!
  Parents first season us: then schoolmasters
  Deliver us to laws; they send us bound
To rules of reason, holy messengers,

Pulpits and Sundays, sorrow dogging sin,   5
  Afflictions sorted,[76] anguish of all sizes,

---

73. *strong holds.* See 2 Cor. 10:4.
74. *by kind.* By nature.
75. See Ezek. 36:26, as well as Jer. 31:33.
76. *sorted.* Assorted.

Fine nets and stratagems to catch us in,
Bibles laid open, millions of surprises,

Blessings beforehand, ties of gratefulness,
   The sound of glory ringing in our ears: *10*
   Without, our shame; within, our consciences;
Angels and grace, eternal hopes and fears.

   Yet all these fences and their whole array
   One cunning bosom-sin blows quite away.

AFFLICTION (I)

When first thou didst entice to thee my heart,
      I thought the service brave:[77]
So many joys I writ down for my part,
      Besides what I might have
Out of my stock of natural delights,   *5*
Augmented with thy gracious benefits.

I looked on thy furniture so fine,
      And made it fine to me;
Thy glorious household stuff did me entwine,
      And 'tice me unto thee.   *10*
Such stars[78] I counted mine: both heav'n and earth
Paid me my wages in a world of mirth.

What pleasures could I want,[79] whose King I served,
      Where joys my fellows were?
Thus argu'd into hopes, my thoughts reserved   *15*
      No place for grief or fear.
Therefore my sudden soul caught at the place,
And made her youth and fierceness seek thy face.

---

77. *brave.* Splendid.
78. *stars.* See Luke 12:33.
79. *want.* Lack.

THE CHURCH

At first thou gav'st me milk and sweetnesses;
      I had my wish and way: *20*
My days were straw'd with flow'rs and happiness;
      There was no month but May.
But with my years sorrow did twist and grow,
And made a party unawares for woe.

My flesh began unto my soul in pain,   *25*
      Sicknesses cleave my bones;
Consuming agues dwell in ev'ry vein,
      And tune my breath to groans.
Sorrow was all my soul; I scarce believed,
Till grief did tell me roundly, that I lived.   *30*

When I got health, thou took'st away my life,
      And more; for my friends die:
My mirth and edge was lost; a blunted knife
      Was of more use than I.
Thus thin and lean without a fence or friend,   *35*
I was blown through with ev'ry storm and wind.

Whereas my birth and spirit rather took
      The way that takes the town;
Thou didst betray me to a ling'ring book,
      And wrap me in a gown.   *40*
I was entangled in the world of strife,
Before I had the power to change my life.

Yet, for I threat'ned oft the siege to raise,
      Not simp'ring[80] all mine age,
Thou often didst with Academic praise   *45*
      Melt and dissolve my rage.
I took thy sweet'ned pill, till I came near;[81]
I could not go away, nor persevere.

---

80. *simp'ring*. Smirking, smiling in a silly, self-conscious manner.
81. *till I came near*. W reads *where* with no punctuation, a reading preferred by modern editors. I find *near* appropriate in the context of the poem's dialectic between "the way that takes to town" and divine service. See Song of Sol. 2:3–4.

Yet lest perchance I should too happy be
  In my unhappiness,   *50*
Turning my purge to food, thou throwest me
  Into more sicknesses.
Thus doth thy power cross-bias me,[82] not making
Thine own gift good, yet me from my ways taking.

Now I am here, what thou wilt do with me   *55*
  None of my books will show:
I read, and sigh, and wish I were a tree;
  For sure then I should grow
To fruit or shade: at least some bird would trust
Her household to me, and I should be just.   *60*

Yet, though thou troublest me, I must be meek;
  In weakness must be stout.[83]
Well, I will change the service, and go seek
  Some other master out.
Ah my dear God! though I am clean forgot,   *65*
Let me not love thee, if I love thee not.

REPENTANCE

 Lord, I confess my sin is great;
 Great is my sin. Oh! gently treat
With thy quick flow'r, thy momentany[84] bloom;
  Whose life still pressing
  Is one undressing,   *5*
A steady aiming at a tomb.

 Man's age is two hours' work, or three:
 Each day doth round about us see.

---

 82. *cross-bias me.* A metaphor from the game of bowls, meaning here "make me change my direction."
 83. *stout.* See Mal. 3:13 ("Your words have been stout against me, saith the Lord.").
 84. *momentany.* W and B read *momentary; momentany* is merely a variant spelling.

Thus are we to delights: but we are all
    To sorrows old,   *10*
    If life be told
From what life feeleth, Adam's fall.

Oh let thy height of mercy then
Compassionate short-breathed men.
Cut me not off for my most foul transgression: *15*
    I do confess
    My foolishness;
My God, accept of my confession.

Sweeten at length this bitter bowl,
Which thou hast pour'd into my soul;   *20*
Thy wormwood[85] turn to health, winds to fair weather:
    For if thou stay,[86]
    I and this day,
As we did rise, we die together.

When thou for sin rebukest man,
Forthwith he waxeth woe and wan:
Bitterness fills our bowels; all our hearts
    Pine, and decay,
    And drop away,
And carry with them th' other parts.   *30*

But thou wilt sin and grief destroy;
That so the broken bones may joy,[87]
And tune together in a well-set song,
    Full of his praises,
    Who dead men raises.   *35*
Fractures well cur'd make us more strong.

---

85. *wormwood.* See Jer. 9:15.
86. *stay.* Stay away.
87. See Ps. 51:8.

GEORGE HERBERT

FAITH

Lord, how couldst thou so much appease
Thy wrath for sin, as when man's sight was dim,
And could see little, to regard his ease,
    And bring by Faith all things to him?

Hungry I was, and had no meat: *5*
I did conceit[88] a most delicious feast;
I had it straight,[89] and did as truly eat,
    As ever did a welcome guest.

There is a rare outlandish root,[90]
Which when I could not get, I thought it here: *10*
That apprehension cur'd so well my foot,
    That I can walk to heav'n well near.

I owed thousands and much more:
I did believe that I did nothing owe,
And liv'd accordingly; my creditor   *15*
    Believes so too, and lets me go.

Faith makes me anything, or all
That I believe is in the sacred story:
And where sin placeth me in Adam's fall,
    Faith sets me higher in his glory.   *20*

If I go lower in the book,
What can be lower than the common manger?
Faith puts me there with him, who sweetly took
    Our flesh and frailty, death and danger.

If bliss had lien in art or strength,   *25*
None but the wise or strong had gained it:
Where now by Faith all arms are of a length;
    One size doth all conditions fit.

---

88. *conceit.* Imagine, conceive.
89. *straight.* Immediately, straightaway.
90. *root.* Christ provides an antidote to the serpent that bruises man's heel (*foot*), as in Gen. 3:15. Hutchinson suggests an allusion to the snake-root of Virginia.

A peasant may believe as much
As a great Clerk,[91] and reach the highest stature.   *30*
Thus dost thou make proud knowledge bend and crouch
    While grace fills up uneven nature.

When creatures had no real light
Inherent in them, thou didst make the sun
Impute a luster, and allow them bright;   *35*
    And in this show, what Christ hath done.

That which before was dark'ned clean[92]
With bushy groves, pricking the looker's eye,
Vanisht away, when Faith did change the scene:
    And then appear'd a glorious sky.   *40*

What though my body run to dust?
Faith cleaves unto it, counting ev'ry grain
With an exact and most particular trust,
    Reserving all for flesh again.[93]

PRAYER (I)

Prayer the Church's banquet, Angels' age,[94]
    God's breath in man returning to his birth,
    The soul in paraphrase,[95] heart in pilgrimage,
The Christian plummet sounding heav'n and earth;

---

91. *clerk.* Cleric; man of learning.
92. *clean.* Wholly, completely.
93. *flesh again.* As in the general resurrection.
94. *Angel's age.* While "man's age" is "threescore years and ten" (Ps. 90:10), after the Resurrection, "Neither can they die any more: for they are equal unto the angels" (Luke 20:36).
95. *the soul in paraphrase.* A paraphrase clarifies by expansion.

Engine against th' Almighty,[96] sinners' tower,   5
   Reversed thunder, Christ-side-piercing spear,
   The six-days world transposing[97] in an hour,
A kind of tune, which all things hear and fear;

Softness, and peace, and joy, and love, and bliss,
   Exalted Manna, gladness of the best,   10
   Heaven in ordinary,[98] man well drest,
The milky way, the bird of Paradise,

   Church-bells beyond the stars heard, the soul's blood,
   The land of spices; something understood.

THE HOLY COMMUNION

Not in rich furniture, or fine array,
   Nor in a wedge of gold,[99]
   Thou, who from me[100] wast sold,
To me dost now thyself convey;
For so thou should'st without me still have been,   5
   Leaving within me sin:

But by the way of nourishment and strength
   Thou creep'st into my breast;
   Making thy way my rest,
And thy small quantities my length;   10
Which spread their forces into every part,
   Meeting sin's force and art.

---

96. *Engine against the Almighty.* See "Artillery," p. 263, l. 25: "Then we are shooters both."

97. *transposing.* Transforming.

98. *ordinary.* In everyday setting or dress.

99. *wedge of gold.* See Josh. 7:21 ("When I saw among the spoils . . . a wedge of gold . . . then I coveted them and took them"). The contrast here is, in part, between the simplicity of Anglican and the elaborateness of Roman Catholic Eucharistic ceremonial.

100. *from me. B* reads "for me."

Yet can these not get over to my soul,
  Leaping the wall that parts
  Our souls and fleshly hearts;   *15*
But as th' outworks,[101] they may control
My rebel flesh, and carrying thy name,
  Affright both sin and shame.

Only thy grace, which with these elements comes,
  Knoweth the ready way,   *20*
  And hath the privy key,
Op'ning the soul's most subtle rooms;
While those to spirits refin'd, at door attend
  Dispatches from their friend.

[PRAYER (II)][102]

Give me my captive soul, or take
  My body also thither.
Another lift like this will make
  Them both to be together.

Before that sin turn'd flesh to stone,   *5*
  And all our lump to leaven;
A fervent sigh might well have blown
  Our innocent earth to heaven.

For sure when Adam did not know
  To sin, or sin to smother;   *10*
He might to heav'n from Paradise go,
  As from one room t'another.

Thou hast restor'd us to this ease
  By this thy heav'nly blood;

---

101. *outworks.* Outer defenses.
102. Title: From *W*, since the spacing in *1633* and *B*, as well as the change in stanza-form, sets these lines off clearly from what goes before. Most modern editions print these lines as lines 25–40 of "The Holy Communion."

Which I can go to, when I please,   *15*
   And leave th' earth to their food.

ANTIPHON (I)[103]

Choir. Let all the world in ev'ry corner sing,
    My God and King.

   Verse. The heav'ns are not too high,
     His praise may thither fly:
     The earth is not too low,   *5*
     His praises there may grow.

Choir. Let all the world in ev'ry corner sing,
    My God and King.

   Verse. The church with psalms must shout,
     No door can keep them out: *10*
     But above all, the heart
     Must bear the longest part.

Choir. Let all the world in ev'ry corner sing,
    My God and King.

LOVE I

Immortal Love, author of this great frame,[104]
   Sprung from that beauty which can never fade;
   How hath man parcel'd out thy glorious name,
And thrown it on that dust which thou hast made,

---

103. *Antiphon.* "A composition, in prose or verse, consisting of verses or passages sung alternatively by two choirs in worship" (Hutchinson).
104. *this great frame.* The universe.

While mortal love doth all the title gain!   5
　Which siding with invention, they together
　Bear all the sway, possessing heart and brain,
(Thy workmanship) and give thee share in neither.

Wit fancies beauty, beauty raiseth wit:
　The world is theirs; they two play out the game,   10
　Thou standing by: and though thy glorious name
Wrought our deliverance from th' infernal pit,

　Who sings thy praise? only a scarf or glove
　Doth warm our hands, and make them write of love.

LOVE II

Immortal Heat, Oh let thy greater flame
　Attract the lesser to it: let those fires,
　Which shall consume the world, first make it tame;
And kindle in our hearts such true desires,

As may consume our lusts, and make thee way.   5
　Then shall our hearts pant thee;[105] then shall our brain
　All her invention on thine Altar lay,
And there in hymns send back thy fire again.

Our eyes shall see thee, which before saw dust;
　Dust blown by wit, till that they both were blind: 10
　Thou shalt recover all thy goods in kind,
Who wert disseized[106] by usurping lust:

All knees shall bow to thee;[107] all wits shall rise,
And praise him who did make and mend our eyes.

------

105. *pant thee*. See Ps. 42:1.
106. *disseized*. Dispossed, usually by force.
107. *All knees shall bow*. See Isa. 45:23.

GEORGE HERBERT

THE TEMPER (I)

How should I praise thee, Lord! how should my rhymes
  Gladly engrave thy love in steel,
  If what my soul doth feel sometimes,
    My soul might ever feel!

Although there were some forty heav'ns, or more,   *5*
  Sometimes I peer above them all;
  Sometimes I hardly reach a score,
    Sometimes to hell I fall.

Oh rack me not to such a vast extent;
  Those distances belong to thee: *10*
  The world's too little for thy tent,
    A grave too big for me.

Wilt thou meet arms with man, that thou dost stretch
  A crumb of dust from heav'n to hell?[108]
  Will great God measure with a wretch?   *15*
    Shall he thy stature spell?

Oh let me, when thy roof my soul hath hid,
  Oh let me roost and nestle there:
  Then of a sinner thou art rid,
    And I of hope and fear.   *20*

Yet take thy way; for sure thy way is best:
  Stretch or contract me thy poor debtor:
  This is but tuning of my breast,
    To make the music better.

Whether I fly with angels, fall with dust,   *25*
  Thy hands made both, and I am there:
  Thy power and love, my love and trust
    Make one place ev'rywhere.

---

108. A dueling tradition is that one does not meet anyone less skilled.

THE TEMPER (II)

It cannot be. Where is that mighty joy,
   Which just now took up all my heart?
   Lord, if thou must needs use thy dart,
Save that, and me; or sin for both destroy.

The grosser world stands to thy word and art;   *5*
   But thy diviner world of grace
   Thou suddenly dost raise and race,[109]
And ev'ry day a new Creator art.

Oh fix thy chair of grace, that all my powers
   May also fix their reverence: *10*
   For when thou dost depart from hence,
They grow unruly, and sit in thy bowers.

Scatter, or bind them all to bend to thee:
   Though elements change, and heaven move,
   Let not thy higher Court remove,   *15*
But keep a standing Majesty in me.

JORDAN (I)[110]

Who says that fictions only and false hair
Become a verse? Is there in truth no beauty?
Is all good structure in a winding stair?
May no lines pass, except they do their duty
   Not to a true, but painted chair?   *5*

Is it no verse, except enchanted groves
And sudden arbors shadow coarse-spun lines?

---

   109. *race.* Raze.
   110. Title: Herbert here links passage through *his* kind of poetry with baptism; see the BCP Baptismal service: "Almighty and everlasting God which of thy great mercy . . . didst sanctify the flood Jordan . . . to the mystical washing away of sin" (Booty, pp. 270–71).

Must purling[111] streams refresh a lover's loves?
Must all be veil'd, while he that reads, divines,
  Catching the sense at two removes?   *10*

Shepherds are honest people; let them sing:
Riddle who list, for me, and pull for Prime:[112]
I envy no man's nightingale or spring;
Nor let them punish me with loss of rhyme,
  Who plainly say, *My God, My King.*   *15*

EMPLOYMENT (I)

  If as a flower doth spread and die,
  Thou wouldst extend me to some good,
Before I were by frost's extremity
    Nipt in the bud;

  The sweetness and the praise were thine;   *5*
  But the extension and the room,
Which in thy garland I should fill, were mine
    At thy great doom.

  For as thou dost impart thy grace,
  The greater shall our glory be.   *10*
The measure of our joys is in this place,
    The stuff with thee.

  Let me not languish then, and spend
  A life as barren to thy praise,
As is the dust, to which that life doth tend,   *15*
    But with delays.

  All things are busy; only I
  Neither bring honey with the bees,

---

111. *purling.* Rippling, murmuring, undulating.
112. *pull for Prime.* Draw for a winning hand in the card game Primero.

Nor flowers to make that, nor the husbandry
    To water these.   *20*

  I am no link of thy great chain,[113]
  But all my company is a weed.
Lord place me in thy consort;[114] give one strain
    To my poor reed.

THE HOLY SCRIPTURES I

Oh Book! infinite sweetness! let my heart
  Suck ev'ry letter, and a honey gain,[115]
  Precious for any grief in any part;
To clear the breast, to mollify all pain.

Thou art all health, health thriving till it make   *5*
  A full eternity: thou art a mass
  Of strange delights, where we may wish and take.
Ladies, look here; this is the thankful glass,

That mends the looker's eyes: this is the well
  That washes what it shows. Who can endear   *10*
  Thy praise too much? thou art heav'ns Lidger[116] here,
Working against the states of death and hell.

  Thou art joy's handsel:[117] heav'n lies flat in thee,
  Subject to ev'ry mounter's bended knee.

---

    113. *great chain.* The Great Chain of Being, the hierarchy of interdependent levels of existence in God's creation.
    114. *consort.* A group of musicians playing together on various instruments.
    115. *honey gain.* See Ps. 119:103.
    116. *Lidger.* An ambassador resident in a foreign court.
    117. *handsel.* A first installment, a pledge of what is to follow.

GEORGE HERBERT

THE HOLY SCRIPTURES II

Oh that I knew how all thy lights combine,
   And the configurations of their glory!
   Seeing not only how each verse doth shine,
But all the constellations of the story.

This verse marks that, and both do make a motion   *5*
   Unto a third, that ten leaves off doth lie:[118]
   Then as dispersed herbs do watch a potion,
These three make up some Christian's destiny:

Such are thy secrets, which my life makes good,
   And comments on thee: for in ev'ry thing   *10*
   Thy words do find me out, and parallels bring,
And in another make me understood.

   Stars are poor books, and oftentimes do miss:
   This book of stars lights to eternal bliss.

WHITSUNDAY

   Listen sweet Dove unto my song,
   And spread thy golden wings in me;
   Hatching my tender heart so long,
Till it get wing, and fly away with thee.

   Where is that fire which once descended   *5*
   On thy Apostles? thou didst then
   Keep open house, richly attended,
Feasting all comers by twelve chosen men.

---

118. See *The Country Parson:* "For all Truth being consonant with itself, and all being penn'd by one of the selfsame Spirit, it cannot be, but an industrious and judicious comparing of place with place must be a singular help for the right understanding of the Scriptures."

Such glorious gifts thou didst bestow,
That th' earth did like a heav'n appear;   *10*
The stars were coming down to know
If they might mend their wages, and serve here.

The sun, which once did shine alone,
Hung down his head, and wisht for night,
When he beheld twelve suns for one   *15*
Going about the world, and giving light.

But since those pipes of gold,[119] which brought
That cordial water to our ground,
Were cut and martyr'd by the fault
Of those, who did themselves through their side wound,   *20*

Thou shutt'st the door, and keep'st within;
Scarce a good joy creeps through the chink:
And if the braves[120] of conqu'ring sin
Did not excite thee, we should wholly sink.

Lord, though we change, thou art the same;   *25*
The same sweet God of love and light:
Restore this day, for thy great name,
Unto his ancient and miraculous right.

GRACE

My stock[121] lies dead, and no increase
Doth my dull husbandry improve:
Oh let thy graces without cease
            Drop from above!

---

119. *those pipes of gold.* The apostles as channels of grace, perhaps with an allusion to Zech. 4:12.

120. *braves.* Challenges, threats.

121. *stock.* The trunk of a tree; see Job 14:7–9 ("there is hope of a tree, if it be cut down, that it will sprout again").

If still the sun should hide his face,   *5*
Thy house would but a dungeon prove,
Thy works night's captives: Oh let grace
        Drop from above!

The dew doth ev'ry morning fall;
And shall the dew outstrip thy Dove?   *10*
The dew, for which grass cannot call,
        Drop from above.

Death is still working like a mole,
And digs my grave at each remove:
Let grace work too, and on my soul   *15*
        Drop from above.

Sin is still hammering my heart
Unto a hardness, void of love:
Let suppl'ing grace, to cross his art,
        Drop from above.   *20*

Oh come! for thou dost know the way.
Or if to me thou wilt not move,
Remove me, where I need not say,
        Drop from above.

PRAISE (I)

To write a verse or two, is all the praise,
        That I can raise:
    Mend my estate in any ways,
        Thou shalt have more.

I go to Church; help me to wings, and I   *5*
        Will thither fly;
    Or, if I mount unto the sky,
        I will do more.

Man is all weakness; there is no such thing
     As Prince or King: *10*
   His arm is short; yet with a sling[122]
     He may do more.

An herb distill'd, and drunk, may dwell next door,
     On the same floor,
   To a brave soul: Exalt the poor,   *15*
     They can do more.

Oh raise me then! Poor bees, that work all day,
     Sting my delay,
   Who have a work, as well as they,
     And much, much more.   *20*

AFFLICTION (II)

     Kill me not ev'ry day,
Thou Lord of life; since thy one death for me
   Is more than all my deaths can be,
     Though I in broken pay[123]
Die over each hour of Methusalem's stay.   *5*

     If all men's tears were let
Into one common sewer, sea, and brine;
   What were they all, compar'd to thine?
     Wherein if they were set,
They would discolor[124] thy most bloody sweat.   *10*

     Thou art my grief alone,
Thou Lord conceal it not: and as thou art
   All my delight, so all my smart:

---

122. *sling.* Such as the one with which David slew Goliath.
123. *in broken pay.* In installments.
124. *discolor.* Take the color out of.

Thy cross took up in one,
By way of imprest,[125] all my future moan.   *15*

MATINS

I cannot ope mine eyes,
But thou art ready there to catch
My morning soul and sacrifice:
Then we must needs for that day make a match.[126]

My God, what is a heart?   *5*
Silver, or gold, or precious stone,
Or star, or rainbow, or a part
Of all these things, or all of them in one?

My God, what is a heart,
That thou shouldst it so eye, and woo,   *10*
Pouring upon it all thy art,
As if that thou hadst nothing else to do?

Indeed man's whole estate
Amounts (and richly) to serve thee:
He did not heav'n and earth create,   *15*
Yet studies them, not him by whom they be.

Teach me thy love to know;
That this new light, which now I see,
May both the work and workman show:
Then by a sunbeam I will climb to thee.   *20*

SIN (II)

Oh that I could a sin once see!
We paint the devil foul, yet he

---

125. *imprest.* Payment in advance.
126. *make a match.* Come to an agreement.

THE CHURCH

Hath some good in him, all agree.
Sin is flat opposite to th' Almighty, seeing
It wants the good of *virtue,* and of *being.*[127]   *5*

But God more care of us hath had:
If apparitions make us sad,
By sight of sin we should grow mad.
Yet as in sleep we see foul death, and live:
So devils are our sins in perspective.[128]   *10*

EVENSONG

Blest be the God of love,
Who gave me eyes, and light, and power this day,
    Both to be busy, and to play.
But much more blest be God above,

    Who gave me sight alone,   *5*
    Which to himself he did deny:
    For when he sees my ways, I die:[129]
But I have got his son, and he hath none.

    What have I brought thee home
For this thy love? have I discharg'd the debt,   *10*
    Which this day's favor did beget?
    I ran; but all I brought, was foam.

    Thy diet, care, and cost
    Do end in bubbles, balls of wind;
    Of wind to thee whom I have crost,   *15*
But balls of wildfire to my troubled mind.

---

127. Exposition of traditional doctrine that evil has no substance, but is a privation or defect or corruption of the good, and thus cannot be seen. We can see evil only in its effects on corrupted good things.

128. *perspective.* A picture made in such a way that it appears distorted unless viewed from a certain angle or point of view.

129. See Psalm 130:3.

Yet still thou goest on,
And now with darkness closest weary eyes,
   Saying to man, *It doth suffice:*
   Henceforth repose; your work is done.   *20*

   Thus in thy Ebony box[130]
Thou dost enclose us, till the day
   Put our amendment in our way,
And give new wheels to our disorder'd clocks.

   I muse, which shows more love,   *25*
The day or night: that is the gale, this th' harbor;
   That is the walk, and this the arbor;
   Or that the garden, this the grove.

   My God, thou art all love.
Not one poor minute scapes thy breast,   *30*
   But brings a favor from above;
And in this love, more than in bed, I rest.

CHURCH MONUMENTS

While that my soul repairs to her devotion,
Here I entomb my flesh, that it betimes
May take acquaintance of this heap of dust;
To which the blast of death's incessant motion,
Fed with the exhalation of our crimes,   *5*
Drive all at last. Therefore I gladly trust

My body to this school, that it may learn
To spell his elements, and find his birth
Written in dusty heraldry and lines;[131]
Which dissolution sure doth best discern,   *10*

---

130. Poisonous liquids were thought to be rendered harmless when enclosed in an ebony box.

131. *lines.* Genealogical patterns.

Comparing dust with dust, and earth with earth.
These[132] laugh at Jet, and Marble put for signs,

To sever the good fellowship of dust,
And spoil the meeting. What shall point out them,[133]
When they shall bow, and kneel, and fall down flat   *15*
To kiss those heaps, which now they have in trust?
Dear flesh, while I do pray, learn here thy stem
And true descent; that when thou shalt grow fat,

And wanton in thy cravings, thou mayest know,
That flesh is but the glass,[134] which holds the dust   *20*
That measures all our time; which also shall
Be crumbled into dust. Mark here below
How tame these ashes are, how free from lust,
That thou mayst fit thy self against thy fall.

CHURCH MUSIC

Sweetest of sweets, I thank you: when displeasure
    Did through my body wound my mind,
You took me thence, and in your house of pleasure
    A dainty lodging me assign'd.

Now I in you without a body move,   *5*
    Rising and falling with your wings:
We both together sweetly live and love,
    Yet say sometimes, *God help poor Kings.*

Comfort,[135] I'll die; for if you post[136] from me,
    Sure I shall do so, and much more: *10*

---

132. *these.* Dust and earth.
133. *them.* The jet and marble monuments, soon themselves to turn to dust.
134. *glass.* Hourglass.
135. *Comfort.* Take comfort.
136. *post.* Travel in haste.

But if I travel in your company,
    You know the way to heaven's door.

CHURCH LOCK AND KEY

I know it is my sin, which locks thine ears,
    And binds thy hands,
Outcrying my requests, drowning my tears;
Or else the chillness of my faint demands.

But as cold hands are angry[137] with the fire,   *5*
    And mend it still;
So I do lay the want of my desire,
Not on my sins, or coldness, but thy will.

Yet hear, Oh God, only for his blood's sake
    Which pleads for me: *10*
For though sins plead too, yet like stones they make
His blood's sweet current much more loud to be.[138]

THE CHURCH FLOOR

Mark you the floor? that square and speckled stone,
    Which looks so firm and strong,
        Is *Patience:*

And th' other black and grave, wherewith each one
    Is checker'd all along,   *5*
        Humility:

---

    137. *cold hands are angry.* Cold hands can be angry in the sense of being inflamed; they can also be impatient with a fire that will not warm them quickly enough.
    138. Stones in a shallow stream cause the current to run more noisily.

THE CHURCH

The gentle rising, which on either hand
    Leads to the Choir above,
        Is *Confidence:*

But the sweet cement, which in one sure band[139]   *10*
    Ties the whole frame, is *Love*
        And *Charity.*

    Hither sometimes Sin steals, and stains
    The marble's neat and curious[140] veins:
But all is cleansed when the marble weeps.   *15*
    Sometimes Death, puffing at the door,
    Blows all the dust about the floor:
But while he thinks to spoil the room, he sweeps.
    Blest be the *Architect,* whose art
    Could build so strong in a weak heart.   *20*

THE WINDOWS

Lord, how can man preach thy eternal word?
    He is a brittle crazy glass:
Yet in thy temple thou dost him afford
    This glorious and transcendent place,
    To be a window, through thy grace.   *5*

But when thou dost anneal in glass[141] thy story,
    Making thy life to shine within
The holy Preacher's; then the light and glory
    More rev'rend grows, and more doth win:
    Which else shows wat'rish, bleak, and thin.   *10*

Doctrine and life, colors and light, in one
    When they combine and mingle, bring

---

139. *one sure band.* See Colossians 3:14.
140. *neat and curious.* Delicate and intricately wrought.
141. *anneal in glass.* Fix the colors by heating the glass after painting.

183

A strong regard and awe: but speech alone
    Doth vanish like a flaring thing,
    And in the ear, not conscience ring.   *15*

TRINITY SUNDAY

Lord, who hast form'd me out of mud,
    And hast redeem'd me through thy blood,
    And sanctifi'd me to do good;

Purge all my sins done heretofore:
    For I confess my heavy score,   *5*
    And I will strive to sin no more.

Enrich my heart, mouth, hands in me,
    With faith, with hope, with charity;
    That I may run, rise, rest with thee.

CONTENT

Peace mutt'ring thoughts, and do not grudge to keep
    Within the walls of your own breast:
Who cannot on his own bed sweetly sleep,
    Can on another's hardly rest.

Gad not abroad at ev'ry quest and call   *5*
    Of an untrained hope or passion.
To court each place or fortune that doth fall,
    Is wantonness in contemplation.

Mark how the fire in flints doth quiet lie,
    Content and warm t' itself alone: *10*
But when it would appear to other's eye,
    Without a knock it never shone.

Give me the pliant mind, whose gentle measure
    Complies and suits with all estates;
Which can let loose to[142] a crown, and yet with pleasure   *15*
    Take up within a cloister's gates.[143]

This soul doth span the world, and hang content
    From either pole unto the center:
Wherein each room of the well-furnisht tent
    He lies warm, and without adventure.   *20*

The brags of life are but a nine days' wonder;
    And after death the fumes that spring
From private bodies, make as big a thunder,
    As those which rise from a huge King.[144]

Only thy Chronicle is lost; and yet   *25*
    Better by worms be all once spent,
Than to have hellish moths still gnaw and fret
    Thy name in books, which may not rent:[145]

When all thy deeds, whose brunt thou feel'st alone,
    Are chaw'd by others' pens and tongue;   *30*
And as their wit is, their digestion,
    Thy nourisht fame is weak or strong.

Then cease discoursing[146] soul, till thine own ground,
    Do not thyself or friends importune.
He that by seeking hath himself once found,   *35*
    Hath ever found a happy fortune.

---

142. *let loose to.* Aim at, as an arrow at a target.

143. *loose a crown, and . . . take up within a cloister's gate.* In 1556, the Emperor Charles V had abdicated and taken up residence in a cloister.

144. The corpse of the corpulent William the Conqueror was reported to have given off an intolerable odor when it was thrust into its narrow stone coffin.

145. *rent.* Rend, tear.

146. *discoursing.* Thinking busily, rapidly passing from one thought to another.

GEORGE HERBERT

THE QUIDDITY[147]

My God, a verse is not a crown,
No point of honor, or gay suit,
No hawk, or banquet, or renown,
Nor a good sword, nor yet a lute:

It cannot vault, or dance, or play; *5*
It never was in *France* or *Spain;*
Nor can it entertain the day
With a great stable[148] or demain:

It is no office, art, or news,
Nor the Exchange, or busy Hall; *10*
But it is that which while I use
I am with thee, and *Most take all.*[149]

HUMILITY

I saw the Virtues sitting hand in hand
In sev'ral ranks upon an azure throne,
Where all the beasts and fowls[150] by their command
Presented tokens of submission.
Humility, who sat the lowest there *5*
To execute their call,
When by the beasts the presents tend'red were,
Gave them about to all.

The angry Lion did present his paw,
Which by consent was giv'n to Mansuetude.[151] *10*
The fearful Hare her ears, which by their law

---

147. Scholastic term for the true nature, or essence, of a thing; also oversubtlety in argument, quirk, quibble.
148. *a great stable.* Both *B* and *W* read "my great."
149. *Most take all.* Since, through verse, the speaker is with God, poetry thus is seen to excel all other goods or human activities.
150. *beasts and fowls.* The natural passions.
151. *Mansuetude.* Gentleness.

Humility did reach to Fortitude.
The jealous Turkey brought his coral chain;[152]
    That went to Temperance.
On Justice was bestow'd the Fox's brain,   *15*
    Kill'd in the way by chance.

At length the Crow bringing the Peacock's plume,
(For he would not) as they beheld the grace
Of that brave gift, each one began to fume,
And challenge it, as proper to his place,   *20*
Till they fell out: which when the beasts espied,
    They leapt upon the throne;
And if the Fox had liv'd to rule their side,
    They had depos'd each one.

Humility, who held the plume, at this   *25*
Did weep so fast, that the tears trickling down
Spoil'd all the train: then saying, *Here it is*
For which ye wrangle, made them turn their frown
Against the beasts: so jointly bandying,[153]
    They drive them soon away;   *30*
And then amerc'd[154] them, double gifts to bring
    At the next Session-day.

FRAILTY

Lord, in my silence how do I despise
    What upon trust
Is styled *honor, riches,* or *fair eyes;*
    But is *fair dust!*
    I surname them *gilded clay,*   *5*
      Dear[155] *earth, fine grass or hay;*

---

152. *coral chain.* The turkey's red wattle, suggesting fleshliness.
153. *bandying.* Banding together.
154. *amerc'd.* Fined.
155. *Dear.* Costly.

In all, I think my foot doth ever tread
    Upon their head.

But when I view abroad both Regiments;[156]
    The world's, and thine: *10*
Thine clad with simpleness, and sad[157] events;
    The other fine,
    Full of glory and gay weeds,
      Brave language, braver deeds:
That which was dust before, doth quickly rise,   *15*
    And prick[158] mine eyes.

Oh brook not this, lest if what even now
    My foot did tread,
Affront[159] those joys, wherewith thou didst endow,
    And long since wed   *20*
    My poor soul, ev'n sick of love:
      It may a Babel prove
Commodious to conquer heav'n and thee
    Planted in me.

CONSTANCY

       Who is the honest man?
   He that doth still and strongly good pursue,
  To God, his neighbor, and himself most true:
       Whom neither force nor fawning can
  Unpin, or wrench from giving all their due.   *5*

       Whose honesty is not
  So loose or easy, that a ruffling wind
  Can blow away, or glittering look it blind:

---

156. *Regiments.* A domain or country under a particular rule.
157. *sad.* Serious.
158. *prick.* Inflame, make to smart.
159. *Affront.* Confront.

Who rides his sure and even trot,
While the world now rides by, now lags behind.   *10*

Who, when great trials come,
Nor seeks, nor shuns them; but doth calmly stay,
Till he the thing and the example weigh:
          All being brought into a sum,
What place or person calls for, he doth pay.   *15*

Whom none can work or woo
To use in anything a trick or sleight;
For above all things he abhors deceit:
          His words and works and fashion too
All of a piece, and all are clear and straight.   *20*

Who never melts or thaws
At close tentations:[160] when the day is done,
His goodness sets not, but in dark can run:
          The sun to others writeth laws,
And is their virtue; Virtue is his Sun.   *25*

Who, when he is to treat
With sick folks, women, those whom passions sway,
Allows for that, and keeps his constant way:
          Whom others' faults do not defeat;
But though men fail him, yet his part doth play.   *30*

Whom nothing can procure,
When the wide world runs bias,[161] from his will
To writhe his limbs, and share, not mend the ill.[162]
          This is the Mark-man, safe and sure,
Who still is right, and prays to be so still.   *35*

---

160. *tentations.* Temptations.
161. *bias.* Obliquely.
162. An image from the game of bowls, the use of "body-english" to attempt to affect the course of the ball after it leaves the hand of the bowler.

GEORGE HERBERT

AFFLICTION (III)

My heart did heave, and there came forth, *Oh God!*
By that I knew that thou wast in the grief,
To guide and govern it to my relief,
   Making a scepter of the rod:
     Hadst thou not had thy part,   *5*
Sure the unruly sigh had broke my heart.

But since thy breath gave me both life and shape,
Thou knowst my tallies;[163] and when there's assign'd
So much breath to a sigh, what's then behind?
   Or if some years with it escape,   *10*
     The sigh then only is
A gale to bring me sooner to my bliss.

Thy life on earth was grief, and thou art still
Constant unto it, making it to be
A point of honor, now to grieve in me,   *15*
   And in thy members suffer ill.
     They who lament one cross,
Thou dying daily,[164] praise thee to thy loss.

THE STAR

Bright spark, shot from a brighter place,
   Where beams surround my Savior's face,
     Canst thou be any where
       So well as there?

Yet, if thou wilt from thence depart,   *5*
   Take a bad lodging in my heart;
     For thou canst make a debtor,
       And make it better.

---

163. *tallies.* Totals, in columns of an account book.
164. *dying daily.* See 1 Cor. 15:31.

THE CHURCH

First with thy fire-work burn to dust
  Folly, and worse than folly, lust: *10*
    Then with thy light refine,
      And make it shine:

So disengag'd from sin and sickness,
  Touch it with thy celestial quickness,
    That it may hang and move   *15*
      After thy love.

Then with our trinity of light,
  Motion, and heat, let's take our flight
    Unto the place where thou
      Before didst bow.   *20*

Get me a standing there, and place
  Among the beams, which crown the face
    Of him, who died to part
      Sin and my heart:

That so among the rest I may   *25*
  Glitter, and curl, and wind as they:
    That winding is their fashion
      Of adoration.

Sure thou wilt joy, by gaining me
  To fly home like a laden bee   *30*
    Unto that hive of beams
      And garland streams.

SUNDAY

  Oh day most calm, most bright,
The fruit of this, the next world's bud,
Th'endorsement of supreme delight,
Writ by a friend, and with his blood;

The couch of time; care's balm and bay:⠀⠀⠀⠀⠀⠀⠀⠀⠀⠀⠀⠀*5*
The week were dark, but for thy light:[165]
⠀⠀Thy torch doth show the way.

⠀⠀The other days and thou
Make up one man; whose face thou art,
Knocking at heaven with thy brow:⠀⠀⠀⠀⠀⠀⠀⠀⠀⠀⠀⠀*10*
The worky-days[166] are the back-part;
The burden of the week lies there,
Making the whole to stoop and bow,
⠀⠀Till thy release appear.

⠀⠀Man had straight forward gone⠀⠀⠀⠀⠀⠀⠀⠀⠀⠀⠀⠀*15*
To endless death: but thou dost pull
And turn us round to look on one,
Whom, if we were not very dull,
We could not choose but look on still;
Since there is no place so alone,⠀⠀⠀⠀⠀⠀⠀⠀⠀⠀⠀⠀*20*
⠀⠀The which he doth not fill.

⠀⠀Sundays the pillars are,
On which heav'n's palace arched lies:
The other days fill up the spare
And hollow room with vanities.⠀⠀⠀⠀⠀⠀⠀⠀⠀⠀⠀⠀*25*
They are the fruitful beds and borders
In God's rich garden: that is bare,[167]
⠀⠀Which parts their ranks and orders.

⠀⠀The Sundays of man's life,
Threaded together on time's string,⠀⠀⠀⠀⠀⠀⠀⠀⠀⠀⠀⠀*30*
Make bracelets to adorn the wife
Of the eternal glorious King.
On Sunday heaven's gate stands ope;
Blessings are plentiful and rife,
⠀⠀More plentiful than hope.⠀⠀⠀⠀⠀⠀⠀⠀⠀⠀⠀⠀*35*

----

165. See Ps. 119:105.
166. *worky-days.* Working days.
167. *that is bare.* The earthen spaces between the flower beds, like the weekly intervals between Sundays, are bare.

This day my Savior rose,
And did enclose this light for his:
That, as each beast his manger knows,
Man might not of his fodder miss.
Christ hath took in this piece of ground,   *40*
And made a garden there for those
    Who want herbs for their wound.[168]

The rest of our Creation
Our great Redeemer did remove
With the same shake, which at his passion   *45*
Did th' earth and all things with it move.[169]
As Samson bore the doors away,[170]
Christ's hands, though nail'd, wrought our salvation,
    And did unhinge that day.[171]

The brightness of that day   *50*
We sullied by our foul offence:
Wherefore that robe we cast away,
Having a new at his expense,
Whose drops of blood paid the full price,
That was requir'd to make us gay,   *55*
    And fit for Paradise.[172]

Thou art a day of mirth:
And where the weekdays trail on ground,
Thy flight is higher, as thy birth.
Oh let me take thee at the bound,   *60*
Leaping with thee from sev'n to sev'n,
Till that we both, being toss'd from earth,
    Fly hand in hand to heav'n!

---

168. *wound.* Because of the medicinal qualities of herbs.
169. Allusion to the account of the Crucifixion in Matt. 27:51.
170. Allusion to Samson's pulling down the gates of Gaza (Judg. 16:3).
171. The rest day of Creation, the seventh day, is unhinged (replaced in the established order of things) by the "Son-day," the first day of the week of Christ's resurrection.
172. See Rev. 7:14.

GEORGE HERBERT

AVARICE

Money, thou bane of bliss, and source of woe,
   Whence com'st thou, that thou art so fresh and fine?
   I know thy parentage is base and low:
Man found thee poor and dirty in a mine.

Surely thou didst so little contribute   5
   To this great kingdom, which thou now hast got,
   That he was fain, when thou wert destitute,
To dig thee out of thy dark cave and grot:[173]

Then forcing thee, by fire he made thee bright:
   Nay, thou hast got the face of man;[174] for we   10
   Have with our stamp and seal transferr'd our right:
Thou art the man,[175] and man but dross to thee.

   Man calleth thee his wealth, who made thee rich;
   And while he digs out thee, falls in the ditch.

$$\textit{Ana-} \left\{ \begin{array}{c} \text{M A R Y} \\ \text{A R M Y} \end{array} \right\} \textit{gram}$$

How well her name an *Army* doth present,
In whom the *Lord of Hosts* did pitch his tent![176]

---

173. *grot.* Grotto.
174. *face to man.* The king's face stamped on coins, perhaps with a reference to Jesus' injunction to "render unto Caesar" (Luke 20:24–25).
175. *Thou art the man.* See 2 Sam. 12:7.
176. *pitch his tent.* The Greek text of John 1:14, translated "the Word was made flesh and dwelt among us" in the KJV, literally reads "the Word became flesh and pitched his tent among us."

THE CHURCH

TO ALL ANGELS AND SAINTS

Oh glorious spirits, who after all your bands[177]
See the smooth face of God, without a frown
      Or strict commands;
Where ev'ry one is king, and hath his crown,
If not upon his head, yet in his hands:[178]   *5*

Not out of envy or maliciousness
Do I forbear to crave your special aid:
      I would address
My vows to thee most gladly, blessed Maid,
And Mother of my God, in my distress.   *10*

Thou art the holy mine, whence came the gold,
The great restorative[179] for all decay
      In young and old;
Thou art the cabinet where the jewel lay:
Chiefly to thee would I my soul unfold: *15*

But now (alas!) I dare not; for our King,
Whom we do all jointly adore and praise,
      Bids no such thing:
And where his pleasure no injunction[180] lays,
('Tis your own case) ye never move a wing.   *20*

All worship is prerogative,[181] and a flower
Of his rich crown, from whom lies no appeal
      At the last hour:
Therefore we dare not from his garland steal,
To make a poesy for inferior power.   *25*

---

177. *bands.* If the "glorious spirits" are the angels, then "bands" are the ranks of angels, their nine orders; if they are the saints, then the "bands" are "the bands (shackles) of
all those sins, which by our frailty we have committed" (BCP, Collect for the twenty-
fourth Sunday after Trinity; see Booty, p. 212).

178. See the vision of the twenty-four elders who cast their golden crowns before
God's throne in Rev. 4:4ff.

179. *restorative.* Gold was believed to have medicinal powers.

180. *injunction.* A command, not a prohibition.

181. *prerogative.* That reserved to a monarch; God, in this case.

Although then others court you, if ye know
What's done on earth, we shall not fare the worse,
    Who do not so;
Since we are ever ready to disburse,
If anyone our Master's hand can show.   *30*

EMPLOYMENT (II)

He that is weary, let him sit.
    My soul would[182] stir
And trade in courtesies and wit,
    Quitting the fur[183]
To cold complexions[184] needing it.   *5*

Man is no star, but a quick coal[185]
    Of mortal fire:
Who blows it not, nor doth control
    A faint desire,
Lets his own ashes choke his soul.   *10*

When th' elements[186] did for place contest
    With him, whose will
Ordain'd the highest to be best;
    The earth sat still,
And by the others is opprest.   *15*

Life is a busyness, not good cheer;
    Ever in wars.
The sun still shineth there or here,
    Whereas the stars
Watch an advantage to appear.   *20*

---

182. *would.* Wishes to.
183. *fur.* Academic dress; warm clothing.
184. *complexions.* Personality states, thought to be caused by different mixtures of the four humors. "Cold" complexions were caused by an excess of phlegm or bile, related to water (cold and wet) or earth (cold and dry).
185. *quick coal.* Live coal.
186. *elements.* The four elements, earth, air, fire, and water.

Oh that I were an Orange tree,
    That busy[187] plant!
Then should I ever laden be,
    And never want
Some fruit for him that dressed me.   *25*

But we are still too young or old;[188]
    The man is gone,
Before we do our wares unfold:
    So we freeze on,
Until the grave increase our cold.   *30*

DENIAL

When my devotions could not pierce
    Thy silent ears;
Then was my heart broken, as was my verse:
    My breast was full of fears
        And disorder.[189]   *5*

My bent thoughts, like a brittle bow,
    Did fly asunder:
Each took his way; some would to pleasures go,
    Some to the wars and thunder
        Of alarms.   *10*

As good go anywhere, they say,
    As to benumb
Both knees and heart, in crying night and day,
    Come, come, my God, Oh come,[190]
        But no hearing.   *15*

---

187. *busy.* Because it bears blossoms and fruit at the same time.
188. *too young or old.* Excuses for inaction.
189. The lack of harmony between man and God is suggested by the absence of rhyme at the end of each stanza save the last, where the restored harmony enables the poet to "mend my rhyme."
190. See Rev. 22:20.

Oh that thou shouldst give dust a tongue
    To cry to thee,
And then not hear it crying! all day long
    My heart was in my knee,
      But no hearing.   20

Therefore my soul lay out of sight,
    Untun'd, unstrung:
My feeble spirit, unable to look right,
    Like a nipt blossom, hung
      Discontented.   25

Oh cheer and tune my heartless breast,
    Defer no time;
That so thy favors granting my request,
    They and my mind may chime,
      And mend my rhyme.   30

CHRISTMAS (I)

All after pleasures as I rid[191] one day,
    My horse and I, both tir'd, body and mind,
    With full cry of affections, quite astray;
I took up in the next inn I could find.

There when I came, whom found I but my dear,   5
    My dearest Lord, expecting[192] till the grief
    Of pleasures brought me to him, ready there
To be all passengers' most sweet relief?

Oh Thou, whose glorious, yet contracted light,
    Wrapt in night's mantle, stole into a manger;   10

---

191. *rid.* Rode.
192. *expecting.* Waiting.

Since my dark soul and brutish is thy right,
To Man of all beasts be not thou a stranger:

Furnish and deck my soul, that thou mayst have
A better lodging, than a rack,[193] or grave.

[CHRISTMAS (II)][194]

The shepherds sing; and shall I silent be?
    My God, no hymn for thee?
My soul's a shepherd too; a flock it feeds
    Of thoughts, and words, and deeds.
The pasture is thy word: the streams, thy grace   *5*
    Enriching all the place.
Shepherd and flock shall sing, and all my powers
    Outsing the daylight hours.
Then we will chide the sun for letting night
    Take up his place and right: *10*
We sing one common Lord; wherefore he should
    Himself the candle hold.
I will go searching, till I find a sun
    Shall stay, till we have done;
A willing shiner, that shall shine as gladly,   *15*
    As frost-nipt suns look sadly.
Then we will sing, and shine all our own day,
    And one another pay:
His beams shall cheer my breast, and both so twine,
Till ev'n his beams sing, and my music shine.   *20*

---

    193. *rack.* A frame of wood to hold fodder for horses and cattle, i.e., the manger of Luke 2:7; also, perhaps, a reference to the Cross.
    194. These lines are usually printed as lines 15–34 of the poem "Christmas"; however, because lines 1–14 of this poem make a complete sonnet, and because of the change in stanza-form and rhyme scheme, I feel justified in dividing the lines into two poems, on analogy with "Holy Baptism" and "Love," above.

GEORGE HERBERT

UNGRATEFULNESS

Lord, with what bounty and rare clemency
 Hast thou redeem'd us from the grave!
  If thou hadst let us run,
 Gladly had man ador'd the sun,[195]
  And thought his god most brave,   *5*
Where now we shall be better gods than he.

Thou hast but two rare cabinets full of treasure,
 The *Trinity,* and *Incarnation:*
  Thou hast unlockt them both,
 And made them jewels to betroth   *10*
  The work of thy creation
Unto thyself in everlasting pleasure.

The statelier cabinet is the *Trinity,*
 Whose sparkling light access denies:
  Therefore thou dost not show   *15*
 This fully to us, till death blow
  The dust into our eyes:
For by that powder thou wilt make us see.[196]

But all thy sweets[197] are packt up in the other;
 Thy mercies thither flock and flow: *20*
  That as the first affrights,
 This may allure us with delights;
  Because this box[198] we know;
For we have all of us just such another.

But man is close, reserv'd, and dark to thee: *25*
 When thou demandest but a heart,
  He cavils instantly.
 In his poor cabinet of bone

---

195. See Matt. 13:43 and Dan. 12:3.
196. Reference to practice of blowing dust into the eyes of a horse or dog to clear them of film.
197. *sweets.* Perfumes.
198. *this box.* Reference to the Incarnation (1.8).

Sins have their box apart,
Defrauding thee, who gavest two for one.[199]   *30*

SIGHS AND GROANS

Oh do not use me
After my sins! look not on my desert,[200]
But on thy glory! then thou wilt reform
And not refuse me: for thou only art
The mighty God, but I a silly worm;   *5*
   Oh do not bruise me!

Oh do not urge me!
For what account can thy ill steward make?
I have abus'd thy stock, destroy'd thy woods,
Suckt all thy magazens:[201] my head did ache,   *10*
Till it found out how to consume thy goods:
   Oh do not scourge me!

Oh do not blind me!
I have deserv'd that an Egyptian night[202]
Should thicken all my powers; because my lust   *15*
Hath still sow'd fig leaves[203] to exclude thy light:
But I am frailty, and already dust;
   Oh do not grind me!

Oh do not fill me
With the turn'd vial[204] of thy bitter wrath!   *20*
For thou hast other vessels full of blood,
A part whereof my Savior empti'd hath,

---

199. *two for one.* In the argument of the poem, God gives "two rare cabinets" and asks only a single heart in return.

200. See Ps. 103:10.

201. *magazens.* Storehouses.

202. *an Egyptian night.* See Exod. 10:22.

203. *fig-leaves.* Used by Adam and Eve to cover their nakedness after the Fall (See Gen. 3:7).

204. *turn'd vial.* See Rev. 15:7.

Ev'n unto death: since he di'd for my good,
    Oh do not kill me!

    But Oh reprieve me!   *25*
For thou hast *life* and *death* at thy command;
Thou art both *Judge* and *Savior, feast* and *rod*,
Cordial and *Corrosive:*[205] put not thy hand
Into the bitter box; but Oh my God,
    My God, relieve me!   *30*

THE WORLD

Love built a stately house; where *Fortune* came,
And spinning fancies, she was heard to say,
That her fine cobwebs did support the frame,
Whereas they were supported by the same:
But *Wisdom* quickly swept them all away.   *5*

Then *Pleasure* came, who liking not the fashion,
Began to make *Balconies, Terraces,*
Till she had weak'ned all by alteration:
But rev'rend *laws*, and many a *proclamation*
Reformed all at length with menaces.   *10*

Then enter'd *Sin,* and with that Sycamore,[206]
Whose leaves first shelt'red man from drought and dew,
Working and winding slyly evermore,
The inward walls and Sommers[207] cleft and tore:
But Grace shor'd these,[208] and cut that as it grew.   *15*

Then *Sin* combin'd with *Death* in a firm band
To raze the building to the very floor:

---

205. *Corrosive.* A caustic remedy.
206. *Sycamore.* In Herbert's day, a variety of fig tree that provided man's first clothes.
207. *Sommers.* Supporting beams.
208. *these.* The walls; *that*, the sycamore.

Which they effected, none could them withstand.
But *Love* and *Grace* took *Glory* by the hand,
And built a braver Palace than before.   *20*

COLOSSIANS 3:3

Our life is hid with Christ in God[209]

My words and thoughts do both express this notion,
That   *Life* hath with the sun a double motion.
The first   *Is* straight, and our diurnal[210] friend,
The other   *Hid,* and doth obliquely bend.
One life is wrapt   *In* flesh, and tends to earth.   *5*
The other winds towards *Him,* whose happy birth
Taught me to live here so,   *That* still one eye
Should aim and shoot at that which *Is* on high:
Quitting   with   daily   labor   all *My* pleasure,
To   gain   at   harvest   an   eternal   *Treasure.*   *10*

VANITY (I)

The fleet Astronomer can bore,
And thread the spheres[211] with his quick-piercing mind:
He views their stations, walks from door to door,
    Surveys, as if he had design'd
To make a purchase there: he sees their dances,   *5*
    And knoweth long before,
Both their full-ey'd aspects,[212] and secret glances.

---

209. The complete verse reads, "For ye are dead, and your life is hid with Christ in God."
210. *diurnal.* Daily.
211. *spheres.* The concentric hollow globes thought to revolve around the earth carrying with them the planets and other heavenly bodies. Each had its own distinctive musical note to add to the harmonious music of the spheres, hence their movement is a dance of regular movement (1.5).
212. *aspects.* Positions of the heavenly bodies in relationship to bodies on earth.

The nimble Diver with his side
Cuts through the working waves, that he may fetch
His dearly-earned pearl, which God did hide   *10*
    On purpose from the vent'rous wretch;
That he might save his life, and also hers,
    Who with excessive pride
Her own destruction and his danger wears.

    The subtle Chymick[213] can divest   *15*
And strip the creature naked, till he find
The callow[214] principles within their nest:
    There he imparts to them his mind,
Admitted to their bedchamber, before
    They appear trim and drest   *20*
To ordinary suitors at the door.

What hath not man sought out and found,
But his dear God? who yet his glorious law
Embosoms in us, mellowing the ground
    With showers and frosts, with love and awe,   *25*
So that we need not say, Where's this command?
    Poor man, thou searchest round
To find out *death*, but missest *life* at hand.

LENT

Welcome dear feast of Lent: who loves not thee,
He loves not Temperance, or Authority,
    But is compos'd of passion.
The Scriptures bid us *fast*; the Church says, *now:*
Give to thy Mother, what thou wouldst allow   *5*
    To ev'ry Corporation.

The humble soul compos'd of love and fear
Begins at home, and lays the burden there,

---

213. *Chymick.* Chemist.
214. *callow.* Bald, without hair; opposite of trim and drest (1.20).

When doctrines disagree.
He says, in things which use hath justly got,   *10*
I am a scandal[215] to the Church, and not
    The Church is so to me.

True Christians should be glad of an occasion
To use their temperance, seeking no evasion,
    When good is seasonable;   *15*
Unless Authority, which should increase
The obligation in us, make it less,
    And Power itself disable.

Besides the cleanness of sweet abstinence,
Quick thoughts and motions at a small expense,   *20*
    A face not fearing light:
Whereas in fullness there are sluttish fumes,
Sour exhalations, and dishonest rheums,
    Revenging[216] the delight.

Then those same pendant[217] profits, which the spring   *25*
And Easter intimate, enlarge the thing,
    And goodness of the deed.
Neither ought other men's abuse of Lent
Spoil the good use; lest by that argument
    We forfeit all our Creed.   *30*

It's true, we cannot reach Christ's forti'th day;
Yet to go part of that religious way,
    Is better than to rest:
We cannot reach our Savior's purity;
Yet are we bid, *Be holy*[218] *ev'n as he.*   *35*
    In both let's do our best.

Who goeth in the way which Christ hath gone,
Is much more sure to meet with him, than one

---

215. *scandal.* Offence, stumbling block.
216. *Revenging.* Exacting appropriate punishment for.
217. *pendant.* Hanging like fruit before it is picked.
218. *Be holy.* See Matt. 5:48.

That travelleth byways:
Perhaps my God, though he be far before,   *40*
May turn, and take me by the hand, and more
    May strengthen my decays.

Yet Lord instruct us to improve our fast
By starving sin and taking such repast,
    As may our faults control: *45*
That ev'ry man may revel at his door,[219]
Not in his parlor; banqueting the poor,
    And among those his soul.

VIRTUE

Sweet day, so cool, so calm, so bright,
The bridal of the earth and sky:
The dew shall weep thy fall tonight;
    For thou must die.

Sweet rose, whose hue angry and brave[220]   *5*
Bids the rash gazer wipe his eye:
Thy root is ever in its grave,
    And thou must die.

Sweet spring, full of sweet days and roses,
A box where sweets[221] compacted lie;   *10*
My music shows ye have your closes,[222]
    And all must die.

Only a sweet and virtuous soul,
Like season'd timber, never gives;
But though the whole world turn to coal,[223]   *15*
    Then chiefly lives.

---

219. *revel at his door.* See Isa. 58:6–7.
220. *brave.* Splendid.
221. *sweets.* Perfumes.
222. *closes.* Musical term for cadences.
223. *coal.* Cinders, glowing coals.

THE CHURCH

THE PEARL. MATTHEW 13: [45–46][224]

I know the ways of Learning; both the head
And pipes that feed the press, and make it run;
What reason hath from nature borrowed,
Or of itself, a good huswife,[225] spun
In laws and policy; what the stars conspire,   *5*
What willing nature speaks, what forc'd by fire;
Both th' old discoveries, and the new-found seas,
The stock and surplus, cause and history:
All these stand open, or I have the keys:
       Yet I love thee.   *10*

I know the ways of Honor, what maintains
The quick returns of courtesy and wit:
In vies of favors whether party gains,
When glory[226] swells the heart, and moldeth it
To all expressions both of hand and eye,   *15*
Which on the world a true-love-knot may tie,
And bear the bundle,[227] wheresoe'er it goes:
How many drams of spirit there must be
To sell my life unto my friends or foes:
       Yet I love thee.   *20*

I know the ways of Pleasure, the sweet strains,
The lullings and the relishes of it;
The propositions[228] of hot blood and brains;
What mirth and music mean; what love and wit
Have done these twenty hundred years, and more: *25*
I know the projects of unbridled store:
My stuff is flesh, not brass; my senses live,
And grumble oft, that they have more in me

---

224. Matt. 13:45–46 reads, "Again, the kingdom of heaven is like unto a merchant man, seeking goodly pearls: Who, when he had found one pearl of great price, went and sold all that he had, and bought it."
225. *huswife.* Housewife, one who manages household with skill and thrift.
226. *glory.* Ambition.
227. *bundle.* Of favor, like a servant.
228. *strains, lullings, relishes, propositions.* Musical terms suggesting tones, melodies, embellishments, parts of musical compositions.

Than he that curbs them being but one to five:
     Yet I love thee.   *30*

I know all these, and have them in my hand;
Therefore not sealed,[229] but with open eyes
I fly to thee, and fully understand
Both the main sale, and the commodities;[230]
And at what rate and price I have thy love;   *35*
With all the circumstances that may move:
Yet through the labyrinths, not my groveling wit,
But thy silk twist let down from heav'n to me,
But both conduct and teach me, how by it
     To climb to thee.   *40*

AFFLICTION (IV)

Broken in pieces all asunder,
     Lord, hunt me not,
     A thing forgot,[231]
Once a poor creature, now a wonder,[232]
     A wonder tortur'd in the space   *5*
     Betwixt this world and that of grace.

My thoughts are all a case of knives,
     Wounding my heart
     With scatter'd smart,
As wat'ring pots give flowers their lives.   *10*
     Nothing their fury can control,
     While they do wound and prick my soul.

All my attendants[233] are at strife,
     Quitting their place

---

229. *sealed.* Term for sewing up a hawk's eyes.
230. *commodities.* Advantages.
231. *a thing forgot.* See Ps. 31:12.
232. *now a wonder.* See Ps. 71:7.
233. *attendants.* His mental and physical faculties.

Unto my face: *15*
Nothing performs the task of life:
    The elements are let loose to fight,
    And while I live, try out their right.

Oh help, my God! let not their plot
      Kill them and me, *20*
      And also thee,
Who art my life: dissolve the knot,
    As the sun scatters by his light
    All the rebellions of the night.

Then shall those powers, which work for grief, *25*
      Enter thy pay,
      And day by day
Labor[234] thy praise, and my relief;
    With care and courage building me,
    Till I reach heav'n, and much more thee. *30*

MAN

    My God, I heard this day,
That none doth build a stately habitation,
    But he that means to dwell therein.
    What house more stately hath there been,
Or can be, than is Man? to whose[235] creation *5*
    All things are in decay.

    For Man is ev'ry thing,
And more: He is a tree, yet bears more fruit;[236]

---

234. *Labor.* Labor for.
235. *to whose.* Compared to.
236. *more fruit.* Thus *W; 1633* and *B* read "no fruit." This is the most difficult textual crux in Herbert, since the authority of the later texts is on the side of "no" while the sense of the passage calls for "more." An editor must take a stand, and here I choose the reading of the earlier ms. See Hutchinson, p. 508, for the fullest extant discussions of the evidence.

A beast, yet is, or should be more:
Reason and speech we only bring.   *10*
Parrots may thank us, if they are not mute,
    They go upon the score.[237]

        Man is all symmetry,
Full of proportions, one limb to another,
    And all to all the world besides: *15*
    Each part may call the farthest, brother:
For head with foot hath private amity,
    And both with moons and tides.[238]

        Nothing hath got so far,
But Man hath caught and kept it, as his prey.   *20*
    His eyes dismount[239] the highest star:
    He is in little all the sphere.
Herbs gladly cure our flesh; because that they
    Find their acquaintance there.

        For us the winds do blow,   *25*
The earth doth rest, heav'n move, and fountains flow.
    Nothing we see, but means our good,
        As our *delight*, or as our *treasure*:
The whole is, either our cupboard of *food*,
        Or cabinet of *pleasure*.   *30*

        The stars have us to bed;
Night draws the curtain, which the sun withdraws;
    Music and light attend our head.
    All things unto our *flesh* are kind
In their *descent* and *being*; to our *mind*   *35*
    In their *ascent* and *cause*.

        Each thing is full of duty:
Waters united are our navigation;

---

237. *go upon the score.* Are indebted to us.
238. This stanza utilizes a medieval and renaissance commonplace, that man is a microcosm, reflecting in the ordering of his members the arrangement of the universe.
239. *dismount.* Bring down from elevated position.

Distinguished,[240] our habitation;
Below, our drink; above, our meat;[241]   *40*
Both are our cleanliness. Hath one such beauty?
    Then how are all things neat?

    More servants wait on Man,
Than he'll take notice of: in ev'ry path
    He treads down that which doth befriend him,   *45*
    When sickness makes him pale and wan.
Oh mighty love! Man is one world, and hath
    Another to attend him.

    Since then, my God, thou hast
So brave a Palace built; Oh dwell in it,   *50*
    That it may dwell with thee at last!
    Till then, afford us so much wit;
That, as the world serves us, we may serve thee,
    And both thy servants be.

ANTIPHON (II)

Chorus. Praised be the God of love,
    Men.   Here below,
    Angels. And here above:
Chorus. Who hath dealt his mercies so,
    Angels. To his friend,   *5*
    Men.   And to his foe;

Chorus. That both grace and glory tend
    Angels. Us of old,
    Men.   And us in th'end.
Chorus. The greatest shepherd of the fold   *10*
    Angels. Us did make,
    Men.   For us was sold.

---

240. *Distinguished.* Reference to God's separation of the waters and the land (Gen. 1:9–10), thus creating for man a proper habitation.
241. *above, our meat.* Rain from above is needed to produce man's food.

Chorus. He our foes in pieces break;
    Angels. Him we touch;
    Men.   And him we take.   *15*
Chorus. Wherefore since that he is such,
    Angels. We adore,
    Men.   And we do crouch.[242]

Chorus. Lord, thy praises should be more.
    Men.   We have none,   *20*
    Angels. And we no store.
Chorus. Praised be the God alone,
    Who hath made of two folds one.

UNKINDNESS

Lord, make me coy[243] and tender to offend:
In friendship, first I think, if that agree,
    Which I intend,
    Unto my friend's intent and end.
I would not use a friend, as I use Thee.   *5*

If any touch my friend, or his good name,
It is my honor and my love to free
    His blasted fame
    From the least spot or thought of blame.
I could not use a friend, as I use Thee.   *10*

My friend may spit upon my curious floor:
Would he have gold? I lend it instantly;
    But let the poor,
    And thou within them starve at door.
I cannot use a friend, as I use Thee.   *15*

---

242. *crouch.* Bow low in reverence.
243. *coy.* Reserved.

THE CHURCH

When that my friend pretendeth[244] to a place,
I quit[245] my interest, and leave it free:
      But when thy grace
    Sues for my heart, I thee displace,
Nor would I use a friend, as I use Thee.   *20*

Yet can a friend what thou has done fulfill?
Oh write in brass, *My God upon a tree*
      His blood did spill
    Only to purchase my good will: *25*
Yet use I not my foes, as I use thee.

LIFE

I made a posey,[246] while the day ran by:
Here will I smell my remnants out, and tie
      My life within this band.
But time did beckon to the flowers, and they
By noon most cunningly did steal away,   *5*
      And wither'd in my hand.

My hand was next to them, and then my heart:
I took, without more thinking, in good part
      Time's gentle admonition:
Who did so sweetly death's sad taste convey,   *10*
Making my mind to smell my fatal day;
      Yet sug'ring the suspicion.

Farewell dear flowers, sweetly your time ye spent,
Fit, while ye liv'd, for smell or ornament,
      And after death for cures.   *15*
I follow straight without complaints or grief,
Since if my scent be good, I care not, if
      It be as short as yours.

---

244. *pretendeth.* Aspires.
245. *quit.* Abandon.
246. *posey.* A bouquet; also, a motto or a poem.

GEORGE HERBERT

SUBMISSION

But that thou art my wisdom, Lord,
  And both mine eyes are thine,
My mind would be extremely stirr'd
  For missing my design.

Were it not better to bestow   5
  Some place and power on me?
Then should thy praises with me grow,
  And share in my degree.

But when I thus dispute and grieve,
  I do resume my sight,   10
And pilf'ring what I once did give,
  Disseize[247] thee of thy right.

How know I, if thou shouldst me raise,
  That I should then raise thee?
Perhaps great places and thy praise   15
  Do not so well agree.

Wherefore unto my gift I stand;
  I will no more advise:
Only do thou lend me a hand,
  Since thou hast both mine eyes.   20

JUSTICE (I)

I cannot skill of these thy ways.
Lord, thou didst make me, yet thou woundest me;
Lord, thou dost wound me, yet thou dost relieve me:
Lord, thou relievest, yet I die by thee:
Lord, thou dost kill me, yet thou dost reprieve me.   5

---

247. *Disseize.* Dispossess.

But when I mark my life and praise,
　Thy justice me most fitly pays:
For, *I do praise thee, yet I praise thee not:*
My prayers mean thee, yet my prayers stray:
I would do well, yet sin the hand hath got:[248]　　　　10
My soul doth love thee, yet it loves delay.
　I cannot skill of these my ways.

CHARMS AND KNOTS

Who read a chapter when they rise,
Shall ne'er be troubled with ill eyes.

A poor man's rod, when thou dost ride,
Is both a weapon and a guide.

Who shuts his hand, hath lost his gold:　　　　5
Who opens it, hath it twice told.

Who goes to bed and doth not pray,
Maketh two nights to ev'ry day.

Who by aspersions throw a stone
At th' head of others, hit their own.　　　　10

Who looks on ground with humble eyes,
Finds himself there, and seeks to rise.

When th' hair is sweet through pride or lust,
The powder doth forget the dust.

Take one from ten, and what remains?　　　　15
Ten still, if sermons go for gains.

In shallow waters heav'n doth show;
But who drinks on, to hell may go.

---

248. *the hand hath got.* Has gotten the upper hand.

GEORGE HERBERT

AFFLICTION (V)

My God, I read this day,
That planted Paradise[249] was not so firm,
As was and is thy floating Ark;[250] whose stay
And anchor thou art only, to confirm
    And strengthen it in ev'ry age,   *5*
    When waves do rise, and tempests rage.

At first we liv'd in pleasure;
Thine own delights thou didst to us impart:
When we grew wanton, thou didst use displeasure
To make us thine: yet that we might not part,   *10*
    As we at first did board with thee,
    Now thou wouldst taste our misery.

There is but joy and grief;
If either will convert us, we are thine:
Some Angels us'd the first; if our relief   *15*
Take up the second, then thy double line
    And sev'ral baits[251] in either kind
    Furnish thy table to thy mind.

Affliction then is ours;
We are the trees, whom shaking fastens more,   *20*
While blust'ring winds destroy the wanton bowers,
And ruffle all their curious knots[252] and store.
    My God, so temper joy and woe,
    That thy bright beams may tame thy bow.[253]

---

249. *planted Paradise*. See Gen. 2:8.
250. *Ark*. In the BCP Baptismal Office, as in other traditional Christian usage, Noah's Ark becomes "the Ark of Christ's Church"; see Booty, p. 271.
251. *baits*. Lures, one of pleasure, the other of weariness.
252. *curious knots*. Intricately designed flower beds in a formal garden.
253. *bow*. The rainbow of Gen. 9:12–17, but also the bow as an instrument of divine punishment.

THE CHURCH

MORTIFICATION

How soon doth man decay!
When clothes are taken from a chest of sweets[254]
    To swaddle infants, whose young breath
        Scarce knows the way;
    Those clouts[255] are little winding sheets,   5
Which do consign and send them unto death.

        When boys go first to bed,
They step into their voluntary graves,
        Sleep binds them fast; only their breath
            Makes them not dead: 10
        Successive nights, like rolling waves,
Convey them quickly, who are bound for death.

        When youth is frank and free,
And calls for music, while his veins do swell,
        All day exchanging mirth and breath   15
            In company;
        That music summons to the knell,[256]
Which shall befriend him at the house of death.[257]

        When man grows staid and wise,
Getting a house and home, where he may move   20
        Within the circle of his breath,
            Schooling his eyes;
        That dumb enclosure maketh love
Unto the coffin, that attends[258] his death.

        When age grows low and weak,   25
Marking his grave, and thawing ev'ry year,
        Till all do melt, and drown his breath
            When he would speak;

---

254. *sweets.* Perfumes.
255. *clouts.* Swaddling clothes.
256. *the knell.* Bell rung, not after death at this time, but when anyone was dying.
257. *house.* W reads "houre."
258. *attends.* Awaits.

217

A chair or litter shows the bier,
Which shall convey him to the house of death.   *30*

Man, ere he is aware,
Hath put together a solemnity,
And drest his hearse,[259] while he has breath
As yet to spare:
Yet Lord, instruct us so to die,   *35*
That all these dyings may be life in death.

DECAY

Sweet were the days, when thou didst lodge with Lot,
Struggle with Jacob, sit with Gideon,
Advise with Abraham,[260] when thy power could not
Encounter Moses' strong complaints and moan:
Thy words were then, *Let me alone.*[261]   *5*

One might have sought and found thee presently
At some fair oak, or bush, or cave, or well.[262]
Is my God this way? No, they would reply:
He is to Sinai gone, as we heard tell:
List, ye may hear great Aaron's bell.[263]   *10*

But now thou dost thyself immure[264] and close
In some one corner of a feeble heart:[265]

259. *hearse.* Bier, not funeral conveyance.
260. See Gen. 19:1, 32:24, 18:33 and Judg. 6:11.
261. Moses, on such familiar terms with God that he could continue to plead with God after being told "let me alone," was finally rewarded for his persistence. See Exod. 32:9–14.
262. God appeared to Gideon near an oak (Judg. 6:11), to Moses in a burning bush (Exod. 3:2), spoke to Elijah in a cave (1 Kings 19:9), and instructed Abraham's servant to meet Rebekah near a well (Gen. 24:11).
263. *great Aaron's bell.* Among Aaron's priestly garments was "a golden bell and a pomegranate" (Exod. 29:34).
264. *immure.* Shut up, enclose.
265. See Luke 17:21.

Where yet both Sin and Satan, thy old foes,
Do pinch and straiten[266] thee, and use much art
   To gain thy thirds[267] and little part.   *15*

I see the world grows old, when as the heat
Of thy great love once spread, as in an urn
Doth closet up itself, and still retreat,
Cold sin still forcing it, till it return,
   And calling Justice, all things burn.   *20*

MISERY

  Lord, let the Angels praise thy name.
Man is a foolish thing, a foolish thing,
  Folly and Sin play all his game.
His house still burns, and yet he still doth sing,
    Man is but grass,[268]   *5*
    He knows it, fill the glass.

  How canst thou brook his foolishness?
Why he'll not lose a cup of drink for thee:
  Bid him but temper his excess;
Not he: he knows, where he can better be,   *10*
    As he will swear,
    Than to serve thee in fear.

  What strange pollutions doth he wed,
And make his own? as if none knew, but he.
  No man shall beat into his head,   *15*
That thou within his curtains drawn canst see:[269]
    They are of cloth,
    Where never yet came moth.

---

266. *straiten.* Shut up in or force into a narrow space.
267. *thirds.* A legal term referring to that part of a deceased husband's property to which his widow was entitled.
268. See Isa. 40:6, "All flesh is grass."
269. See Ps. 139:2.

The best of men, turn but thy hand
For one poor minute, stumble at a pin: *20*
   They would not have their actions scann'd,
Nor any sorrow tell them that they sin,
      Though it be small,
      And measure not their fall.

   They quarrel[270] thee, and would give over   *25*
The bargain made to serve thee: but thy love
   Holds them unto it, and doth cover
Their follies with the wing of thy mild Dove,
      Not suff'ring those
      Who would, to be thy foes.   *30*

   My God, Man cannot praise thy name:
Thou art all brightness, perfect purity;
   The sun holds down his head for shame,
Dead with eclipses, when we speak of thee:
      How shall infection   *35*
      Presume on thy perfection?

   As dirty hands foul all they touch,
And those things most, which are most pure and fine:
   So our clay hearts, ev'n when we crouch[271]
To sing thy praises, make them less divine.   *40*
      Yet either this,
      Or none thy portion is.

   Man cannot serve thee; let him go,
And serve the swine: there, there is his delight:
   He doth not like this virtue, no;   *45*
Give him his dirt to wallow in all night:
      These Preachers make
      His head to shoot and ache.

   Oh foolish man! where are thine eyes?
How hast thou lost them in a crowd of cares?   *50*

---

270. *quarrel.* Find fault with, dispute God's right to command.
271. *crouch.* Bow low in reverence.

THE CHURCH

Thou pull'st the rug, and wilt not rise,
No, not to purchase the whole pack of stars:
    There let them shine,
    Thou must go sleep, or dine.

The bird that sees a dainty bower   *55*
Made in the tree, where she was wont to sit,
    Wonders and sings, but not his power
Who made the arbor: this exceeds her wit.
        But Man doth know
        The spring, whence all things flow: *60*

And yet as though he knew it not,
His knowledge winks, and lets his humors reign;
    They make his life a constant blot,
And all the blood of God to run in vain.
        Ah wretch! what verse   *65*
        Can thy strange ways rehearse?

Indeed at first Man was a treasure,
A box of jewels, shop of rarities,
    A ring, whose posey[272] was, *My pleasure:*
He was a garden in a Paradise: *70*
        Glory and grace
        Did crown his heart and face.

But sin hath fool'd him. Now he is
A lump of flesh, without a foot or wing
    To raise him to the glimpse of bliss: *75*
A sick toss'd vessel, dashing on each thing;
        Nay, his own shelf:[273]
        My God, I mean myself.

---

272. *posey.* Motto.
273. *shelf.* Reef, sand bar, or submerged ledge of rock.

GEORGE HERBERT

JORDAN (II)[274]

When first my lines of heav'nly joys made mention,
Such was their luster, they did so excel,
That I sought out quaint words, and trim invention;[275]
My thoughts began to burnish,[276] sprout, and swell,
Curling with metaphors a plain intention,   5
Decking the sense, as if it were to sell.

Thousands of notions in my brain did run,
Off'ring their service, if I were not sped:
I often blotted what I had begun;
This was not quick[277] enough, and that was dead.   10
Nothing could seem too rich to clothe the sun,
Much less those joys which trample on his head.

As flames do work and wind, when they ascend,
So did I weave myself into the sense.
But while I bustled, I might hear a friend   15
Whisper, *How wide*[278] *is all this long pretense!*
There is in love a sweetness ready penn'd:
Copy out only that, and save expense.

[PRAYER (III)][279]

Of what an easy quick access,
My blessed Lord, art thou! how suddenly
    May our requests thine ear invade!
To show that state dislikes not easyness,
If I but lift mine eyes, my suit is made: 5
Thou canst no more not hear, than thou canst die.

---

274. On meaning of title, see note on "Jordan (I)" above, p. 171.
275. *invention*. Technical term in rhetoric, meaning the finding of suitable subject matter.
276. *burnish*. Spread out, grow in strength and vigor.
277. *quick*. Lively.
278. *wide*. Wide of the mark.
279. In most editions, "Prayer (II)."

Of what supreme almighty power
Is thy great arm which spans the east and west,
   And tacks the center to the sphere![280]
By it do all things live their measur'd hour: *10*
We cannot ask the thing, which is not there,
Blaming the shallowness of our request.

Of what unmeasurable love
Art thou possest, who, when thou couldst not die,
   Wert fain to take our flesh and curse,[281]   *15*
And for our sakes in person sin reprove,
That by destroying that which tied thy purse,
Thou mightst make sure for liberality!

Since then these three wait on thy throne,
Ease, Power, and *Love;* I value prayer so,   *20*
   That were I to leave all but one,
Wealth, fame, endowments, virtues, all should go;
I and dear prayer would together dwell,
And quickly gain, for each inch lost, an ell.[282]

OBEDIENCE

   My God, if writings may
   Convey[283] a Lordship any way
Whither the buyer and the seller please;
   Let it not thee displease,
If this poor paper do as much as they.   *5*

   On it my heart doth bleed
   As many lines as there doth need
To pass[284] itself and all it hath to thee,

---

280. *sphere.* The sphere, the apparent outermost limit of space, is everywhere equidistant from its center, which is the earth.

281. *curse.* See Gal. 3:13.

282. *ell.* A measure of length, amounting to 45 inches.

283. *Convey.* Legal term; to transfer by deed or other legal process.

284. *pass.* Convey legally.

To which I do agree,
And here present it as my special deed. *10*

If that hereafter Pleasure
Cavil,[285] and claim her part and measure,
As if this passed with a reservation,[286]
Or some such words in fashion;
I here exclude the wrangler from thy treasure. *15*

Oh let thy sacred will
All thy delight in me fulfill!
Let me not think an action mine own way,
But as thy love shall sway,
Resigning up the rudder to thy skill. *20*

Lord, what is man to thee,
That thou shouldst mind a rotten tree?
Yet since thou canst not choose but see my actions;
So great are thy perfections,
Thou mayest as well my actions guide, as see. *25*

Besides, thy death and blood
Show'd a strange love to all our good:
Thy sorrows were in earnest; no faint proffer,
Or superficial offer
Of what we might not take, or be withstood. *30*

Wherefore I all forego:
To one word only I say, No:
Where in the deed there was an intimation
Of a *gift* or *donation*,
Lord, let it now by way of *purchase*[287] go. *35*

He that will pass his land,
As I have mine, may set his hand

---

285. *Cavil*. Raise frivolous objections.
286. *reservation*. Clause of a deed by which the right to some property to be conveyed to another is reserved or retained by oneself.
287. *purchase*. Possession of lands by deed or agreement.

And heart unto this deed, when he hath read;
    And make the purchase spread
To both our goods, if he to it will stand.   *40*

    How happy were my part,
  If some kind man would thrust his heart
Into these lines; till in heav'n's court of rolls[288]
    They were by winged souls
Ent'red for both, far above their desert!   *45*

CONSCIENCE

    Peace prattler, do not lour:[289]
Not a fair look, but thou dost call it foul:
Not a sweet dish, but thou dost call it sour:
    Music to thee doth howl.
  By list'ning to thy chatting fears   *5*
  I have both lost mine eyes and ears.

    Prattler, no more, I say:
My thoughts must work, but like a noiseless sphere;
Harmonious peace must rock them all the day:
    No room for prattlers there.   *10*
  If thou persistest, I will tell thee,
  That I have physic[290] to expel thee.

    And the receipt shall be
My Savior's blood: whenever at his board
I do but taste it, straight it cleanseth me,   *15*
    And leaves thee not a word;
  No, not a tooth or nail to scratch,
  And at my actions carp, or catch.

---

288. *court of rolls.* Registry of legal documents.
289. *lour.* Frown, scowl, look angry.
290. *physic.* Medicine.

Yet it thou talkest still,
Besides my physic, know there's some for thee: *20*
Some wood and nails to make a staff or bill[291]
    For those that trouble me:[292]
  The bloody cross of my dear Lord
  Is both my physic and my sword.

SION[293]

Lord, with what glory wast thou serv'd of old,
When Solomon's temple stood and flourished!
  Where most things were of purest gold;
  The wood was all embellished
With flowers and carvings, mystical and rare: *5*
All show'd the builders, crav'd the seer's care.

Yet all this glory, all this pomp and state
Did not affect thee much, was not thy aim;
  Something there was, that sow'd debate:
  Wherefore thou quitt'st thy ancient claim: *10*
And now thy Architecture meets with sin;
For all thy frame and fabric is within.

There thou art struggling with a peevish heart,
Which sometimes crosseth thee, thou sometimes it:
  The fight is hard on either part. *15*
  Great God doth fight, he doth submit.
All Solomon's sea of brass and world of stone[294]
Is not so dear to thee as one good groan.

And truly brass and stones are heavy things,
Tombs for the dead, not temples fit for thee: *20*

---

291. *bill.* Halberd, spear.
292. See Ps. 23:4–5.
293. See Acts 7:47–48.
294. Solomon "made a molten Sea" of brass (1 Kings 7:23), and his temple "was built of stone" (1 Kings 6:7).

But groans are quick, and full of wings,
    And all their motions upward be;
And ever as they mount, like larks they sing;
    The note is sad, yet music for a king.

HOME

Come Lord, my head doth burn, my heart is sick,
    While thou dost ever, ever stay:[295]
Thy long deferrings wound me to the quick,
    My spirit gaspeth night and day.
        Oh show thyself to me,   *5*
        Or take me up to thee!

How canst thou stay, considering the pace
    The blood did make, which thou didst waste?
When I behold it trickling down thy face,
    I never saw thing make such haste.   *10*
        Oh show thyself to me,
        Or take me up to thee!

When man was lost, thy pity lookt about
    To see what help in th' earth or sky:
But there was none; at least no help without:[296]   *15*
    The help did in thy bosom lie.
        Oh show thyself to me,
        Or take me up to thee!

There lay thy son: and must he leave that nest,
    That hive of sweetness, to remove   *20*
Thraldom[297] from those, who would not at a feast
    Leave one poor apple for thy love?
        Oh show thyself to me,
        Or take me up to thee!

---

295. *stay* (also lines 7, 31, 67, 76). Stay away.
296. See Isa. 59:16.
297. *Thraldom.* State of captivity or bondage.

He did, he came: Oh my Redeemer dear,   25
   After all this canst thou be strange?
So many years baptiz'd, and not appear?
   As if thy love could fail or change.
      Oh show thyself to me,
      Or take me up to thee!   30

Yet if thou stayest still, why must I stay?
   My God, what is this world to me?
This world of woe? hence all ye clouds, away,
   Away; I must get up and see.
      Oh show thyself to me,   35
      Or take me up to thee!

What is this weary world; this meat and drink,
   That chains us by the teeth so fast?
What is this womankind, which I can wink
   Into a blackness and distaste?   40
      Oh show thyself to me,
      Or take me up to thee!

With one small sigh thou gav'st me th' other day
   I blasted all the joys about me:
And scowling on them as they pin'd away,   45
   Now come again, said I, and flout me.
      Oh show thyself to me,
      Or take me up to thee!

Nothing but drought and dearth, but bush and brake,
   Which way soe're I look, I see.   50
Some may dream merrily, but when they wake,
   They dress themselves and come to thee.
      Oh show thyself to me,
      Or take me up to thee!

We talk of harvests; there are no such things,   55
   But when we leave our corn and hay:
There is no fruitful year, but that which brings
   The last and lov'd, though dreadful day.

Oh show thyself to me,
Or take me up to thee!

Oh loose this frame, this knot of man untie!   *60*
   That my free soul may use her wing,
Which now is pinion'd with mortality,
   As an entangled, hamper'd thing.
     Oh show thyself to me,   *65*
     Or take me up to thee!

What have I left, that I should stay and groan?
   The most of me to heav'n is fled:
My thoughts and joys are all packt up and gone,
   And for their old acquaintance plead.   *70*
     Oh show thyself to me,
     Or take me up to thee!

Come dearest Lord, pass not this holy season,
   My flesh and bones and joints do pray:
And ev'n my verse, when by the rhyme and reason   *75*
   The word is, *Stay,* says ever, *Come.*[298]
     Oh show thyself to me,
     Or take me up to thee!

THE BRITISH CHURCH

I joy, dear Mother, when I view
Thy perfect lineaments, and hue
     Both sweet and bright.

Beauty in thee takes up her place,
And dates her letters from thy face,[299]   *5*
     When she doth write.

---

   298. The rhyme demands "stay," but the speaker urges, "come."
   299. The church of England in Herbert's day dated the first day of the year as March 25, the Feast of the Annunciation, or Lady Day.

A fine aspect in fit array,
Neither too mean, nor yet too gay,
    Shows who is best.

Outlandish looks may not compare: *10*
For all they either painted are,
    Or else undrest.

She on the hills,[300] which wantonly
Allureth all in hope to be
    By her preferr'd,   *15*

Hath kiss'd so long her painted shrines,
That ev'n her face by kissing shines,
    For her reward.

She in the valley[301] is so shy
Of dressing, that her hair doth lie   *20*
    About her ears:

While she avoids her neighbor's pride,
She wholly goes on th' other side,
    And nothing wears.

But dearest Mother, (what those miss)   *25*
The mean[302] thy praise and glory is,
    And long may be.

Blessed be God, whose love it was
To double-moat[303] thee with his grace,
    And none but thee.   *30*

---

300. *She on the hills.* The Roman Catholic Church.
301. *She in the valley.* Genevan Calvinism.
302. *the mean.* The Anglican *"via media."*
303. *double-moat.* The British Church is protected against both ostentation and nudity.

THE QUIP[304]

The merry world did on a day
With his train-bands[305] and mates agree
To meet together, where I lay,
And all in sport to jeer at me.

First, Beauty crept into a rose,   *5*
Which when I pluckt not, Sir, said she,
Tell me, I pray, Whose hands are those?
But thou shalt answer, Lord, for me.[306]

Then Money came, and chinking still,
What tune is this, poor man? said he: *10*
I heard in Music you had skill.
But thou shalt answer, Lord, for me.

Then came brave Glory puffing by
In silks that whistled, who but he?
He scarce allow'd me half an eye.   *15*
But thou shalt answer, Lord, for me.

Then came quick Wit and Conversation,
And he would needs a comfort be,
And, to be short, make an oration.
But thou shalt answer, Lord, for me.   *20*

Yet when the hour of thy design
To answer these fine things shall come;
Speak not at large, say, I am thine:
And then they have their answer home.

---

304. Title means both "sharp remarks" and "verbal equivocations."
305. *train-bands.* Abbreviation of trained bands, the citizen-soldiers of London; here, referring to all society (also 11, 12, 16, 20).
306. *But thou shalt answer, Lord, for me.* See Ps. 38:15, "For in thee, O Lord, have I put my trust; thou shalt answer for me, oh Lord my God."

GEORGE HERBERT

VANITY (II)

Poor silly soul, whose hope and head lies low;
Whose flat delights on earth do creep and grow;
To whom the stars shine not so fair, as eyes;
Nor solid work, as false embroideries;
Hark and beware, lest what you now do measure   *5*
And write for sweet, prove a most sour displeasure.

    Oh hear betimes, lest thy relenting
        May come too late!
    To purchase heaven for repenting,
        Is no hard rate.   *10*
    If souls be made of earthly mold,
        Let them love gold;
        If born on high,
    Let them unto their kindred fly:
    For they can never be at rest,   *15*
    Till they regain their ancient nest.
Then silly soul take heed; for earthly joy
Is but a bubble, and makes thee a boy.

THE DAWNING[307]

Awake sad heart, whom sorrow ever drowns;
  Take up thine eyes, which feed on earth;
Unfold thy forehead gather'd into frowns:
  Thy Savior comes, and with him mirth:
    Awake, awake;   *5*
And with a thankful heart his comforts take.
  But thou dost still lament, and pine, and cry;
  And feel his death, but not his victory.

Arise sad heart; if thou dost not withstand,
  Christ's resurrection thine may be: *10*

---

307. Of Easter Day.

Do not by hanging down break from the hand,
  Which as it riseth, raiseth thee:
      Arise, arise;
And with his burial linen dry thine eyes:
  Christ left his graveclothes, that we might, when grief   *15*
  Draws tears, or blood, not want an handkerchief.[308]

JESU

J E S U is in my heart, his sacred name
Is deeply carved there: but th'other week
A great affliction broke the little frame,
Ev'n all to pieces: which I went to seek:
And first I found the corner, where was *J*,   *5*
After, where *E S*, and next where *U* was graved.
When I had got these parcels, instantly
I sat me down to spell them, and perceived
That to my broken heart he was *I ease you*,[309]
     And to my whole is *J E S U.*   *10*

BUSINESS

     Canst be idle? canst thou play,
     Foolish soul who sinn'd today?

Rivers run, and springs each one
Know their home, and get them gone:
Hast thou tears, or hast thou none?   *5*

If, poor soul, thou hast no tears,
Would thou hadst no faults or fears!
Who hath these, those ill forebears.

---

308. *handkerchief.* Not modern usage, but the biblical sense of a miraculous means of healing; see Acts 19:11–12.
  309. *I ease you.* The differentiation of *I* and *J* was not complete in Herbert's time, thus permitting this play on the spelling of Jesus' name.

Winds still work: it is their plot,
Be the season cold, or hot: *10*
Hast thou sighs, or hast thou not?

If thou hast no signs or groans,
Would thou hadst no flesh and bones!
Lesser pains 'scape greater ones.
   But if yet thou idle be,   *15*
   Foolish soul, Who di'd for thee?

Who did leave his Father's throne,
To assume thy flesh and bone;
Had he life, or had he none?

If he had not liv'd for thee,   *20*
Thou hadst di'd most wretchedly;
And two deaths[310] had been thy fee.[311]

He so far thy good did plot,
That his own self he forgot.
Did he die, or did he not?   *25*

If he had not di'd for thee,
Thou hadst liv'd in misery.
Two lives[312] worse than ten deaths be.
   And hath any space of breath
   'Twixt his sins and Savior's death?   *30*

He that loseth gold, though dross,
Tells to all he meets, his cross:
He that sins, hath he no loss?

He that finds a silver vein,
Thinks on it, and thinks again,   *35*
Brings thy Savior's death no gain?

---

310. *two deaths.* The natural death of the body and the "second death" of Rev. 21:8.
311. *fee.* Reward.
312. *two lives.* One here, the other hereafter, alike in misery.

THE CHURCH

Who in heart not ever kneels,
Neither sin nor Savior feels.

DIALOGUE

Sweetest Savior, if my soul
  Were but worth the having,
Quickly should I then control
  Any thought of waving.[313]
But when all my care and pains   *5*
Cannot give the name of gains
To thy wretch so full of stains;
What delights or hope remains?

What (child) is the balance thine,
  Thine the poise and measure?   *10*
If I say, Thou shalt be mine;
  Finger not my treasure.
What the gains in having thee
Do amount to, only he,
Who for man was sold, can see;   *15*
That transferr'd th' accounts to me.

But as I can see no merit,
  Leading to this favor:
So the way to fit me for it,
  Is beyond my savor.[314]   *20*
As the reason then is thine;
So the way is none of mine:[315]
I disclaim the whole design:
Sin disclaims and I resign.

That is all, if that I could   *25*
  Get without repining;

---

313. *waving*. Declining the offer; waiving.
314. *savor*. Perception, understanding.
315. See John 14:6.

And my clay my creature would
  Follow my resigning.
That as I did freely part
With my glory and desert,[316]
Left all joys to feel all smart—
Ah! no more: thou break'st my heart.

                                    30

DULLNESS

Why do I languish thus, drooping and dull,
    As if I were all earth?
Oh give me quickness, that I may with mirth
    Praise thee brim-full!

The wanton lover in a curious strain   *5*
    Can praise his fairest fair;
And with quaint metaphors her curled hair
    Curl o'er again.

Thou art my loveliness, my life, my light,
    Beauty alone to me: *10*
Thy bloody death and undeserv'd, makes thee
    Pure red and white.[317]

When all perfections as but one appear,
    That those thy form doth show,
The very dust, where thou dost tread and go,   *15*
    Makes beauties here.

Where are my lines then? my approaches? views?
    Where are my window-songs?[318]
Lovers are still pretending,[319] and ev'n wrongs
    Sharpen their Muse: *20*

---

316. *desert.* Excellence, worthiness; pronounced to rhyme with "part."
317. *Pure red and white.* Usual poetic description of the beauty of the beloved in secular love poetry, but see also Song of Solomon 5:10, "My beloved is white and ruddy."
318. *window-songs.* Serenades.
319. *pretending.* Seeking favor, wooing.

But I am lost in flesh, whose sug'red lies
    Still mock me, and grow bold:
Sure thou didst put a mind there, if I could
    Find where it lies.

Lord, clear[320] thy gift, that with a constant wit   *25*
    I may but look towards thee:
Look only; for to *love* thee, who can be,
    What angel fit?

LOVE-JOY

As on a window late I cast mine eye,
I saw a vine drop grapes with *J* and *C*
Anneal'd[321] on every bunch. One standing by
Ask'd what it meant. I (who am never loth
To spend[322] my judgment) said, It seem'd to me   *5*
To be the body[323] and the letters both
Of *Joy* and *Charity.* Sir, you have not miss'd,
The man replied; It figures *JESUS CHRIST.*

PROVIDENCE[324]

Oh sacred Providence, who from end to end
Strongly and sweetly movest![325] shall I write,
And not of thee, through whom my fingers bend
To hold my quill? shall they not do thee right?

---

320. *clear.* Discharge a debt or promise.
321. *anneal'd.* Fixed the colors by heating the glass after painting.
322. *spend.* Utter.
323. *body.* The stem or main part of a tree.
324. Title: Allusions here to Job 38 and Ps. 104, entitled in the KJV "A meditation upon the mighty power, and wonderful providence of God."
325. See Wisd. 8:1, "Wisdom reacheth from one end to another mightily: and sweetly doth she order things." See also lines 31, 38–39.

Of all the creatures both in sea and land   *5*
Only to Man thou hast made known thy ways,
And put the pen alone into his hand,
And made him Secretary of thy praise.

Beasts fain would sing; birds ditty to their notes;[326]
Trees would be tuning on their native lute   *10*
To thy renown: but all their hands and throats
Are brought to Man, while they are lame and mute.

Man is the world's high Priest: he doth present
The sacrifice for all; while they below
Unto the service mutter an assent,   *15*
Such as springs use that fall, and winds that blow.

He that to praise and laud thee doth refrain,
Doth not refrain unto himself alone,
But robs a thousand who would praise thee fain,[327]
And doth commit a world of sin in one.   *20*

The beasts say, Eat me: but, if beasts must teach,
The tongue is yours to eat, but mine to praise.
The trees say, Pull me: but the hand you stretch,
Is mine to write, as it is yours to raise.

Wherefore, most sacred Spirit, I here present   *25*
For me and all my fellows praise to thee:
And just it is that I should pay the rent,
Because the benefit accrues to me.

We all acknowledge both thy power and love
To be exact, transcendent, and divine;   *30*
Who dost so strongly and so sweetly move,
While all things have their will, yet none but thine.

---

326. *birds ditty to their notes.* Birds would readily fit words to their songs.
327. *fain.* Gladly, willingly.

For either thy *command*, or thy *permission*
Lay hands on all: they are thy *right* and *left*.
The first puts on with speed and expedition;   *35*
The other curbs sin's stealing pace and theft.

Nothing escapes them both; all must appear,
And be dispos'd, and dress'd, and tun'd by thee,
Who sweetly temper'st[328] all. If we could hear
Thy skill and art, what music would it be!   *40*

Thou art in small things great, not small in any:
Thy even praise can neither rise, nor fall.
Thou art in all things one, in each thing many:
For thou art infinite in one and all.

Tempests are calm to thee; they know thy hand,   *45*
And hold it fast, as children do their fathers,
Which cry and follow. Thou hast made poor sand
Check the proud sea, ev'n when it swells and gathers.[329]

Thy cupboard serves the world: the meat is set,
Where all may reach: no beast but knows his feed.   *50*
Birds teach us hawking; fishes have their net:[330]
The great prey on the less, they on some weed.

Nothing ingend'red doth prevent[331] his meat:
Flies have their table spread, ere they appear.
Some creatures have in winter what to eat;   *55*
Others do sleep, and envy not their cheer.[332]

How finely dost thou times and seasons spin,
And make a twist checker'd with night and day!
Which as it lengthens winds, and winds us in,
As bowls go on, but turning all the way.   *60*

---

328. *temper'st.* Tune, bring into harmony.
329. See Jer. 5:22; Job 38:11.
330. *their net.* The mouths of the fishes are like nets.
331. *prevent.* Anticipate.
332. *cheer.* Winter provisions of those in 1.55.

Each creature hath a wisdom for his good.
The pigeons feed their tender offspring, crying,
When they are callow; but withdraw their food
When they are fledge, that need may teach them flying.

Bees work for man; and yet they never bruise   65
Their master's flower, but leave it, having done,
As fair as ever, and as fit to use;
So both the flower doth stay, and honey run.

Sheep eat the grass, and dung the ground for more:
Trees after bearing drop their leaves for soil: 70
Springs vent their streams, and by expense get store:
Clouds cool by heat, and baths by cooling boil.

Who hath the virtue to express[333] the rare
And curious virtues[334] both of herbs and stones?
Is there an herb for that? Oh that thy care   75
Would show a root, that gives expressions!

And if an herb hath power, what have the stars?
A rose, besides his beauty, is a cure.[335]
Doubtless our plagues and plenty, peace and wars
Are there much surer than our art is sure.   80

Thou hast hid metals: man may take them thence;
But at his peril: when he digs the place,
He makes a grave; as if the thing had sense,
And threat'ned man, that he should fill the space.

Ev'n poisons praise thee. Should a thing be lost?   85
Should creatures want for want of heed their due?
Since where are poisons, antidotes are most:
The help stands close, and keeps the fear in view.

---

333. *express.* Describe; also, squeeze out.
334. *virtues.* Healing properties.
335. *cure.* Roses were thought to have medicinal properties.

THE CHURCH

The sea, which seems to stop the traveler,
Is by a ship the speedier passage made.
The winds, who think they rule the mariner,
Are rul'd by him, and taught to serve his trade.

And as thy house is full, so I adore
Thy curious art in marshalling thy goods.
The hills with health abound; the vales with store;
The South with marble; North with furs and woods.

Hard things are glorious; easy things good cheap.
The common all men have; that which is rare,
Men therefore seek to have, and care to keep.
The healthy frosts with summer fruits compare.

Light without wind is glass: warm without weight
Is wool and furs: cool without closeness, shade:
Speed without pains, a horse: tall without height,
A servile hawk: low without loss, a spade.

All countries have enough to serve their need:
If they seek fine things, thou dost make them run
For their offense; and then dost turn their speed
To be commerce and trade from sun to sun.

Nothing wears clothes, but Man; nothing doth need
But he to wear them. Nothing useth fire,
But Man alone, to show his heav'nly breed:
And only he hath fuel in desire.

When th' earth was dry, thou mad'st a sea of wet:
When that lay gather'd, thou didst broach the mountains:
When yet some places could no moisture get,
The winds grew[336] gard'ners, and the clouds good fountains.

_90_

_95_

_100_

_105_

_110_

_115_

---

336. *grew.* Grew into.

241

Rain, do not hurt my flowers; but gently spend
Your honey drops: press not to smell them here:
When they are ripe, their odor will ascend,
And at your lodging with their thanks appear.   120

How harsh are thorns to[337] pears! and yet they make
A better hedge, and need less reparation.
How smooth are silks compared with a stake,
Or with a stone! yet make no good foundation.

Sometimes thou dost divide thy gifts to man,   125
Sometimes unite. The Indian nut[338] alone
Is clothing, meat and trencher, drink and can,[339]
Boat, cable, sail and needle, all in one.

Most herbs that grow in brooks, are hot and dry.
Cold fruits warm kernels help against the wind.   130
The lemon's juice and rind cure mutually.
The whey of milk doth loose, the milk doth bind.

Thy creatures leap not, but express a feast,
Where all the guests sit close, and nothing wants.
Frogs marry[340] fish and flesh; bats, bird and beast;   135
Sponges, nonsense and sense; mines, th' earth and plants.

To show thou art not bound, as if thy lot
Were worse than ours, sometimes thou shiftest hands.
Most things move th' under-jaw; the Crocodile not.
Most things sleep lying; th' Elephant leans or stands.   140

But who hath praise enough? nay, who hath any?
None can express thy works, but he that knows them:
And none can know thy works, which are so many,
And so complete, but only he that owes[341] them.

---

337. *to.* Compared to.
338. *Indian nut.* Coconut.
339. *can.* Drinking can.
340. *marry.* Form a link between.
341. *owes.* Owns.

All things that are, though they have sev'ral ways,   *145*
Yet in their being join with one advise[342]
To honor thee: and so I give thee praise
In all my other hymns, but in this twice.[343]

Each thing that is, although in use and name
It go for one, hath many ways in store   *150*
To honor thee; and so each hymn thy fame
Extolleth mány ways, yet this one more.

HOPE

I gave to Hope a watch of mine: but he
     An anchor gave to me.[344]
Then an old prayer book I did present:
     And he an optic[345] sent.
With that I gave a vial full of tears: *5*
     But he a few green ears:
Ah Loiterer! I'll no more, no more I'll bring:
     I did expect a ring.[346]

SIN'S ROUND

Sorry I am, my God, sorry I am,
That my offenses course it in a ring.
My thoughts are working like a busy flame,

---

342. *advise.* Opinion, judgment.
343. *twice.* Herbert offers praise as a poet and as "the worlds High Priest" (see lines 13–14, 25–26).
344. See Heb. 6:19; "Which hope we have as an anchor of the soul." There may be a reference here to Donne's having had made, shortly before his death, a number of seals bearing the figure of Christ crucified on an anchor as an emblem of hope, one of which was given to Herbert (see Walton, *Life of Herbert*, p. 274).
345. *optic.* Telescope.
346. *ring.* Perhaps a reference to the sign given in marriage of the union between Christ and his Church.

Until their cockatrice[347] they hatch and bring:
And when they once have perfected their draughts,   *5*
My words take fire from my inflamed thoughts.

My words take fire from my inflamed thoughts,
Which spit it forth like the Sicilian hill.[348]
They vent[349] the wares, and pass them with their faults,
And by their breathing ventilate the ill.   *10*
But words suffice not, where are lewd intentions:
My hands do join to finish the inventions.

My hands do join to finish the inventions:
And so my sins ascend three stories high,
As Babel grew, before there were dissentions.   *15*
Yet ill deeds loiter not: for they supply
New thoughts of sinning: wherefore, to my shame,
Sorry I am, my God, sorry I am.

TIME

Meeting with Time, Slack thing, said I,
Thy scythe is dull; whet it for shame.
No marvel Sir, he did reply,
If it at length deserve some blame:
   But where one man would have me grind it,   *5*
   Twenty for one too sharp do find it.

Perhaps some such of old did pass,
Who above all things lov'd this life;
To whom thy scythe a hatchet was,
Which now is but a pruning-knife.   *10*
   Christ's coming hath made man thy debtor,
   Since by thy cutting he grows better.

---

347. *cockatrice.* Mythical creature, hatched from a cock's egg by a serpent, thought to kill with its breath. See also Isa. 59:5.

348. *Sicilian hill.* Mount Etna, a volcano.

349. *vent.* Discharge, with suggestion of *vend*, to sell.

And in his blessing thou art blest:
For where thou only wert before
An executioner at best;   *15*
Thou art a gard'ner now, and more,
   An usher to convey our souls
   Beyond the utmost stars and poles.

And this is that makes life so long,
While it detains us from our God.   *20*
Ev'n pleasures here increase the wrong,
And length of days lengthen the rod.
   Who wants[350] the place, where God doth dwell,
   Partakes already half of hell.

Of what strange length must that needs be,   *25*
Which ev'n eternity excludes!
Thus far Time heard me patiently:
Then chafing said, This man deludes:
   What do I here before his door?
   He doth not crave less time, but more.   *30*

GRATEFULNESS

Thou that hast giv'n so much to me,
Give one thing more, a grateful heart.
See how thy beggar works on thee
      By art.

He makes thy gifts occasion more,   *5*
And says, If he in this be crost,[351]
All thou hast giv'n him heretofore
      Is lost.

---

350. *wants.* Lacks.
351. *crost.* Crossed.

But thou didst reckon, when at first
Thy word our hearts and hands did crave,   *10*
What it would come to at the worst
   To save.

Perpetual knockings at thy door,
Tears sullying thy transparent rooms,
Gift upon gift, much would have more,   *15*
   And comes.

This not withstanding, thou wentst on,
And didst allow us all our noise:
Nay, thou hast made a sigh and groan
   Thy joys.   *20*

Not that thou hast not still above
Much better tunes, than groans can make;
But that these country airs thy love
   Did take.³⁵²

Wherefore I cry, and cry again;   *25*
And in no quiet canst thou be,
Till I a thankful heart obtain
   Of thee:

Not thankful, when it pleaseth me;
As if thy blessings had spare days: *30*
But such a heart, whose pulse may be
   Thy praise.

PEACE

Sweet Peace, where dost thou dwell? I humbly crave,
   Let me once know.
  I sought thee in a secret cave,
   And ask'd, if Peace were there.

---

352. *take.* Captivate.

246

A hollow wind did seem to answer, No: *5*
    Go seek elsewhere.

I did; and going did a rainbow note:
    Surely, thought I,
  This is the lace of Peace's coat:
    I will search out the matter.   *10*
But while I lookt, the clouds immediately
    Did break and scatter.

Then went I to a garden, and did spy
    A gallant flower,
  The crown Imperial: Sure, said I,   *15*
    Peace at the root must dwell.
But when I digg'd, I saw a worm devour
    What show'd so well.

At length I met a rev'rend good old man,
    Whom when for Peace   *20*
  I did demand, he thus began:
    There was a Prince of old[353]
At Salem dwelt, who liv'd with good increase
    Of flock and fold.

He sweetly liv'd; yet sweetness did not save   *25*
    His life from foes.
  But after death out of his grave
    There sprang twelve stalks of wheat:[354]
Which many wond'ring at, got some of those
    To plant and set.   *30*

It prosper'd strangely, and did soon disperse
    Through all the earth:
  For they that taste it do rehearse,
    That virtue[355] lies therein,

---

    353. *a Prince of old.* Melchizedek, seen in Heb. 6:20 as a type of Christ as High Priest, brought bread and wine to Abraham (Gen. 14:18).
    354. *twelve stalks.* Jesus' apostles.
    355. *virtue.* Power, potency.

A secret virtue bringing peace and mirth   *35*
      By flight of sin.

Take of this grain, which in my garden grows,
      And grows for you;
    Make bread of it: and that repose
      And peace which ev'ry where   *40*
With so much earnestness you do pursue,
      Is only there.

CONFESSION

    Oh what a cunning guest
Is this same grief! within my heart I made
   Closets; and in them many a chest;
   And like a master in my trade,
In those chests, boxes; in each box, a till:[356]   *5*
Yet grief knows all, and enters when he will.

    No screw, no piercer can
Into a piece of timber work and wind,
   As God's afflictions into man,
   When he a torture hath design'd.   *10*
They are too subtle for the subtlest hearts;
And fall, like rheums,[357] upon the tend'rest parts.

    We are the earth; and they,
Like moles within us, heave, and cast about:
   And till they foot[358] and clutch their prey,   *15*
   They never cool, much less give out.
No smith can make such locks but they have keys:
Closets are halls to them; and hearts, highways.

---

   356. *till.* A closed compartment within a larger box, used to keep valuables more safely.

   357. *rheums.* Mucous, discharge from the eyes or nose.

   358. *foot.* Seize with claws.

Only an open breast[359]
Doth shut them out, so that they cannot enter;   *20*
   Or, if they enter, cannot rest,
   But quickly seek some new adventure.
Smooth open hearts no fast'ning have; but fiction
Doth give a hold and handle to affliction.

   Wherefore my faults and sins,   *25*
Lord, I acknowledge; take thy plagues away:
   For since confession pardon wins,
   I challenge here the brightest day,
The clearest diamond: let them do their best,
They shall be thick and cloudy to[360] my breast.   *30*

GIDDINESS

Oh, what a thing is man! how far from power,
   From set'led peace and rest!
He is some twenty sev'ral men at least
   Each sev'ral hour.

One while he counts of heav'n, as of his treasure: *5*
   But then a thought creeps in,
And calls him coward, who for fear of sin
   Will lose a pleasure.

Now he will fight it out, and to the wars;
   Now eat his bread in peace,   *10*
And snudge[361] in quiet: now he scorns increase;
   Now all day spares.

He builds a house, which quickly down must go,
   As if a whirlwind blew
And crusht the building: and it's partly true,   *15*
   His mind is so.

---

359. *open breast.* Through confession, the heart is protected from its adversaries.
360. *to.* I.e., compared to.
361. *snudge.* Remain snug and quiet; also, be stingy.

Oh what a sight were Man, if his attires
    Did alter with his mind;
And like a Dolphin's[362] skin, his clothes combin'd
    With his desires!   *20*

Surely if each one saw another's heart,
    There would be no commerce,
No sale or bargain pass: all would disperse,
    And live apart.

Lord, mend or rather make us: one creation   *25*
    Will not suffice our turn:
Except thou make us daily, we shall spurn
    Our own salvation.

THE BUNCH OF GRAPES[363]

Joy, I did lock thee up: but some bad man
    Hath let thee out again:
And now, methinks, I am where I began
    Sev'n years ago: one vogue[364] and vein,
    One air of thoughts usurps my brain.   *5*
I did toward Canaan draw; but now I am
Brought back to the Red sea, the sea of shame.

For as the Jews of old by God's command
    Travel'd, and saw no town,
So now each Christian hath his journeys spann'd:[365]   *10*
    Their story pens and sets us down.
    A single deed is small renown.

---

362. *Dolphin.* Hutchinson suggests Herbert here means not the porpoise-like mammal, but the dorado, a mackerel-like fish that changes color rapidly when taken out of the water.

363. Title: The Israelites crossing the Red Sea becomes our story because we wander with them in the wilderness and achieve the Promised Land instead of the "cluster of grapes" found at Eschol (Num. 13:23) or Noah's vine (Gen. 9:20).

364. *vogue.* General course or tendency.

365. *spann'd.* Measured out.

God's works are wide, and let in future times;
His ancient justice overflows our crimes.

Then have we too our guardian fires and clouds;[366]   *15*
    Our Scripture-dew[367] drops fast:
We have our sands and serpents, tents and shrouds;[368]
    Alas! our murmurings come not last.
    But where's the cluster? where's the taste
Of mine inheritance? Lord, if I must borrow,   *20*
Let me as well take up their joy, as sorrow.

But can he want the grape, who hath the wine?
    I have their fruit and more.
Blessed be God, who prosper'd *Noah's* vine,[369]
    And made it bring forth grapes' good store.   *25*
    But much more him I must adore,
Who of the Law's sour juice sweet wine did make,
Ev'n God himself, being pressed for my sake.

LOVE UNKNOWN[370]

Dear Friend, sit down, the tale is long and sad:
And in my faintings I presume your love
Will more comply, than help. A Lord I had,
And have, of whom some grounds which may improve,
I hold for two lives, and both lives in me.   *5*
To him I brought a dish of fruit one day,
And in the middle plac'd my heart. But he
    (I sigh to say)
Lookt on a servant, who did know his eye
Better than you know me, or (which is one)   *10*

---

366. See Exod. 13:21.
367. *Scripture-dew.* See Num. 11:19.
368. *shrouds.* Shelters, especially temporary ones.
369. *Noah's vine.* The people of God (see Ps. 80:8), redeemed by the "true vine" (see John 15:1).
370. See Psalm 51.

Than I myself. The servant instantly
Quitting the fruit, seiz'd on my heart alone,
And threw it in a font, wherein did fall
A stream of blood, which issu'd from the side
Of a great rock:[371] I well remember all,   *15*
And have good cause: there it was dipt and dy'd,
And washt, and wrung: the very wringing yet
Enforceth tears. *Your heart was foul, I fear.*
Indeed 'tis true. I did and do commit
Many a fault more than my lease will bear;   *20*
Yet still askt pardon, and was not deni'd.
But you shall hear. After my heart was well,
And clean and fair, as I one eventide
      (I sigh to tell)
Walkt by myself abroad, I saw a large   *25*
And spacious furnace flaming, and thereon
A boiling caldron, round about whose verge
Was in great letters set *AFFLICTION*.
The greatness show'd the owner. So I went
To fetch a sacrifice out of my fold,   *30*
Thinking with that, which I did thus present,
To warm his love, which I did fear grew cold.
But as my heart did tender it, the man
Who was to take it from me, slipt[372] his hand,
And threw my heart into the scalding pan;   *35*
My heart, that brought it (do you understand?)
The offerer's heart. *Your heart was hard, I fear.*
Indeed 'tis true. I found a callous matter
Began to spread and to expatiate[373] there:
But with a richer drug, than scalding water,   *40*
I bath'd it often, ev'n with holy blood,
Which at a board, while many drunk bare wine,
A friend did steal into my cup for good,
Ev'n taken inwardly, and most divine

---

371. *rock*. The rock struck by Moses (Exod. 17:6) is explained typologically in 1 Cor. 10:4 ("our fathers ... drank of that spiritual Rock that followed them: and that Rock was Christ").

372. *slipt*. Inserted stealthily.

373. *expatiate*. Laid at full length.

To supple hardnesses.[374] But at the length   *45*
Out of the caldron getting, soon I fled
Unto my house, where to repair the strength
Which I had lost, I hasted to my bed.
But when I thought to sleep out all these faults
      (I sigh to speak)   *50*
I found that some had stuff'd the bed with thoughts,
I would say *thorns*. Dear, could my heart not break,
When with my pleasures ev'n my rest was gone?
Full well I understood, who had been there:
For I had giv'n the key to none, but one: *55*
It must be he. *Your heart was dull, I fear.*
Indeed a slack and sleepy state of mind
Did oft possess me, so that when I pray'd,
Though my lips went, my heart did stay behind.
But all my scores were by another paid,   *60*
Who took the debt upon him. *Truly, Friend,*
For ought I hear, your Master shows to you
More favor than you wot of. Mark the end.
The Font did only, what was old, renew:
The Caldron suppled, what was grown too hard: *65*
The Thorns did quicken, what was grown too dull:
All did but strive to mend, what you had marr'd.
Wherefore be cheer'd, and praise him to the full
Each day, each hour, each moment of the week,
Who fain would have to be new, tender, quick.   *70*

MAN'S MEDLEY[375]

    Hark, how the birds do sing,
        And woods do ring.
All creatures have their joy: and man hath his.
    Yet if we rightly measure,
        Man's joy and pleasure   *5*
Rather hereafter, than in present, is.

---

   374. *To supple hardnesses.* To make hardnesses supple.
   375. Title: *Medley.* A combination or mixture; also, a cloth woven with wools of different colors or shades.

To this life things of sense
    Make their pretense:
In th' other Angels have a right by birth:
    Man ties them both alone,[376]
      And makes them one,
With th' one hand touching heav'n, with th' other earth.

    In soul he mounts and flies,
      In flesh he dies.
He wears a stuff whose thread is coarse and round,[377]
    But trimm'd with curious lace,
      And should take place
After[378] the trimming, not the stuff and ground.[379]

    Not, that he may not here
      Taste of the cheer,
But as birds drink, and straight lift up their head,
    So must he sip and think
      Of better drink
He may attain to, after he is dead.

    But as his joys are double;
      So is his trouble.
He hath two winters,[380] other things but one:
    Both frosts and thoughts do nip,
      And bite his lip;
And he of all things fears two deaths[381] alone.

    Yet ev'n the greatest griefs
      May be reliefs,
Could he but take them right, and in their ways.
    Happy is he, whose heart
      Hath found the art
To turn his double pains to double praise.

10

15

20

25

30

35

---

376. Only man shares the joys of both heaven and earth.
377. *round.* Technical term for cloth made of thick thread.
378. *After.* According to.
379. *ground.* Cloth used as basis for embroidery or decoration.
380. *two winters.* I.e., both physical ("frosts") and spiritual ("thoughts").
381. *two deaths,* I.e., both natural and eternal.

THE CHURCH

THE STORM

If as the winds and waters here below
    Do fly and flow,
My sighs and tears as busy were above;
    Sure they would move
And much affect thee, as tempestuous times   *5*
Amaze poor mortals, and object[382] their crimes.

Stars have their storms,[383] ev'n in a high degree,
    As well as we.
A throbbing conscience spurred by remorse
    Hath a strange force: *10*
It quits the earth, and mounting more and more,
Dares to assault, and besiege thy door.

There it stands knocking, to thy music's wrong,
    And drowns the song.
Glory and honor are set by till it   *15*
    An answer get.
Poets have wrong'd poor storms: such days are best;
They purge the air without, within the breast.

PARADISE[384]

I bless thee, Lord, because I   G R O W
Among thy trees, which in a   R O W
To thee both fruit and order   O W.

What open force, or hidden   C H A R M
Can blast my fruit, or bring me H A R M,   *5*
While the enclosure is thine   A R M?

---

382. *object.* Accuse.
383. *storms.* Meteor-showers.
384. Here, the rhyme scheme suggests the process of pruning trees.

GEORGE HERBERT

Enclose me still for fear I   S T A R T.
Be to me rather sharp and   T A R T,
Than let me want thy hand and   A R T.

When thou dost greater judgments S P A R E,   *10*
And with thy knife but prune and   P A R E,
Ev'n fruitful trees more fruitful   A R E.

Such sharpness shows the sweetest F R·I E N D:
Such cuttings rather heal than   R E N D:
And such beginnings touch their   E N D.   *15*

THE METHOD

           Poor heart, lament.
For since thy God refuseth still,
There is some rub,[385] some discontent,
           Which cools his will.

           Thy Father *could*   *5*
Quickly effect, what thou dost move;[386]
For he is *Power:* and sure he *would;*
           For he is *Love.*

           Go search this thing,
Tumble thy breast, and turn thy book.[387]   *10*
If thou hadst lost a glove or ring,
           Wouldst thou not look?

           What do I see
Written above there? *Yesterday*
I did behave me carelessly,   *15*
           When I did pray.

---

385. *rub.* An impediment (technical term from game of bowls).
386. *move.* Urge.
387. *turn thy book.* Search through "book of life" page by page.

And should God's ear
To such indifferents[388] chained be,
Who do not their own motions hear?
    Is God less free?   20

    But stay! what's there?
Late when I would have something done,
I had a motion to forebear,
    Yet I went on.

    And should God's ear,   25
Which needs not man, be tied to those
Who hear not him, but quickly hear
    His utter foes?

    Then once more pray:
Down with thy knees, up with thy voice.   30
Seek pardon first, and God will say,
    Glad heart rejoice.

DIVINITY

As men, for fear the stars should sleep and nod,
    And trip at night, have spheres[389] suppli'd;
As if a star were duller than a clod,
    Which knows his way without a guide:

Just so the other heav'n they also serve,   5
    Divinity's transcendent sky:
Which with the edge of wit they cut and carve.
    Reason triumphs, and faith lies by.[390]

---

388. *indifferents.* Those so little concerned that they do not pay attention to their own petitions.
389. *spheres.* Concentric hollow globes that rotate around the earth and carry the heavenly bodies, in Ptolemaic astronomy.
390. *lies by.* Is unused.

Could not that wisdom, which first broacht[391] the wine,
  Have thicken'd it with definitions?   *10*
And jagg'd[392] his seamless coat, had that been fine,
  With curious questions and divisions?

But all the doctrine, which he taught and gave,
  Was clear as heav'n, from whence it came.
At least those beams of truth, which only save,   *15*
  Surpass in brightness any flame.

Love God, and love your neighbor. Watch and pray.
  Do as ye would be done unto.[393]
Oh dark instructions; ev'n as dark as day!
  Who can these Gordian knots undo?   *20*

But he doth bid us take his blood for wine.
  Bid what he please; yet I am sure,
To take and taste what he doth there design,
  Is all that saves, and not obscure.

Then burn thy Epicycles,[394] foolish man;   *25*
  Break all thy spheres, and save thy head.
Faith needs no staff of flesh, but stoutly can
  To heav'n alone both go, and lead.

---

391. *broacht.* Opened.
392. *jagg'd.* Slashed or pinked by way of ornament.
393. See Matt. 22:37–40; Luke 21:36; Mark 13:33, 14:38; Matt. 7:12.
394. *Epicycles.* In Ptolemaic astronomy, each of the seven planets was thought to move in a small circle, the center of which moved in a larger circle around the earth; this scheme was used to account for discrepancies between observable planetary movement and the philosophical need to preserve planetary motion in circles.

THE CHURCH

EPHESIANS 4:30

Grieve not the Holy Spirit, & c.[395]

And art thou grieved, sweet and sacred Dove,
    When I am sour,
    And cross thy love?
Grieved for me? the God of strength and power
  Griev'd for a worm, which when I tread,   *5*
  I pass away and leave it dead?

Then weep mine eyes, the God of love doth grieve:
    Weep foolish heart,
    And weeping live:
For death is dry as dust. Yet if ye part,[396]   *10*
  End as the night, whose sable hue
  Your sins express; melt into dew.

When saucy mirth shall knock or call at door,
    Cry out, Get hence,
    Or cry no more.   *15*
Almighty God doth grieve, he puts on sense:
  I sin not to my grief alone,
  But to my God's, too; he doth groan.

Oh take thy lute, and tune it to a strain,
    Which may with thee   *20*
    All day complain.
There can no discord but in ceasing be.
  Marbles can weep; and surely strings
  More bowels have, than such hard things.[397]

---

395. Eph. 4:30 reads, "And grieve not the holy Spirit of God, whereby ye are sealed unto the day of redemption."

396. *part*. Die.

397. Lute strings were made of cat-gut; Herbert here links this fact to the traditional view that the bowels were the seat of tender emotions like pity and compassion.

Lord, I adjudge myself to tears and grief,   *25*
    Ev'n endless tears
    Without relief.
If a clear spring for me no time forebears,
  But runs, although I be not dry;
  I am no Crystal,[398] what shall I?   *30*

Yet if I wail not still, since still to wail
    Nature denies;
    And flesh would fail,
If my deserts were masters of mine eyes:
  Lord, pardon, for thy son makes good   *35*
  My want of tears with store of blood.

THE FAMILY

What doth this noise of thoughts within my heart
    As if they had a part?
What do these loud complaints and pulling[399] fears,
  As if there were no rule or ears?

But, Lord, the house and family are thine,   *5*
    Though some of them repine.
Turn out these wranglers, which defile thy seat:
  For where thou dwellest all is neat.

First Peace and Silence all disputes control,
    Then Order plays the soul;   *10*
And giving all things their set forms and hours,
  Makes of wild woods sweet walks and bowers.

Humble Obedience near the door doth stand,
    Expecting a command:
Than whom in waiting nothing seems more slow,   *15*
  Nothing more quick when she doth go.

---

398. *Crystal.* Fig., pure, clear water.
399. *pulling.* Puling; whining, weakly querulous.

Joys oft are there, and griefs as oft as joys;
    But griefs without a noise;
Yet speak they louder, than distemper'd fears.
    What is so shrill as silent tears?   *20*

This is thy house, with these it doth abound:
    And where these are not found,
Perhaps thou com'st sometimes, and for a day;
    But not to make a constant stay.

THE SIZE[400]

    Content thee, greedy heart.
Modest and moderate joys to those, that have
Title to more hereafter when they part,
    Are passing brave.
Let th' upper springs into the low   *5*
Descend and fall, and thou dost flow.

    What though some have a fraught[401]
Of cloves and nutmegs, and in cinnamon sail;
If thou hast wherewithal to spice a draught,
    When griefs prevail;   *10*
And for the future time art heir
To th' Isle of spices, is't not fair?

    To be in both worlds full
Is more than God was, who was hungry here.
Wouldst thou his laws of fasting disanull?   *15*
    Enact good cheer?
Lay out thy joy, yet hope to save it?
Wouldst thou both eat thy cake, and have it?

    Great joys are all at once;
But little do reserve themselves for more: *20*

---

400. Title: State, condition, or status.
401. *fraught.* Load.

Those have their hopes; these what they have renounce,
    And live on score:[402]
  Those are at home; these journey still,
  And meet the rest on Sion's hill.

    Thy Savior sentenc'd joy,   25
And in the flesh condemn'd it as unfit,
At least in lump: for such doth oft destroy;
    Whereas a bit
Doth 'tice[403] us on to hopes of more,
And for the present health restore.   30

    A Christian's state and case
Is not a corpulent, but a thin and spare,
Yet active strength: whose long and bony face
    Content and care
Do seem to equally divide,   35
Like a pretender,[404] not a bride.

    Wherefore sit down, good heart;
Grasp not at much, for fear thou losest all.
If comforts fell according to desert,
  They would great frosts and snows destroy: 40
  For we should count, Since the last joy.

    Then close again the seam,
Which thou hast open'd: do not spread thy robe
In hope of great things. Call to mind thy dream,
    An earthly globe,   45
On whose meridian[405] was engraven.
These seas are tears, and heav'n the haven.

---

402. *score.* Credit.
403. *tice.* Entice.
404. *pretender.* Suitor, wooer.
405. *meridian.* A brass ring from which a globe is suspended.

THE CHURCH

ARTILLERY[406]

As I one ev'ning sat before my cell,
Me thoughts[407] a star did shoot into my lap.
I rose, and shook my clothes, as knowing well,
That from small fires comes oft no small mishap.
    When suddenly I heard one say,   *5*
    Do as thou usest, disobey,
    Expel good motions from thy breast,
Which have the face of fire, but end in rest.

I, who had heard of music in the spheres,
But not of speech in stars, began to muse: *10*
But turning to my God, whose ministers[408]
The stars and all things are; If I refuse,
    Dread Lord, said I, so oft my good;
    Then I refuse not ev'n with blood
    To wash away my stubborn thought: *15*
For I will do, or suffer what I ought.

But I have also stars and shooters[409] too,
Born where thy servants both artilleries use.
My tears and prayers night and day do woo,
And work up to thee; yet thou dost refuse.   *20*
    Not, but I am (I must say still)
    Much more oblig'd to do thy will,
    Than thou to grant mine: but because
Thy promise now hath ev'n set thee thy laws.

Then we are shooters both, and thou dost deign   *25*
To enter combat with us, and contest
With thine own clay. But I would parley fain:

---

406. Title: See Saint Paul's military imagery in Eph. 6:13ff.
407. *Me thoughts.* I thought.
408. *ministers.* See Ps. 104:4.
409. *shooters.* Shooting stars; also, those who use artillery.

263

Shun not my arrows, and behold my breast.
  Yet if thou shunnest, I am thine:
  I must be so, if I am mine.   *30*
  There is no articling[410] with thee:
I am but finite, yet thine infinitely.

CHURCH RENTS AND SCHISMS

Brave rose,[411] (alas!) where art thou? in the chair
Where thou didst lately so triumph and shine,
A worm doth sit, whose many feet and hair
Are the more foul, the more thou wert divine.
This, this hath done it, this did bite the root   *5*
And bottom of the leaves: which when the wind
Did once perceive, it blew them under foot,
Where rude unhallow'd steps do crush and grind
  Their beauteous glories. Only shreds of thee,
  And those all bitten, in thy chair I see.   *10*

Why doth my Mother blush? is she the rose,
And shows it so? Indeed Christ's precious blood
Gave you a color once; which when your foes
Thought to let out, the bleeding did you good,
And made you look much fresher than before,   *15*
But when debates and fretting jealousies
Did worm and work within you more and more,
Your color faded, and calamities
  Turned your ruddy into pale and bleak:
  Your health and beauty both began to break.   *20*

Then did your sev'rall parts unloose and start:[412]
Which when your neighbors saw, like a north wind,
They rushed in, and cast them in the dirt
Where Pagans tread. Oh Mother dear and kind,

---

410. *articling.* Arranging by treaty or other legal document.
411. *Rose.* See Song of Sol. 2:1 for the Church as the "rose of Sharon."
412. *start.* Explode.

Where shall I get me eyes enough to weep,   *25*
As many eyes as stars? since it is night,
And much of Asia and Europe fast asleep,
And ev'n all Africk; would at least I might
  With these two poor ones lick up all the dew,
  Which falls by night, and pour it out for you!   *30*

JUSTICE (II)

Oh dreadful Justice, what a fright and terror
      Wast thou of old,[413]
      When sin and error
  Did show and shape thy looks to me,
  And through their glass discolor thee!   *5*
He that did but look up, was proud and bold.

The dishes of thy balance[414] seem'd to gape,
      Like two great pits;
      The beam and scape[415]
  Did like some tort'ring engine show: *10*
  Thy hand above did burn and glow,
Danting[416] the stoutest hearts, the proudest wits.

But now that Christ's pure veil[417] presents the sight,
      I see no fears:
      Thy hand is white,   *15*
  Thy scales like buckets, which attend
  And interchangeably descend,
Lifting to heaven from this well of tears.

---

413. *of old.* The old Law, now replaced by the new law of love through Christ's mediation.
414. *balance.* Scale of justice.
415. *scape.* The upright shaft of a balance.
416. *Danting.* Daunting; overcoming, subduing.
417. *Christ's pure veil.* See Heb. 10:20 for Christ's flesh as veil in opposition to the multicolored veil of Solomon's Temple (2 Chron. 3:14).

For where before thou still didst call on me,
     Now I still touch   *20*
       And harp on thee.
  God's promises have made thee mine;
  Why should I justice now decline?
Against me there is none, but for me much.

THE PILGRIMAGE

I travel'd on, seeing the hill, where lay
     My expectation.
  A long it was and weary way.
  The gloomy cave of Desperation
I left on th' one, and on the other side   *5*
     The rock of Pride.

And so I came to Fancy's meadow strow'd
     With many a flower:
  Fair would I here have made abode,
  But I was quicken'd by my hour.   *10*
So to Care's copse I came, and there got through
     With much ado.

That led me to the wild of Passion, which
     Some call the wold;[418]
  A wasted place, but sometimes rich.   *15*
  Here I was robb'd of all my gold,
Save one good Angel,[419] which a friend had ti'd
     Close to my side.

At length I got unto the gladsome hill,
     Where lay my hope,   *20*
  Where lay my heart; and climbing still,
  When I had gain'd the brow and top,
A lake of brackish waters on the ground
     Was all I found.

---

418. *wold*. Open country, moorland.
419. *Angel*. A gold coin, also a guardian angel.

With that abash'd and struck with many a sting   *25*
      Of swarming fears,
    I fell, and cried, Alas my King;
    Can both the way and end be tears?
Yet taking heart I rose, and then perceiv'd
      I was deceiv'd: *30*

My hill was further: so I flung away,
      Yet heard a cry
    Just as I went, *None goes that way*
    And lives: If that be all, said I,
After so foul a journey death is fair,   *35*
      And but a chair.[420]

THE HOLDFAST[421]

I threat'ned to observe the strict decree
    Of my dear God with all my power and might.
    But I was told by one, it could not be;
Yet I might trust in God to be my light.

Then will I trust, said I, in him alone.   *5*
    Nay, ev'n to trust in him, was also his:
    We must confess, that nothing is our own.
Then I confess that he my succor is:

But to have nought is ours, not to confess
    That we have nought. I stood amaz'd at this,   *10*
    Much troubled, till I heard a friend express,
That all things were more ours by being his.
    What Adam had, and forfeited for all,
    Christ keepeth now, who cannot fail or fall.[422]

---

420. *chair.* A sedan-chair, a comfortable mode of transportion.
421. Title: See Ps. 73:27.
422. See 1 Cor. 15:22.

GEORGE HERBERT

COMPLAINING

Do not beguile my heart,
    Because thou art
My power and wisdom. Put me not to shame,
    Because I am
Thy clay that weeps, thy dust that calls.   *5*

Thou art the Lord of glory:
    The deed and story
Are both thy due: but I a silly fly,
    That live or die
According as the weather falls.   *10*

Art thou all justice, Lord?
    Shows not thy word
More attributes? Am I all throat or eye,
    To weep or cry?
Have I no parts but those of grief?   *15*

Let not thy wrathful power
    Afflict my hour,
My inch of life: or let thy gracious power
    Contract my hour,
That I may climb and find relief.   *20*

THE DISCHARGE[423]

Busy inquiring heart, what wouldst thou know?
    Why dost thou pry,
And turn, and leer, and with a lickerous[424] eye
    Look high and low;
And in thy lookings stretch and grow?   *5*

---

423. Title: A document releasing one from an obligation.
424. *lickerous.* Desiring what is pleasant, with sexual overtones.

Has thou not made thy counts,[425] and summ'd up all?
 Did not thy heart
Give up the whole, and with the whole depart?[426]
 Let what will fall:
 That which is past who can recall?   *10*

Thy life is God's, thy time to come is gone,
 And is his right.
He is thy night at noon: he is at night
 Thy noon alone.
 The crop is his, for he hath sown.   *15*

And well it was for thee, when this befell,
 That God did make
Thy business his, and in thy life partake:
 For thou canst tell,
 If it be his once, all is well.   *20*

Only the present is thy part and fee.[427]
 And happy thou,
If, though thou didst not beat thy future brow,
 Thou couldst well see
 What present things requir'd of thee.   *25*

They ask enough; why shouldst thou further go?
 Raise not the muddle
Of future depths, but drink the clear and good.
 Dig not for woe
 In times to come; for it will grow.   *30*

Man and the present fit: if he provide,[428]
 He breaks the square.
This hour is mine: if for the next I care,
 I grow too wide,
 And do encroach upon death's side.   *35*

---

425. *counts.* Accounts.
426. *with the whole depart.* Part with all.
427. *fee.* Allotted portion.
428. *provide.* Plan for the future; see Luke 12:22–40.

For death each hour environs and surrounds.
      He that would know
And care for future chances, cannot go
      Unto those grounds,
    But through a Churchyard which them bounds.   40

Things present shrink and die: but they that spend
      Their thoughts and sense
On future grief, do not remove it thence,
      But it extend,
    And draw the bottom out an end.[429]   45

God chains the dog till night: wilt loose the chain,
      And wake thy sorrow?
Wilt thou forestall it, and now grieve tomorrow,
      And then again
    Grieve over freshly all thy pain?   50

Either grief will not come: or if it must,
      Do not forecast.
And while it cometh, it is almost past.
      Away distrust:
    My God hath promis'd, he is just.   55

PRAISE (II)[430]

King of Glory, King of Peace,
      I will love thee;
And that love may never cease,
      I will move thee.

Thou has granted my request,   5
      Thou hast heard me:
Thou didst note my working breast,
      Thou hast spar'd me.

---

429. *draw the bottom out an end.* Reach the end of a skein of thread.
430. Title: See Ps. 116.

THE CHURCH

Wherefore with my utmost art
    I will sing thee,   *10*
And the cream of all my heart
    I will bring thee.

Though my sins against me cried,
    Thou didst clear me;
And alone, when they replied,   *15*
    Thou didst hear me.

Sev'n whole days, not one in seven,
    I will praise thee.
In my heart, though not in heaven,
    I can raise thee.   *20*

Thou grew'st soft and moist with tears,
    Thou relentedst:
And when Justice call'd for fears,
    Thou dissentedst.

Small it is, in this poor sort   *25*
    To enroll[431] thee:
Ev'n eternity is too short
    To extol thee.

AN OFFERING

Come, bring thy gift. If blessings were as slow
As men's returns, what would become of fools?
What hast thou there? a heart? but is it pure?
Search well and see; for hearts have many holes.
Yet one pure heart is nothing to bestow: *5*
In Christ two natures met to be thy cure.

Oh that within us hearts had propagation,
Since many gifts do challenge many hearts!

---

431. *enroll.* Record with honor, celebrate.

Yet one, if good, may title[432] to a number;
And single things grow fruitful by deserts.   *10*
In public judgments one may be a nation,
And fence a plague, while others sleep and slumber.

But all I fear is lest thy heart displease,
As neither good, nor one: so oft divisions
Thy lusts have made, and not thy lusts alone;   *15*
Thy passions also have their set partitions.
These parcel out thy heart: recover these,
And thou mayst offer many gifts in one.

There is a balsam, or indeed a blood,
Dropping from heav'n, which doth both cleanse and close   *20*
All sorts of wounds; of such strange force it is.
Seek out this All-heal,[433] and seek no repose,
Until thou find and use it to thy good:
Then bring thy gift, and let thy hymn be this;

     Since my sadness   *25*
     Into gladness
Lord thou dost convert,
     Oh accept
     What thou hast kept,
As thy due desert.   *30*

     Had I many,
     Had I any,
(For this heart is none)
     All were thine
     And none of mine: *35*
Surely thine alone.

---

432. *may title.* May hold title.
433. *All-heal.* A general curative for all wounds.

                    Yet thy favor
                    May give savor
         To this poor oblation;
                    And it raise   *40*
                    To be thy praise,
         And be my salvation.

LONGING

                    With sick and famisht eyes,
         With doub'ling knees and weary bones,
                    To thee my cries,
                    To thee my groans,
         To thee my sighs, my tears ascend: *5*
                    No end?

                    My throat, my soul is hoarse;
         My heart is wither'd like a ground
                    Which thou dost curse.[434]
                    My thoughts turn round,[435]   *10*
         And make me giddy; Lord, I fall,
                    Yet call.

                    From thee all pity flows.
         Mothers are kind, because thou art,
                    And dost dispose   *15*
                    To them a part:
         Their infants, them; and they suck thee
                    More free.

                    Bowels of pity, hear!
         Lord of my soul, love of my mind,   *20*

---

434. See Gen. 3:17.
435. See Ps. 86:1.

Bow down thine ear!
Let not the wind
Scatter my words, and in the same
Thy name!

Look on my sorrows round! 25
Mark well my furnace! Oh what flames,
What heats abound!
What griefs, what shames!
Consider, Lord; Lord, bow thine ear,
And hear! 30

Lord Jesu, thou didst bow
Thy dying head upon the tree:
Oh be not now
More dead to me!
Lord hear! *Shall he that made the ear,* 35
*Not hear?*436

Behold, thy dust doth stir,
It moves, it creeps, it aims at thee:
Wilt thou defer
To succor me, 40
Thy pile of dust, wherein each crumb
Says, Come?

To thee help appertains.
Hast thou left all things to their course,
And laid the reins
Upon the horse? 45
Is all lockt? hath a sinner's plea
No key?

Indeed the world's thy book,
Where all things have their leaf assign'd: 50
Yet a meek look
Hath interlin'd.437

---

436. See Ps. 94:9.
437. *interlin'd.* Come between the lines.

Thy board is full, yet humble guests
    Find nests.

    Thou tarriest, while I die,   *55*
And fall to nothing: thou dost reign,
     And rule on high,
     While I remain
In bitter grief: yet am I styl'd
    Thy child.   *60*

    Lord, didst thou leave thy throne,
Not to relieve? how can it be,
     That thou art grown
     Thus hard to me?
Were sin alive, good cause there were   *65*
    To bear.

    But now both sin is dead,
And all thy promises live and bide.
     That wants his head;
     These speak and chide,   *70*
And in thy bosom pour my tears,
    As theirs.

    Lord J E S U, hear my heart,
Which hath been broken now so long,
     That ev'ry part   *75*
     Hath got a tongue!
Thy beggars grow; rid them away
    Today.

    My love, my sweetness, hear!
By these thy feet, at which my heart   *80*
     Lies all the year,
     Pluck out thy dart,
And heal my troubled breast which cries,
    Which dies.

GEORGE HERBERT

THE BAG

Away despair; my gracious Lord doth hear.
  Though winds and waves assault my keel,
  He doth preserve it: he doth steer,
  Ev'n when the boat seems most to reel.
  Storms are the triumph of his art: 5
Well may he close his eyes, but not his heart.[438]

Hast thou not heard, that my Lord JESUS di'd?
  Then let me tell thee a strange story.
  The God of power, as he did ride
  In his majestic robes of glory,   10
  Resolv'd to light; and so one day
He did descend, undressing all the way.

The stars his tire[439] of light and rings obtain'd,
  The cloud his bow, the fire[440] his spear,
  The sky his azure mantle gain'd.   15
  And when they ask'd, what he would wear;
  He smil'd and said as he did go,
He had new clothes amaking here below.

When he was come, as travelers are wont,
  He did repair unto an inn.   20
  Both then, and after, many a brunt
  He did endure to cancel sin:
  And having giv'n the rest before,
Here he gave up his life to pay our score.

But as he was returning, there came one   25
  That ran upon him with a spear.
  He, who came hither all alone,
  Bringing nor man, nor arms, nor fear,
  Receiv'd the blow upon his side,
And straight he turn'd, and to his brethren cried,   30

---

438. See Matt. 8:24.
439. *tire*. Form of tiara, headdress.
440. *fire*. Lightning.

If ye have anything to send or write,
   (I have no bag, but here is room)
Unto my father's hands and sight
   (Believe me) it shall safely come.
   That I shall mind, what you impart;   *35*
Look, you may put it very near my heart.

Or if hereafter any of my friends
   Will use me in this kind, the door
Shall still be open; what he sends
   I will present, and somewhat more,   *40*
   Not to his hurt. Sighs will convey
Anything to me. Hark despair, away.

THE JEWS

   Poor nation, whose sweet sap, and juice
Our cyens[441] have purloin'd, and left you dry:
Whose streams we got by the Apostles' sluice,
And use in baptism, while ye pine and die:
   Who by not keeping once, became a debtor;   *5*
     And now by keeping lose the letter:[442]

   Oh that my prayers! mine, alas!
Oh that some Angel might a trumpet sound;
At which the Church falling upon her face
Should cry so loud, until the trump were drown'd,[443]   *10*
   And by that cry of her dear Lord obtain,
     That your sweet sap might come again![444]

---

441. *cyens.* I.e., scions, slips for grafting.

442. See Rom. 7:6 and Gal. 5:3; Jews remain bound as debtors to the old law, while Christians are free by the new law of love. By keeping the law now, and not accepting Christ as the Messiah, Jews stand to lose everything.

443. Conversion of the Jews was traditionally expected as a sign of the imminence of the Last Judgment.

444. See Job 14:7–9.

GEORGE HERBERT

THE COLLAR[445]

I struck the board, and cried, No more.
    I will abroad.
What? shall I ever sigh and pine?
My lines and life are free; free as the rode,
    Loose as the wind, as large as store.[446]   *5*
    Shall I be still in suit?[447]
Have I no harvest but a thorn
To let me blood, and not restore
What I have lost with cordial[448] fruit?
    Sure there was wine   *10*
Before my sighs did dry it: there was corn
    Before my tears did drown it.
Is the year only lost to me?
    Have I no bays to crown it?
No flowers, no garlands gay? all blasted?   *15*
    All wasted?
Not so, my heart: but there is fruit,
    And thou hast hands.
    Recover all thy sigh-blown age
On double pleasures: leave thy cold dispute   *20*
Of what is fit, and not. Forsake thy cage,
    Thy rope of sands,
Which petty thoughts have made, and made to thee
    Good cable, to enforce and draw,
    And be thy law,   *25*
While thou didst wink and wouldst not see.
    Away; take heed:
    I will abroad.
Call in thy death's head there: tie up thy fears.
    He that forbears   *30*
    To suit and serve his need,
      Deserves his load.

---

445. Title: Suggests restraint, perhaps also choler, caller; see Matt. 11:29–30 for Christ's yoke; *not* clerical collar.
446. *store.* Abundance.
447. *in suit.* A petitioner, suitor.
448. *cordial.* Invigorating.

But as I rav'd and grew more fierce and wild
    At every word,
Me thoughts I heard one calling, *Child:*   *35*
    And I replied, *My Lord.*

THE GLIMPSE

    Whither away delight?
Thou cam'st but now; wilt thou so soon depart,
    And give me up to night?
For many weeks of ling'ring pain and smart
But one half hour of comfort for my heart?   *5*

    Methinks delight should have
More skill in music, and keep better time.
    Wert thou a wind or wave,
They quickly go and come with lesser crime:
Flowers look about, and die not in their prime.   *10*

    Thy short abode and stay
Feeds not, but adds to the desire of meat.
    Lime[449] begg'd of old (they say)
A neighbor spring to cool his inward heat;
Which by the spring's access grew much more great.   *15*

    In hope of thee my heart
Pickt here and there a crumb, and would not die;
    But constant to his part,
When as my fears foretold this, did reply,
A slender thread a gentle guest will tie.   *20*

    Yet if the heart that wept
Must let thee go, return when it doth knock.
    Although thy heap be kept
For future times, the droppings of the stock
May oft break forth, and never break the lock.   *25*

---

449. *Lime.* Quicklime, whose heat is increased by water.

  If I have more to spin,
The wheel shall go, so that thy stay[450] be short.
  Thou knowst how grief and sin
Disturb the work. Oh make me not their sport,
Who by thy coming may be made a court!   *30*

ASSURANCE

  Oh spiteful bitter thought!
Bitterly spiteful thought! Couldst thou invent
So high a torture? Is such poison bought?
Doubtless, but in the way of punishment,
  When wit contrives to meet with thee,   *5*
  No such rank poison can there be.

  Thou said'st but even now,
That all was not so fair, as I conceiv'd,
Betwixt my God and me; that I allow
And coin large hopes; but, that I was deceiv'd: *10*
  Either the league was broke, or near it;
  And, that I had great cause to fear it.

  And what to this? what more
Could poison, if it had a tongue, express?
What is thy aim? wouldst thou unlock the door *15*
To cold despairs, and gnawing pensiveness?
  Wouldst thou raise devils? I see, I know,
  I writ thy purpose long ago.

  But I will to my Father,
Who heard thee say it. Oh most gracious Lord, *20*
If all the hope and comfort that I gather,
Were from myself, I had not half a word,
  Not half a letter to oppose
  What is objected by my foes.

---

450. *stay*. Absence.

But thou art my desert: *25*
And in this league, which now my foes invade,
Thou art not only to perform thy part,
But also mine; as when the league was made
    Thou didst at once thyself indite,
    And hold my hand, while I did write.   *30*

    Wherefore if thou canst fail,
Then can thy truth and I: but while rocks stand,
And rivers stir, thou canst not shrink or quail:
Yea, when both rocks and all things shall disband,
    Then shalt thou be my rock and tower,   *35*
    And make their ruin praise thy power.

    Now foolish thought go on,
Spin out thy thread, and make thereof a coat
To hide thy shame: for thou hast cast a bone[451]
Which bounds on thee, and will not down thy throat: *40*
    What for itself love once began,
    Now love and truth will end in man.

THE CALL

Come, my Way, my Truth, my Life:
Such a Way, as gives us breath:
Such a Truth, as ends all strife:
And such a Life, as killeth death.

Come, my Light, my Feast, my Strength: *5*
Such a Light, as shows a feast:
Such a Feast, as mends in length:
Such a Strength, as makes his guest.

Come, my Joy, my Love, my Heart:
Such a Joy, as none can move: *10*
Such a Love, as none can part:
Such a Heart, as joys in love.

---

451. *bone.* Bone of contention.

GEORGE HERBERT

CLASPING OF HANDS

Lord, thou art mine, and I am thine,
If mine I am: and thine much more,
Than I or ought, or can be mine.
Yet to be thine, doth me restore;
So that again I now am mine, 5
And with advantage mine the more.
Since this being mine, brings with it thine,
And thou with me dost thee restore.
    If I without thee would be mine,
    I neither should be mine nor thine. 10

Lord, I am thine, and thou art mine:
So mine thou art, that something more
I may presume thee mine, than thine.
For thou didst suffer to restore
Not thee, but me, and to be mine, 15
And with advantage mine the more.
Since thou in death wast none of thine,
Yet then as mine didst me restore.
    Oh be mine still! still make me thine!
    Or rather make no Thine and Mine! 20

PRAISE (III)

    Lord, I will mean and speak thy praise,
        Thy praise alone.
My busy heart shall spin it all my days:
    And when it stops for want of store,
Then will I wring it with a sigh or groan, 5
        That thou mayst yet have more.

    When thou dost favor any action,
        It runs, it flies:
All things concur to give it a perfection.
    That which had but two legs before, 10
When thou dost bless, hath twelve: one wheel doth rise
        To twenty then, or more.

But when thou dost on business blow,
    It hangs, it clogs:
Not all the teams of Albion[452] in a row   *15*
   Can hale or draw it out of door.
Legs are but stumps, and Pharaoh's wheels but logs,[453]
    And struggling hinders more.

Thousands of things do thee employ
    In ruling all   *20*
This spacious globe: Angels must have their joy,
   Devils their rod, the sea his shore,
The winds their stint:[454] and yet when I did call,
    Thou heardst my call, and more.

I have not lost one single tear: *25*
    But when mine eyes
Did weep to heav'n, they found a bottle[455] there
   (As we have boxes for the poor)
Ready to take them in; yet of a size
    That would contain much more.   *30*

But after thou hadst slipt a drop
    From thy right eye,
(Which there did hang like streamers[456] near the top
   Of some fair church, to show the sore
And bloody battle which thou once didst try)   *35*
    The glass was full and more.

Wherefore I sing. Yet since my heart,
    Though press'd, runs thin;
Oh that I might some other hearts convert,
   And so take up at use[457] good store: *40*
That to thy chests there might be coming in
    Both all my praise, and more!

---

452. *Albion.* Classical name for Britain.
453. See Exod. 14:25.
454. *stint.* Limit.
455. *bottle.* See Ps. 56:8.
456. *streamers.* Flags hung from church towers after a victory.
457. *use.* Interest.

GEORGE HERBERT

JOSEPH'S COAT[458]

Wounded I sing, tormented I indite,
Thrown down I fall into a bed, and rest:
Sorrow hath chang'd its note: such is his will,
Who changeth all things, as him pleaseth best.
    For well he knows, if but one grief and smart   *5*
Among my many had his full career,
Sure it would carry with it ev'n my heart,
And both would run until they found a bier
    To fetch the body; both being due to grief.
But he hath spoil'd the race; and giv'n to anguish   *10*
One of Joy's coats, 'ticing[459] it with relief
To linger in me, and together languish.
    I live to show his power, who once did bring
    My *joys* to *weep*, and now my *griefs* to *sing*.

THE PULLEY[460]

    When God at first made man,
Having a glass of blessings standing by;
Let us (said he) pour on him all we can:
Let the world's riches, which dispersed lie,
    Contract into a span.   *5*

    So strength first made a way;
Then beauty flow'd, then wisdom, honor, pleasure:
When almost all was out, God made a stay,
Perceiving that alone of all his treasure
    Rest in the bottom lay.   *10*

---

458. Title: See Gen. 37:3; Joseph's coat, symbolic of a father's love, suggests in its multicolored fabric the varieties of life's experiences, the humanity taken on by God in Christ. The Body of Christ becomes for the speaker one of "Joy's coats, which affords relief for his own sufferings."

459. *ticing.* Enticing.

460. Title: The poem transfigures the legend of Pandora's box, from which were released all man's woes, leaving only Hope behind.

For if I should (said he)
Bestow this jewel also on my creature,
He would adore my gifts instead of me,
And rest in Nature, not the God of Nature:
    So both should losers be.   *15*

    Yet let him keep the rest,
But keep them with repining restlessness:
Let him be rich and weary, that at least,
If goodness lead him not, yet weariness
    May toss him to my breast.   *20*

THE PRIESTHOOD

Blest Order, which in power dost so excel,
That with th' one hand thou liftest to the sky,
And with the other throwest down to hell
In thy just censures;[461] fain would I draw nigh,
Fain put thee on, exchanging my lay-sword   *5*
    For that of th' holy Word.

But thou art fire, sacred and hallow'd fire;
And I but earth and clay:[462] should I presume
To wear thy habit, the severe attire
My slender compositions might consume.   *10*
I am both foul and brittle; much unfit
    To deal in holy Writ.

Yet have I often seen, by cunning hand
And force of fire, what curious things are made
Of wretched earth. Where once I scorn'd to stand,   *15*
That earth is fitted by the fire and trade
Of skillful artists, for the boards of those
    Who make the bravest shows.

---

461. See Matt. 16:19.
462. *earth and clay.* See Jer. 18:6; Isa. 64:8; and Rom. 9:21–23.

But since those great ones, be they ne're so great,
Come from the earth, from whence those vessels come;   *20*
So that at once both feeder, dish, and meat
Have one beginning and one final sum:
I do not greatly wonder at the sight,
      If earth in earth delight.

But th' holy men of God such vessels are,   *25*
As serve him up, who all the world commands:
When God vouchsafeth to become our fare,
Their hands convey him, who conveys their hands.
Oh what pure things, most pure must those things be,
      Who bring my God to me!   *30*

Wherefore I dare not, I, put forth my hand
To hold the Ark,[463] although it seem to shake
Through th' old sins and new doctrines of our land.
Only, since God doth often vessels make
Of lowly matter for high uses meet,   *35*
      I throw me at his feet.

There will I lie, until my Maker seek
For some mean stuff whereon to show his skill:
Then is my time. The distance of the meek
Doth flatter power. Lest good come short of ill   *40*
In praising might, the poor do by submission
      What pride by opposition.

THE SEARCH

Whither, Oh, whither art thou fled,
      My Lord, my Love?
My searches are my daily bread;
      Yet never prove.

---

463. *To hold the Ark.* See 2 Sam. 6:6.

My knees pierce th' earth, mine eyes the sky;   *5*
    And yet the sphere
And center both to me deny
    That thou art there.

Yet can I mark how herbs below
    Grow green and gay,   *10*
As if to meet thee they did know,
    While I decay.

Yet can I mark how stars above
    Simper[464] and shine,
As having keys unto thy love,   *15*
    While poor I pine.

I sent a sigh to seek thee out,
    Deep drawn in pain,
Wing'd like an arrow: but my scout
    Returns in vain.   *20*

    I tun'd another (having store)
    Into a groan;
Because the search was dumb before:
    But all was one.

Lord, dost thou some new fabric mold,   *25*
    Which favor wins,
And keeps thee present, leaving th' old
    Unto their sins?

Where is my God? what hidden place
    Conceals thee still?   *30*
What covert dare eclipse thy face?
    Is it thy will?

Oh let not that of anything;[465]
    Let rather brass,

---

464. *simper.* Twinkle.
465. *of anything.* Above all.

Or steel, or mountains be thy ring,   *35*
    And I will pass.

Thy will such an entrenching is,
    As passeth thought:
To it all strength, all subtleties
    Are things of naught.   *40*

Thy will such a strange distance is,
    As that to it
East and West touch, the poles do kiss,
    And parallels meet.

Since then my grief must be as large,   *45*
    As is thy space,
Thy distance from me; see my charge,[466]
    Lord, see my case.

Oh take these bars, these lengths away;
    Turn, and restore me: *50*
Be not Almighty, let me say,
    Against, but for me.

When thou dost turn, and wilt be near;
    What edge so keen,
What point so piercing can appear   *55*
    To come between?

For as thy absence doth excel
    All distance known:
So doth thy nearness bear the bell,[467]
    Making two one.   *60*

---

466. *charge.* Burden.
467. *bear the bell.* Take precedence.

THE CHURCH

GRIEF

Oh who will give me tears? Come all ye springs,
Dwell in my head and eyes: come clouds, and rain:[468]
My grief hath need of all the wat'ry things,
That nature hath produc'd. Let ev'ry vein
Suck up a river to supply mine eyes,   *5*
My weary weeping eyes too dry for me,
Unless they get new conduits, new supplies
To bear them out, and with my state agree.
What are two shallow fords, two little spouts
Of a less world? the greater is but small,   *10*
A narrow cupboard for my griefs and doubts,
Which want provision in the midst of all.
Verses, ye are too fine a thing, too wise
For my rough sorrows: cease, be dumb and mute,
Give up your feet[469] and running to mine eyes,   *15*
And keep your measures for some lover's lute,
Whose grief allows him music and a rhyme:
For mine excludes both measure, tune, and time.
        Alas, my God!

THE CROSS

    What is this strange and uncouth thing?
To make me sigh, and seek, and faint, and die,
Until I had some place, where I might sing,
    And serve thee; and not only I,
But all my wealth and family might combine   *5*
To set thy honor up, as our design.

    And then when after much delay,
Much wrestling, many a combat, this dear end,

---

468. See Jer. 9:1.
469. *feet.* A pun on metrical feet.

So much desir'd, is giv'n, to take away
    My power to serve thee; to unbend   *10*
All my abilities, my designs confound,
And lay my threat'nings bleeding on the ground.

    One ague dwelleth in my bones,
Another in my soul (the memory
What I would do for thee, if once my groans   *15*
    Could be allow'd for harmony)
I am in all a weak disabled thing,
Save in the sight thereof, where strength doth sting.

    Besides, things sort not to my will,
Ev'n when my will doth study thy renown: *20*
Thou turnest th' edge of all things on me still,
    Taking me up to throw me down:
So that, ev'n when my hopes seem to be sped,[470]
I am to grief alive, to them as dead.

    To have my aim, and yet to be   *25*
Further from it than when I bent my bow;
To make my hopes my torture, and the fee
    Of all my woes another woe,
Is in the midst of delicates to need,
And ev'n in Paradise to be a weed.   *30*

    Ah my dear Father, ease my smart!
These contrarieties crush me: these cross actions
Do wind a rope about, and cut my heart:
    And yet since these thy contradictions
Are properly a cross felt by thy Son,   *35*
With but four words, my words, *Thy will be done.*

---

470. *sped.* Brought to a successful conclusion.

THE CHURCH

THE FLOWER[471]

How fresh, Oh Lord, how sweet and clean
Are thy returns! ev'n as the flowers in spring;
　　To which, besides their own demean,[472]
The late-past frosts tributes of pleasure bring.
　　　　Grief melts away
　　　　Like snow in May,
　　As if there were no such cold thing.

Who would have thought my shrivel'd heart
Could have recover'd greenness? It was gone
　　Quite underground; as flowers depart
To see their mother-root, when they have blown;
　　　　Where they together
　　　　All the hard weather,
　　Dead to the world, keep house unknown.

These are thy wonders, Lord of power,
Killing and quick'ning,[473] bringing down to hell
　　And up to heaven in an hour;
Making a chiming of a passing-bell.
　　　　We say amiss,
　　　　This or that is:
　　Thy word is all, if we could spell.

Oh that I once past changing were,
Fast in thy Paradise, where no flower can wither!
　　Many a spring I shoot up fair,
Off'ring at[474] heav'n, growing and groaning thither:
　　　　Nor doth my flower
　　　　Want a spring shower,
　　My sins and I joining together:

5
10
15
20
25

---

　　471. As Patrick notes, the shape of each stanza of this poem suggests the outline of a flower.
　　472. *demean*. Demeanor.
　　473. *quick'ning*. Giving life to.
　　474. *Off'ring at*. Aiming at.

But while I grow in a straight line,
Still upwards bent, as if heav'n were mine own,   *30*
    Thy anger comes, and I decline:
What frost to that? what pole is not the zone,
        Where all things burn,
        When thou dost turn,
    And the least frown of thine is shown?   *35*

    And now in age I bud again,
After so many deaths I live and write;
    I once more smell the dew and rain,
And relish versing: Oh my only light,
        It cannot be   *40*
        That I am he
    On whom thy tempests fell all night.

    These are thy wonders, Lord of love,
To make us see we are but flowers that glide;[475]
    Which when we once can find and prove,[476]   *45*
Thou hast a garden for us, where to bide.
        Who would be more,
        Swelling through store,
    Forfeit their Paradise by their pride.

DOTAGE

False glozing[477] pleasures, casks[478] of happiness,
Foolish night-fires,[479] women's and children's wishes,
Chases in Arras,[480] gilded emptiness,
Shadows well mounted, dreams in a career,[481]

---

475. *glide.* Slip away gently.
476. *prove.* Experience.
477. *glozing.* Flattering, cajoling.
478. *casks.* Caskets, containers.
479. *Foolish night-fires.* Will o'the wisps.
480. *Chases in Arras.* Hunting scenes displayed in tapestries.
481. *in a career.* Fully developed.

Embroider'd lies, nothing between two dishes; 5
    These are the pleasures here.
True earnest sorrows, rooted miseries,
Anguish in grain,[482] vexations ripe and blown,
Sure-footed griefs, solid calamities,
Plain demonstrations, evident and clear, 10
Fetching their proofs ev'n from the very bone;
    These are the sorrows here.
But oh the folly of distracted men,
Who griefs in earnest, joys in jest pursue;
Preferring, like brute beasts, a loathsome den 15
Before a court, ev'n that above so clear,
Where are no sorrows, but delights more true,
    Than miseries are here!

THE SON

Let foreign nations of their language boast,
What fine variety each tongue affords:
I like our language, as our men and coast:[483]
Who cannot dress it well, want wit, not words.
How neatly do we give one only name 5
To parents' issue and the sun's bright star!
A son is light and fruit; a fruitful flame
Chasing[484] the father's dimness, carr'd far
From the first man in th' East, to fresh and new
Western discov'ries of posterity. 10
So in one word our Lord's humility
We turn upon him in a sense most true:
    For what Christ once in humbleness began,
    We him in glory call, *The Son of Man.*

---

482. *in grain.* Indelible, firmly established.
483. *coast.* Region, country.
484. *chasing.* Dispelling.

GEORGE HERBERT

A TRUE HYMN

    My joy, my life, my crown!
  My heart was meaning all the day,
    Somewhat it fain would say:
And still it runneth mutt'ring up and down
With only this, *My joy, my life, my crown.*   *5*

    Yet slight not these few words:
  If truly said, they may take part
    Among the best in art.
The fineness which a hymn or psalm affords,
Is, when the soul unto the lines accords.   *10*

    He who craves all the mind,
  And all the soul, and strength, and time,
    If the words only rhyme,
Justly complains, that somewhat is behind[485]
To make his verse, or write a hymn in kind.   *15*

    Whereas if th' heart be moved,
  Although the verse be somewhat scant,
    God doth supply the want.
As when th' heart says (sighing to be approved)
Oh, could I love! and stops: God writeth, *Loved.*   *20*

THE ANSWER

My comforts drop and melt away like snow:
I shake my head, and all the thoughts and ends,
Which my fierce youth did bandy, fall and flow
Like leaves about me; or like summer friends,
Flies of estates and sunshine. But to all,   *5*
Who think me eager, hot, and undertaking,
But in my prosecutions slack and small;

---

485. *behind.* Lacking.

As a young exhalation,[486] newly waking,
Scorns his first bed of dirt, and means the sky;
But cooling by the way, grows pursie[487] and slow,   *10*
And set'ling to a cloud, doth live and die
In that dark state of tears: to all, that so
    Show me, and set me, I have one reply,
    Which they that know the rest, know more than I.

A DIALOGUE ANTHEM

Christian.   *Death.*

Christian.   Alas, poor Death, where is thy glory?
          Where is thy famous force, thy ancient sting?[488]
Death.   *Alas poor mortal, void of story,*
          Go spell and read how I have kill'd thy King.
Christian.   Poor death! and who was hurt thereby?[489]   *5*
          Thy curse being laid on him, makes thee accurst.
Death.   *Let losers talk: yet thou shalt die;*
          These arms shall crush thee.
Christian: Spare not, do thy worst.
          I shall be one day better than before:
          Thou so much worse, that thou shalt be no more.   *10*

THE WATER COURSE

Thou who dost dwell and linger here below,
Since the condition of this world is frail,
Where of all plants afflictions soonest grow;

---

486. *exhalation.* A vapor rising from damp ground.
487. *pursie.* Swollen, puffy.
488. See 1 Cor. 15:55.
489. See Gal. 3:13.

GEORGE HERBERT

If troubles overtake thee, do not wail:

For who can look for less, that loveth $\begin{cases} \text{Life.} \\ \text{Strife.} \end{cases}$ *5*

But rather turn the pipe, and water's course
To serve thy sins, and furnish thee with store
Of sov'reign tears, spring from true remorse:
That so in pureness thou mayest him adore,

Who gives to man, as he sees fit $\begin{cases} \text{Salvation.} \\ \text{Damnation.} \end{cases}$ *10*

SELF-CONDEMNATION[490]

    Thou who condemnest Jewish hate,
For choosing Barabbas a murderer
      Before the Lord of Glory;
    Look back upon thine own estate,
Call home thine eye (that busy wanderer)   *5*
      That choice may be thy story.

    He that doth love, and love amiss
This world's delights before true Christian joy,
      Hath made a Jewish choice:
    The world an ancient murderer is;   *10*
Thousands of souls it hath and doth destroy
      With her enchanting voice.

    He that hath made a sorry wedding
Between his soul and gold, and hath preferr'd
      False gain before the true,   *15*
    Hath done what he condemns in reading:
For he hath sold for money his dear Lord,
      And is a Judas-Jew.

---

490. Title: See Luke 23:18–19.

THE CHURCH

Thus we prevent the last great day,
And judge ourselves. That light, which sin and passion   *20*
    Did before dim and choke,
When once those snuffs are ta'en away,
Shines bright and clear, ev'n unto condemnation,
    Without excuse or cloak.

BITTER-SWEET

Ah my dear angry Lord,
Since thou dost love, yet strike;
Cast down, yet help afford;
Sure I will do the like.
I will complain, yet praise;
I will bewail, approve:
And all my sour-sweet days
I will lament, and love.

THE GLANCE

When first thy sweet and gracious eye
Vouchsaf'd ev'n in the midst of youth and night
To look upon me, who before did lie
    Welt'ring in sin;
  I felt a sug'red strange delight,   *5*
Passing all cordials made by any art,
Bedew, embalm, and overrun my heart,
    And take it in.

Since that time many a bitter storm
My soul hath felt, ev'n able to destroy,   *10*
Had the malicious and ill-meaning harm
    His swing and sway:
  But still thy sweet original joy
Sprung from thine eye, did work within my soul,

And surging griefs, when they grew bold, control,   *15*
    And got[491] the day.

  If thy first glance so powerful be,
A mirth but open'd and seal'd up again;
What wonders shall we feel, when we shall see
    Thy full-ey'd love!   *20*
  When thou shalt look us out of pain,
And one aspect of thine spend in delight
More than a thousand suns disburse in light,
    In heav'n above.

THE 23rd PSALM

The God of love my shepherd is,
    And he that doth me feed:
While he is mine, and I am his,
    What can I want or need?

He leads me to the tender grass,   *5*
    Where I both feed and rest;
Then to the streams that gently pass:
    In both I have the best.

Or if I stray, he doth convert
    And bring my mind in frame:[492]   *10*
And all this not for my desert,
    But for his holy name.

Yea, in death's shady black abode
    Well may I walk, not fear:
For thou art with me; and thy rod   *15*
    To guide, thy staff to bear.

---

491. *got.* Won.
492. *in frame.* In an appropriate order.

Nay, thou dost make me sit and dine,
  Ev'n in my enemy's sight:
My head with oil, my cup with wine
  Runs over day and night.   *20*

Surely thy sweet and wondrous love
  Shall measure all my days;
And as it never shall remove,
  So neither shall my praise.

MARY MAGDALENE[493]

When blessed Mary wip'd her Savior's feet,
(Whose precepts she had trampled on before)
And wore them for a jewel on her head,
  Showing his steps should be the street,
  Wherein she thenceforth evermore   *5*
With pensive humbleness would live and tread:

She being stain'd herself, why did she strive
To make him clean, who could not be defil'd?
Why kept she not her tears for her own faults,
  And not his feet? Though we could dive   *10*
  In tears like seas, our sins are pil'd
Deeper than they, in words, and works, and thoughts.

Dear soul, she knew who did vouchsafe and deign
To bear her filth; and that her sins did dash
Ev'n God himself: wherefore she was not loath, *15*
  As she had brought wherewith to stain,
  So to bring in wherewith to wash:
And yet in washing one, she washed both.

---

493. Title: See Luke 7:37–38.

AARON[494]

Holiness on the head,
  Light and perfections on the breast,
Harmonious bells below, raising the dead
  To lead them unto life and rest.
    Thus are true Aarons drest.   5

Profaneness in my head,
  Defects and darkness in my breast,
A noise[495] of passions ringing me for dead
  Unto a place where is no rest.
    Poor priest thus am I drest.   10

Only another head
  I have, another heart and breast,
Another music, making live not dead,
  Without whom I could have no rest:
    In him I am well drest.   15

Christ is my only head,
  My alone only heart and breast,
My only music, striking me ev'n dead;
  That to the old man I may rest,
    And be in him new drest.[496]   20

So holy in my head,
  Perfect and light in my dear breast,
My doctrine tun'd by Christ, (who is not dead,
  But lives in me while I do rest)
    Come people; Aaron's drest.   25

---

494. Title: See Exod. 28.
495. *noise.* A band of musicians.
496. See Col. 3:9–10 and Gal. 2:20.

THE CHURCH

THE ODOR. 2 CORINTHIANS 2[497]

How sweetly doth *My Master* sound! *My Master!*
    As Ambergris[498] leaves a rich scent
        Unto the taster:
    So do these words a sweet content,
An oriental fragrancy, *My Master.*   *5*

With these all day I do perfume my mind,
    My mind ev'n thrust into them both;
        That I might find
    What cordials make this curious broth,
This broth of smells, that feeds and fats my mind.   *10*

My Master, shall I speak? Oh that to thee
    My servant were a little so,
        As flesh may be;
    That these two words might creep and grow
To some degree of spiciness to thee!   *15*

Then should the Pomander,[499] which was before
    A speaking sweet, mend by reflection,
        And tell me more:
    For pardon of my imperfection
Would warm and work it sweeter than before.   *20*

For when *My Master*, which alone is sweet,
    And ev'n in my unworthiness pleasing,
        Shall call and meet,
    My servant, as thee not displeasing,
That call is but the breathing of the sweet.   *25*

---

497. Title: 2 Cor. 2:15–16 reads, "we are unto God a sweet savor of Christ, in them that are saved, and in them that perish: to the one we are the savor of death unto death; and to the other the savor of life unto life."

498. *Ambergris.* A secretion of the sperm whale used in perfume.

499. *Pomander.* A scent ball that releases its odor when warmed or squeezed.

This breathing would with gains by sweet'ning me
    (As sweet things traffic when they meet)
        Return to thee.
    And so this new commerce and sweet
Should all my life employ, and busy me.   *30*

THE FOIL[500]

    If we could see below
The sphere of virtue, and each shining grace
    As plainly as that above doth show;
This were the better sky, the brighter place.

    God hath made stars the foil   *5*
To set off virtues; griefs to set off sinning:
    Yet in this wretched world we toil,
As if grief were not foul, nor virtue winning.

THE FORERUNNERS

The harbingers[501] are come. See, see their mark;
White is their color, and behold my head.
But must they have my brain? must they dispark[502]
Those sparkling notions, which therein were bred?
    Must dullness turn me to a clod?   *5*
Yet have they left me, *Thou art still my God.*[503]

---

500. Title: A foil is a kind of dueling sword, as well as a thin piece of metal put under a gem-stone to enhance and display its brilliance.

501. *harbingers*. Those sent in front of a royal progress (thus "forerunners") to secure lodgings by chalking the doors; here, the mark of approaching death is the whiteness of the speaker's hair.

502. *dispark*. Turn out of a park.

503. See Ps. 31:14.

Good men ye be, to leave me my best room,
Ev'n all my heart, and what is lodged there:
I pass not,[504] I, what of the rest become,
So *Thou art still my God*, be out of fear.   *10*
　　　He will be pleased with that ditty;
And if I please him, I write fine and witty.

Farewell sweet phrases, lovely metaphors.
But will ye leave me thus? when ye before
Of stews and brothels only knew the doors,   *15*
Then did I wash you with my tears, and more,
　　　Brought you to Church well drest and clad:
My God must have my best, ev'n all I had.

Lovely enchanting language, sugar-cane,
Honey of roses, whither wilt thou fly?   *20*
Hath some fond lover tic'd[505] thee to thy bane?
And wilt thou leave the Church, and love a sty?
　　　Fie, thou wilt soil thy broider'd[506] coat,
And hurt thyself, and him that sings the note.

Let foolish lovers, if they will love dung,   *25*
With canvas, not with arras clothe their shame:
Let folly speak in her own native tongue.
True beauty dwells on high: ours is a flame
　　　But borrow'd thence to light us thither.
Beauty and beauteous words should go together.   *30*

Yet if you go, I pass not;[507] take your way:
For, *Thou art still my God,* is all that ye
Perhaps with more embellishment can say.
Go birds of spring: let winter have his fee,
　　　Let a bleak paleness chalk the door,   *35*
So all within be livelier than before.

---

504. *pass not.* Am not concerned about.
505. *tic'd.* Enticed.
506. *broider'd.* Embroidered.
507. *pass not.* Care not.

GEORGE HERBERT

THE ROSE[508]

Press me not to take more pleasure
    In this world of sug'red lies,
And to use a larger measure
    Than my strict, yet welcome size.[509]

First, there is no pleasure here: 5
    Color'd[510] griefs indeed there are,
Blushing woes, that look as clear
    As if they could beauty spare.

Or if such deceits there be,
    Such delights I meant to say;   10
There are no such things to me,
    Who have pass'd my right away.

But I will not much oppose
    Unto what you now advise:
Only take this gentle rose,   15
    And therein my answer lies.

What is fairer than a rose?
    What is sweeter? yet it purgeth.[511]
Purgings enmity disclose,
    Enmity forebearance[512] urgeth.   20

If then all that worldlings prize
    Be contracted to a rose;
Sweetly there indeed it lies,
    But it biteth in the close.

So this flower doth judge and sentence   25
    Worldly joys to be a scourge:

---

508. Title: See Song of Sol. 2:1.
509. *size.* Status.
510. *Color'd.* Disguised.
511. *purgeth.* Roses were thought to have purgative qualities.
512. *forbearance.* Abstinence.

For they all produce repentance.
    And repentance is a purge.

But I health, not physic choose:
    Only though I you oppose,   *30*
Say that fairly I refuse,
    For my answer is a rose.

DISCIPLINE

Throw away thy rod,
Throw away thy wrath:
    Oh my God,
Take the gentle path.

For my heart's desire   *5*
Unto thine is bent:
    I aspire
To a full consent.

Not a word or look
I affect to own,   *10*
    But by book,
And thy book alone.

Though I fail, I weep:
Though I halt in pace,
    Yet I creep   *15*
To the throne of grace.

Then let wrath remove;
Love will do the deed:
    For with love
Stony hearts will bleed.   *20*

Love is swift of foot;
Love's a man of war,[513]

---

513. See Exod. 15:3.

And can shoot,
And can hit from far.

Who can 'scape his bow?   *25*
That which wrought on thee,
        Brought thee low,
Needs must work on me.

Throw away thy rod;
Though man frailties hath,   *30*
        Thou art God:
Throw away thy wrath.

THE INVITATION

Come ye hither all, whose taste
        Is your waste;
Save your cost, and mend your fare.[514]
God is here prepar'd and drest,
        And the feast,   *5*
God, in whom all dainties are.

Come ye hither all, whom wine
        Doth define,[515]
Naming you not to your good:
Weep what ye have drunk amiss,   *10*
        And drink this,
Which before ye drink is blood.

Come ye hither all, whom pain
        Doth arraign,
Bringing all your sins to sight: *15*
Taste and fear not: God is here
        In this cheer,
And on sin doth cast the fright.

---

514. See Isa. 55:1–2.
515. *define*. Characterize.

Come ye hither all, whom joy
      Doth destroy,   *20*
While ye graze without your bounds:
Here is joy that drowneth quite
      Your delight,
As a flood the lower grounds.

Come ye hither all, whose love   *25*
      Is your dove,
And exalts you to the sky:
Here is love, which having breath
      Ev'n in death,
After death can never die.   *30*

Lord I have invited all,
      And I shall
Still invite, still call to thee:
For it seems but just and right
      In my sight,   *35*
Where is all, there all should be.

THE BANQUET

Welcome sweet and sacred cheer,
      Welcome dear;
With me, in me, live and dwell:
For thy neatness[516] passeth sight,
      Thy delight
Passeth tongue to taste or tell.

Oh what sweetness from the bowl
      Fills my soul,
Such as is, and makes divine!
Is some star (fled from the sphere)   *10*
      Melted there,
As we sugar melt in wine?

---

516. *neatness.* Purity, elegance, precise effectiveness.

Or hath sweetness in the bread
      Made a head[517]
To subdue the smell of sin;   *15*
Flowers, and gums, and powders giving
      All their living,
Lest the enemy should win?

Doubtless, neither star nor flower
      Hath the power   *20*
Such a sweetness to impart:
Only God, who gives perfumes,
      Flesh assumes,
And with it perfumes my heart.

But as Pomanders and wood   *25*
      Still are good,
Yet being bruis'd are better scented:
God, to show how far his love
      Could improve,
Here, as broken, is presented.   *30*

When I had forgot my birth,
      And on earth
In delights of earth was drown'd;
God took blood, and needs would be
      Spilt with me,   *35*
And so found me on the ground.

Having rais'd me to look up,
      In a cup
Sweetly he doth meet my taste.
But I still being low and short,   *40*
      Far from court,
Wine becomes a wing at last.

For with it alone I fly
      To the sky:

---

517. *Made a head.* Pressed forward in opposition.

Where I wipe mine eyes, and see   *45*
What I seek, for what I sue;
    Him I view,
Who hath done so much for me.

Let the wonder of this pity
    Be my ditty,   *50*
And take up my lines and life:
Harken under pain of death,
    Hands and breath;
Strive in this, and love the strife.

THE POESY[518]

    Let wits contest,
And with their words and poesies windows fill:
    Less than the least
Of all thy mercies,[519] is my poesy still.

    This on my ring,   *5*
This by my picture, in my book I write:
    Whether I sing,
Or say, or dictate, this is my delight.

    Invention rest,
Comparisons go play, wit use thy will: *10*
    Less than the least
Of all God's mercies, is my poesy still.

---

518. Title: A short motto; also, poetry.
519. Herbert's own motto; see Gen. 32:10 and Eph. 3:8.

GEORGE HERBERT

A PARODY[520]

Soul's joy, when thou art gone,
    And I alone,
      Which cannot be,
Because thou dost abide with me,
    And I depend on thee;   *5*

Yet when thou dost suppress
    The cheerfulness
      Of thy abode,
And in my powers not stir abroad,
    But leave me to my load: *10*

Oh what a damp and shade
    Doth me invade!
      No stormy night
Can so afflict or so affright,
    As thy eclipsed light.   *15*

Ah Lord! do not withdraw,
    Lest want of awe
      Make Sin appear;
And when thou dost but shine less clear,
    Say, that thou art not here.   *20*

And then what life I have,
    While Sin doth rave,
      And fals'ly boast,
That I may seek, but thou art lost;
    Thou and alone thou know'st.   *25*

Oh what a deadly cold
    Doth me infold!
      I half believe,

---

520. Title: A parody is a poem that takes another poem as its point of departure and puts that poem to another use; here, Herbert "parodies" a poem attributed to William Herbert, third Earl of Pembroke and a relative of George's, and turns its secular tribute to an earthly "Soul's joy" into a sacred address to God.

That Sin says true: but while I grieve,
 Thou com'st and dost relieve.   *30*

THE ELIXIR[521]

 Teach me, my God and King,
  In all things thee to see,
And what I do in anything,
  To do it as for thee:

 Not rudely, as a beast,   *5*
  To run into an action;
But still to make thee prepossest,[522]
  And give it his perfection.

 A man that looks on glass,
  On it may stay his eye;   *10*
Or if he pleaseth, through it pass,
  And then the heav'n espy.

 All may of thee partake:
  Nothing can be so mean,
Which with his tincture[523] (for thy sake) *15*
  Will not grow bright and clean.

 A servant with this clause
  Makes drudgery divine:
Who sweeps a room, as for thy laws,
  Makes that and th' action fine.   *20*

 This is the famous stone
  That turneth all to gold:

---

 521. Title: The elixer is identified in 1.21 with the philosopher's stone, claimed by alchemists to turn base metals into gold.
 522: *still to make thee prepossest.* Always to give thee a prior claim.
 523. *tincture.* Alchemical term for a supposed spiritual principal or immaterial substance whose qualities may be infused into material things.

GEORGE HERBERT

For that which God doth touch[524] and own
    Cannot for less be told.

A WREATH

A wreathed garland of deserved praise,
Of praise deserved, unto thee I give,
I give to thee, who knowest all my ways,
My crooked winding ways, wherein I live,
Wherein I die, not live: for life is straight,   *5*
Straight as a line, and ever tends to thee,
To thee, who art more far above deceit,
Than deceit seems above simplicity.
Give me simplicity, that I may live,
So live and like, that I may know thy ways,   *10*
Know them and practice them: then shall I give
For this poor wreath, give thee a crown of praise.

DEATH

Death, thou wast once an uncouth hideous thing,
      Nothing but bones,
    The sad effect of sadder groans:
Thy mouth was open, but thou couldst not sing.

For we consider'd thee as at some six   *5*
      Or ten years hence,
    After the loss of life and sense,
Flesh being turn'd to dust, and bones to sticks.

We lookt on this side of thee, shooting short;
      Where we did find   *10*

---

524. *touch.* Test with a touchstone to determine quality of gold.

The shells of fledge[525] souls left behind,
Dry dust, which sheds no tears, but may extort.

But since our Savior's death did put some blood
      Into thy face;
   Thou art grown fair and full of grace,   *15*
Much in request, much sought for, as a good.

For we do now behold thee gay and glad,
      As at doomsday;
   When souls shall wear their new array,
And all thy bones with beauty shall be clad.   *20*

Therefore we can go die as sleep, and trust
      Half that we have
   Unto an honest faithful grave;
Making our pillows either down, or dust.

DOOMSDAY

      Come away,
    Make no delay.
Summon all the dust to rise,
Till it stir, and rub the eyes;
While this member jogs the other,   *5*
Each one whisp'ring, *Live you brother?*

      Come away,
    Make this the day.
Dust, alas, no music feels,
But thy trumpet: then it kneels,   *10*

---

525. *fledge.* Ready for flight, as birds leave their shells behind when they fly from the nest.

As peculiar notes and strains
Cure Tarantula's raging pains.[526]

     Come away,
      Oh make no stay!
Let the graves make their confession,[527]   *15*
Lest at length they plead possession:
Flesh's stubbornness may have
Read that lesson to the grave.

     Come away,
      Thy flock doth stray.   *20*
Some to winds their body lend,
And in them may drown a friend:
Some in noisome vapors grow
To a plague and public woe.

     Come away,   *25*
      Help our decay.
Man is out of order hurl'd,
Parcel'd out to all the world.
Lord, thy broken consort[528] raise,
And the music shall be praise.   *30*

JUDGMENT

Almighty Judge, how shall poor wretches brook
     Thy dreadful look,
Able a heart of iron to appall,

---

526. *Tarantula's raging pains.* Hutchinson notes that "Tarantism, an hysterical malady, was supposed to be caused by the bite of the wolf-spider, or tarantula and to be cured by music and wild dancing."

527. *graves make their confession.* I.e., that they do not actually possess permanently the bodies they hold.

528. *consort.* Group of musicians.

When thou shalt call
    For ev'ry man's peculiar book?   *5*

What others mean to do, I know not well;
    Yet I hear tell,
That some will turn thee to some leaves therein
    So void of sin,
    That they in merit shall excel.   *10*

But I resolve, when thou shalt call for mine,
    That to decline,
And thrust a Testament into thy hand:
    Let that be scann'd.
    There thou shalt find my faults are thine.   *15*

HEAVEN

Oh who will show me those delights on high?
    Echo.   *I.*
Thou Echo, thou art mortal, all men know.
    Echo.   *No.*
Wert thou not born among the trees and leaves?   *5*
    Echo.   *Leaves.*
And are there any leaves, that still abide?
    Echo.   *Bide.*
What leaves are they? impart the matter wholly.
    Echo.   *Holy.*   *10*
Are holy leaves the Echo then of bliss?
    Echo.   *Yes.*
Then tell me, what is that supreme delight?
    Echo.   *Light.*
Light to the mind: what shall the will enjoy?   *15*
    Echo.   *Joy.*
But are there cares and business with the pleasure?
    Echo.   *Leisure.*
Light, joy, and leisure; but shall they persevere?
    Echo.   *Ever.*   *20*

GEORGE HERBERT

LOVE (III)

Love bade me welcome: yet my soul drew back,
  Guilty of dust and sin.
But quick-ey'd Love, observing me grow slack
  From my first entrance in,
Drew nearer to me, sweetly questioning,   *5*
  If I lack'd anything.

A guest, I answer'd, worthy to be here:
  Love said, You shall be he.
I the unkind, ungrateful? Ah my dear,
  I cannot look on thee.   *10*
Love took my hand, and smiling did reply,
  Who made the eyes but I?

Truth Lord, but I have marr'd them: let my shame
  Go where it doth deserve.
And know you not, says Love, who bore the blame?   *15*
  My dear, then I will serve.
You must sit down, says Love, and taste my meat:
  So I did sit and eat.

FINIS.

Glory be to God on high, and on earth
peace, good will towards men.[529]

---

529. *Finis.* This two-line conclusion is the beginning of the *Gloria in excelsis*, directed by the Book of Common Prayer to be said or sung at the end of the service of Holy Communion; see Booty, p. 265.

THE CHURCH MILITANT

Almighty Lord, who from thy glorious throne
Seest and rulest all things ev'n as one:
The smallest ant or atom knows thy power,
Known also to each minute of an hour:
Much more do Commonweals acknowledge thee,   *5*
And wrap their policies in thy decree,
Complying with thy counsels, doing nought
Which doth not meet with an eternal thought.
But above all, thy Church and Spouse doth prove
Not the decrees of power, but bands of love.   *10*
Early didst thou arise to plant this vine,
Which might the more endear[1] it to be thine.
Spices come from the East; so did thy Spouse,
Trim as the light, sweet as the laden boughs
Of *Noah's* shady vine,[2] chaste as the dove;   *15*
Prepar'd and fitted to receive thy love.
The course was westward, that the sun might light
As well our understanding as our sight.
Where th' Ark did rest, there *Abraham* began
To bring the other Ark from *Canaan.*   *20*
Moses pursu'd this; but King *Solomon*
Finish'd and fixt the old religion.[3]
When it grew loose, the Jews did hope in vain
By nailing Christ to fasten it again.
But to the Gentiles he bore cross and all,   *25*
Rending with earthquakes the partition wall:[4]
Only whereas the Ark in glory shone,
Now with the cross, as with a staff, alone,

---

1. *endear.* Bind by obligations of gratitude.
2. Here Herbert combines images of the Church as spouse from the Song of Solomon, the bride of Rev. 21:2, and the vineyard of Gen. 9:20 with the tradition of Israel as a vine (Ps. 80:8).
3. Herbert, following traditional readings, here identifies the place that Noah's ark landed after the Flood with the place Abraham started his journey toward Egypt and the Promised Land with the Ark of the Covenant, which was ultimately to be "fixt" in the wall of the Temple at Jerusalem by Solomon. See Gen. 8:4, 11:31, 12:10; Exod. 37:1; 1 Sam. 5:1; and 2 Chron. 3:1.
4. *partition wall.* See Eph. 2:14.

Religion, like a pilgrim, westward bent,
Knocking at all doors, ever as she went.   *30*
Yet as the sun, though forward be his flight,
Listens behind him, and allows some light,
Till all depart: so went the Church her way,
Letting, while one foot stept, the other stay
Among the eastern nations for a time,   *35*
Till both removed to the western clime.
To *Egypt* first she came, where they did prove
Wonders of anger once, but now of love.
The ten Commandments there did flourish more
Than the ten bitter plagues had done before.   *40*
Holy *Macarius* and great *Anthony*⁵
Made *Pharaoh Moses,* changing th' history.
Goshen was darkness, *Egypt* full of lights,
Nilus for monsters brought forth Israelites.
Such power hath mighty Baptism to produce   *45*
For⁶ things misshapen, things of highest use.
How dear to me, Oh God, thy counsels are!
        *Who may with thee compare?*⁷
Religion thence fled into *Greece,* where arts
Gave her the highest place in all men's hearts.   *50*
Learning was pos'd, Philosophy was set,⁸
Sophisters taken in a fisher's net.
Plato and *Aristotle* were at a loss,
And wheel'd about again to spell *Christ-Cross.*⁹
Prayers chas'd syllogisms into their den,   *55*
And *Ergo*¹⁰ was transform'd into *Amen.*
Though *Greece* took horse as soon as *Egypt* did,
And *Rome* as both; yet *Egypt* faster rid,

---

5. Macarius and Anthony were hermits in Upper Egypt in the fourth century A.D.; here, Herbert indicates that Egypt now brings forth Christians instead of frogs, as in the story of the Plagues (Exod. 10:21–23, 8:1–14).

6. *for.* Instead of (also in lines 44 and 127).

7. Herbert's refrain in this poem is from Ps. 89:6 and Ps. 139:17 in the Great Bible, and BCP, versions.

8. *pos'd . . . set.* Puzzled, defeated.

9. *Christ-Cross.* A name for the alphabet, because a cross was prefixed to hornbook primers; philosophers had to learn to spell all over again after the advent of Christ.

10. *Ergo.* Therefore.

And spent her period and prefixed time
Before the other. *Greece* being past her prime,   *60*
Religion went to *Rome,* subduing those,
Who, that they might subdue, made all their foes.
The Warrior his dear scars no more resounds,[11]
But seems to yield Christ hath the greater wounds,
Wounds willingly endur'd to work his bliss,   *65*
Who by an ambush lost his Paradise.
The great heart stoops, and taketh from the dust
A sad repentance, not the spoils of lust:
Quitting his spear, lest it should pierce again
Him in his members, who for him was slain.   *70*
The Shepherd's hook grew to a scepter here,
Giving new names and numbers to the year.[12]
But th' Empire dwelt in *Greece,* to comfort them
Who were cut short in *Alexander's* stem.[13]
In both of these Prowess and Arts did tame   *75*
And tune men's hearts against[14] the Gospel came:
Which using, and not fearing skill in th' one,
Or strength in th' other, did erect her throne.
Many a rent and struggling th' Empire knew,
(As dying things are wont) until it flew   *80*
At length to *Germany,* still westward bending,
And there the Church's festival attending:
That as before Empire and Arts made way,
(For no less Harbingers would serve than they)
So they might still, and point us out the place   *85*
Where first the Church should raise her downcast face.
Strength levels grounds, Art makes a garden there;
Then showers Religion, and makes all to bear.
Spain in the Empire shar'd with *Germany,*
But *England* in the higher victory: *90*
Giving the Church a crown to keep her state,
And not go less than she had done of late.

---

11. *resounds.* Proclaims, celebrates.
12. Reference to introduction of Christian calendar.
13. Reference to revival of glory of Roman empire when Constantine moved the capital to Byzantium from Rome in A.D. 330.
14. *against.* Before.

Constantine's British line[15] meant this of old,
And did this mystery wrap up and fold
Within a sheet of paper,[16] which was rent   *95*
From time's great Chronicle, and hither sent.
Thus both the Church and Sun together ran
Unto the farthest old meridian.[17]
How dear to me, Oh God, thy counsels are!
    Who may with thee compare?   *100*
Much about one and the same time and place,
Both where and when the Church began her race,
Sin did set out of Eastern *Babylon*,
And travel'd westward also: journeying on
He chid the Church away, where're he came,   *105*
Breaking her peace, and tainting her good name.
At first he got to *Egypt*, and did sow
Gardens of gods, which ev'ry year did grow
Fresh and fine deities. They were at great cost,
Who for a god clearly a sallet[18] lost.   *110*
Ah, what a thing is man devoid of grace,
Adoring garlic[19] with an humble face,
Begging his food of that which he may eat,
Starving the while he worshippeth his meat!
Who makes a root his god, how low is he,   *115*
If God and man be sever'd infinitely!
What wretchedness can give him any room,
Whose house is foul, while he adores his broom?[20]
None will believe this now, though money be
In us the same transplanted foolery.   *120*
Thus Sin in *Egypt* sneaked for a while;

---

15. *Constantine's British line.* Constantine was reputed to have a British mother; he was proclaimed emperor of Britain at York in A.D. 306, thus setting a precedent for royal protection of the English church.

16. *a sheet of paper.* The "Donation of Constantine," held by writers of the Renaissance to be a forgery, gave great temporal power to the Church.

17. *meridian.* The highest point of the sun's progress across the sky, thus the point just before its decline.

18. *sallet.* Salad, vegetable eaten raw.

19. *Adoring garlic.* The Israelites, after leaving Egypt, missed the garlic; see Num. 11:15.

20. *adores his broom.* This worshiper of the vegetable gods neglects to use what would otherwise have kept his house clean.

His highest was an ox or crocodile,
And such poor game. Thence he to *Greece* doth pass,
And being craftier much than Goodness was,
He left behind him garrisons of sins   *125*
To make good that which ev'ry day he wins.
Here Sin took heart, and for a garden-bed
Rich shrines and oracles he purchased:
He grew a gallant, and would needs foretell
As well what should befall, as what befell.   *130*
Nay, he became a poet,[21] and would serve
His pills of sublimate[22] in that conserve.
The world came both with hands and purses full
To this great lottery, and all would pull.[23]
But all was glorious cheating, brave deceit,   *135*
Where some poor truths were shuffled for a bait
To credit him, and to discredit those
Who after him should braver truths disclose.
From *Greece* he went to *Rome:* and as before
He was a God, now he's an Emperor.   *140*
Nero and others lodg'd him bravely there,
Put him in trust to rule the Roman sphere.
Glory was his chief instrument of old:
Pleasure succeeded straight, when that grew cold.
Which soon was blown to such a mighty flame,   *145*
That though our Savior did destroy the game,
Disparking[24] oracles, and all their treasure,
Setting affliction to encounter pleasure;
Yet did a rogue[25] with hope of carnal joy
Cheat the most subtle nations. Who so coy,   *150*
So trim, as *Greece* and *Egypt?* yet their hearts
Are given over, for their curious arts,
To such Mahometan[26] stupidities,
As the old heathen would deem prodigies.

---

21. *a poet.* Greek oracles were often delivered in verse.
22. *sublimate.* A poison (mercuric chloride) in a medicinal *conserve* is concealed by the pill's sugar coating.
23. *pull.* Draw, as in choose a lottery number.
24. *Disparking.* Expelling.
25. *a rogue.* Mohammed.
26. *Mahometan.* Mohammedan.

How dear to me, Oh God, thy counsels are!   *155*
    Who may with thee compare?
Only the West and *Rome* do keep them free
From this contagious infidelity.
And this is all the Rock, whereof they boast,
As *Rome* will one day find unto her cost.   *160*
Sin being not able to extirpate[27] quite
The Churches here, bravely resolv'd one night
To be a Churchman too, and wear a Mitre:
The old debauched ruffian would turn writer.
I saw him in his study, where he sate[28]   *165*
Busy in controversies sprung of late.
A gown and pen became him wondrous well:
His grave aspect had more of heav'n than hell:
Only there was a handsome picture by,
To which he lent a corner of his eye.[29]   *170*
As Sin in *Greece* a Prophet was before,
And in old *Rome* a mighty Emperor;
So now being Priest he plainly did profess
To make a jest of Christ's three offices:[30]
The rather since his scatter'd jugglings were   *175*
United now in one both time and sphere.
From *Egypt* he took pretty deities,
From *Greece* oracular infallibilities,
And from old *Rome* the liberty of pleasure,
By free dispensings of the Church's treasure.   *180*
Then in memorial of his ancient throne
He did surname his palace, *Babylon.*[31]
Yet that he might the better gain all nations,
And make that name good by their transmigrations;
From all these places, but at divers times,   *185*
He took fine vizards[32] to conceal his crimes:

---

27. *extirpate.* Root out.
28. *sate.* I.e., Sat.
29. A reference to the Renaissance popes and their patronage of the arts.
30. *Christ's three offices.* Prophet, King, Priest, here perverted by Sin (ll. 171–73, 177–80, 187–88).
31. *Babylon.* A recurring biblical image of the evil city; see Rev. 17:5.
32. *vizards.* Masks.

From *Egypt* Anchorism[33] and retiredness,
Learning from *Greece*, from old *Rome* stateliness:
And blending these he carri'd all men's eyes,
While Truth sat by, counting his victories: *190*
Whereby he grew apace and scorn'd to use
Such force as once did captivate[34] the Jews;
But did bewitch, and finely work each nation
Into a voluntary transmigration.
All post to *Rome:* Princes submit their necks   *195*
Either t' his public foot or private tricks.
It did not fit his gravity to stir,
Nor his long journey, nor his gout and fur.
Therefore he sent out able ministers,
Statesmen within, without doors cloisterers: *200*
Who without spear, or sword, or other drum
Than what was in their tongue, did overcome;
And having conquer'd, did so strangely rule,
That the whole world did seem but the Pope's mule.[35]
As new and old *Rome* did one Empire twist;   *205*
So both together are one Antichrist,
Yet with two faces, as their *Janus* was;
Being in this their old crackt looking glass.
How dear to me, Oh God, thy counsels are!
    Who may with thee compare?   *210*
Thus Sin triumphs in Western *Babylon;*
Yet not as Sin, but as Religion.
Of his two thrones he made the latter best,
And to defray his journey from the east.
Old and new *Babylon* are to hell and night,   *215*
As is the moon and sun to heav'n and light.
When th' one did set, the other did take place,
Confronting equally the law and grace.
They are hell's landmarks, Satan's double crest:[36]

---

33. *Anchorism.* Life of retirement and seclusion from the world; reference to beginning of monasticism.
34. *captivate.* Make captive.
35. *the Pope's mule.* A purple slipper worn by the Pope; reference here is to the kiss ceremonially bestowed upon his "public foot" (1. 196).
36. *double crest.* One may, by special royal grant, bear the surname and coat of arms of another family in addition to one's own.

They are Sin's nipples,[37] feeding th' east and west.   *220*
But as in vice the copy still exceeds
The pattern, but not so in virtuous deeds;
So though Sin made his latter seat the better,
The latter Church is to the first a debtor.
The second Temple could not reach the first: *225*
And the late reformation never durst
Compare with ancient times and purer years;
But in the Jews and us deserveth tears.
Nay, it shall ev'ry year decrease and fade,
Till such a darkness do the world invade   *230*
At Christ's last coming, as his first did find:
Yet must there such proportions be assign'd
To these diminishings, as is between
The spacious world and *Jewery* to be seen.
Religion stands on tip-toe in our land,   *235*
Ready to pass to the *American* strand.[38]
When height of malice, and prodigious lusts,
Impudent sinning, witchcrafts, and distrusts
(The marks of future bane) shall fill our cup
Unto the brim, and make our measure up;   *240*
When *Seine* shall swallow *Tiber*, and the *Thames*
By letting in them both, pollutes her streams:
When *Italy* of us shall have her will,
And all her calendar of sins fulfill;
Whereby one may foretell, what sins next year   *245*
Shall both in *France* and *England* domineer:
Then shall Religion to *America* flee:
They have their times of Gospel, ev'n as we.
My God, thou dost prepare for them a way
By carrying first their gold from them away:[39]   *250*
For gold and grace did never yet agree:
Religion always sides with poverty.
We think we rob them, but we think amiss:
We are more poor, and they more rich by this.

---

37. *Sin's Nipples*. Inversion of motif from Song of Sol. of the breasts of the beloved (4:5; 7:3), interpreted as the two Testaments or two Sacraments, sources of eternal life.

38. Walton states that these lines caused difficulty in getting *The Temple* licensed for publication by the Cambridge Vice-Chancellor (*Lives*, p. 315).

39. Reference to expeditions to new world in search of gold.

Thou wilt revenge their quarrel, making grace   *255*
To pay our debts, and leave our ancient place
To go to them, while that which now their nation
But lends to us, shall be our desolation.
Yet as the Church shall thither westward fly,
So Sin shall trace and dog her instantly: *260*
They have their period also and set times
Both for their virtuous actions and their crimes.
And where of old the Empire and the Arts
Usher'd the Gospel ever in men's hearts,
Spain hath done one;[40] when Arts perform the other,   *265*
The Church shall come, and Sin the Church shall smother:
That when they have accomplished the round,
And met in th' east their first and ancient sound,[41]
Judgment may meet them both and search them round.
Thus do both lights, as well in Church as Sun,   *270*
Light one another, and together run.
Thus also Sin and Darkness follow still
The Church and Sun with all their power and skill.
But as the Sun still goes both west and east;
So also did the Church by going west   *275*
Still eastward go; because it drew more near
To time and place, where judgment shall appear.
How dear to me, Oh God, thy counsels are!
    Who may with thee compare?

L'ENVOY

King of Glory, King of Peace,[42]
With the one make war to cease;[43]
With the other bless thy sheep,
Thee to love, in thee to sleep.

---

40. *Spain hath done one.* Spain illustrates one way of spreading the gospel through its missionary efforts in South America.
41. *sound.* Inlet, haven.
42. Repeated from "Praise (II)."
43. See Ps. 46:9.

Let not Sin devour thy fold, 5
Bragging that thy blood is cold,
That thy death is also dead,
While his conquests daily spread;
That thy flesh hath lost his food,
And thy Cross is common wood. 10
Choke him, let him say no more,
But reserve his breath in store,
Till thy conquests and his fall
Make his sighs to use it all,
And then bargain with the wind 15
To discharge what is behind.

Blessed be God alone,
Thrice blessed Three in One.

FINIS.

POEMS NOT INCLUDED IN *THE TEMPLE*

THE HOLY COMMUNION.

Oh Gracious Lord how shall I know
Whether in these gifts thou be so
   As thou art ev'rywhere;
Or rather so, as thou alone
Tak'st all the Lodging, leaving none   *5*
   For thy poor creature there?

First I am sure, whether bread stay
Or whether Bread do fly away
   Concerneth bread, not me.
But that both thou, and all thy train,   *10*
Be there, to thy truth, and my gain,
   Concerneth me and Thee.

And if in coming to thy foes
Thou dost come first to them, that shows
   The haste of thy good will.   *15*
Or if that thou two stations makest
In Bread and me, the way thou takest
   Is more, but for me still.

Then of this also I am sure
That thou didst all those pains endure   *20*
   To abolish Sin, not Wheat.
Creatures are good, and have their place;
Sin only, which did all deface
   Thou drivest from his seat.

I could believe an Impanation[1]   *25*
At the rate of an Incarnation

---

1. *Impanation.* A theory of the Eucharistic presence of Christ that argues that Christ takes the bread and wine into a union with himself like that union he achieved between human and divine natures at the Incarnation; this theory is the obverse of transubstantia-

If thou hadst died for Bread.
But that which made my soul to die,
My flesh, and fleshly villany,
   That also made thee dead.   *30*

That Flesh is there, mine eyes deny:
And what should flesh but flesh descry,
   The noblest sense of five?
If glorious bodies pass the sight,
Shall they be food and strength and might   *35*
   Even there, where they deceive?

Into my soul this cannot pass;
Flesh (though exalted) keeps his grass
   And cannot turn to soul.
Bodies and Minds are different Spheres   *40*
Nor can they change their bounds and meres,[2]
   But keep a constant Pole.

This gift of all gifts is the best,
Thy flesh the least that I request.
   Thou took'st that pledge from me: *45*
Give me not that I had before,
Or give me that, so I have more;
   My God, give me all Thee.

LOVE

Thou art too hard for me in Love:
There is no dealing with thee in that Art:
   That is thy Masterpiece I see
   When I contrive and plot to prove
Something that may be conquest on my part   *5*
   Thou still, Oh Lord, outstrippest me.

---

tion, which asserts that the essence of bread and wine become the body and blood, their accidental appearance and other tactile and sensory qualities remaining intact.
   2. *meres.* Boundaries; also, marks indicating boundaries.

Sometimes, when as I wash, I say
And shrewdly, as I think, Lord, wash my soul
  More spotted than my flesh can be.
But then there comes into my way   *10*
Thy ancient baptism, which when I was foul
  And knew it not, yet cleansed me.

I took a time when thou didst sleep[3]
Great waves of trouble combating my breast:
  I thought it brave to praise thee then,   *15*
  Yet then I found, that thou didst creep
Into my heart with joy, giving more rest
  Than flesh did lend thee, back again,

Let me but once the conquest have
Upon the matter 'twill thy conquest prove: *20*
  If thou subdue mortality
  Thou do'st no more, than doth the grave:
Whereas, if I o'ercome thee and thy Love
  Hell, Death and Devil come short of me.

TRINITY SUNDAY

  He that is one,
    Is none.
  Two reacheth thee
  In some degree.
  Nature and Grace   *5*
With Glory may attain thy Face.
  Steel and a flint strike fire,
    Wit and desire
  Never to thee aspire,
Except life catch and hold those fast.   *10*
  That which belief
Did not confess in the first Thief[4]

---

3. See Mark 4:37.
4. *the first Thief.* Satan.

His fall can tell,
From Heaven, through Earth, to Hell.
   Let two of those alone   *15*
      To them that fall,
Who God and Saints and Angels loose at last.
    He that has one,
        Has all.

EVENSONG

The Day is spent, and hath his will on me:
  I and the Sun have run our races,
  I went the slower, yet more paces,
    For I decay not he.

Lord, make my Losses up, and set me free: *5*
  That I, who cannot now by day
  Look on his daring brightness, may
    Shine then more bright than he.

If thou defer this light, then shadow me:
  Lest that the Night, earth's gloomy shade   *10*
  Fouling her nest, my earth invade,
    As if shades knew not Thee.

But thou art Light and darkness both together:
  If that be dark we cannot see:
  The sun is darker than a Tree,   *15*
    And thou more dark than either.

Yet Thou art not so dark, since I know this,
  But that my darkness may touch thine:
  And hope, that may teach it to shine,
    Since Light thy Darkness is.   *20*

Oh let my Soul, whose keys I must deliver
  Into the hands of senseless Dreams

Which know not thee, suck in thy beams
    And wake with thee forever.

THE KNELL

    The Bell doth toll;
Lord, help thy servant whose perplexed Soul
    Doth wishly[5] look
    On either hand
And sometimes offers, sometimes makes a stand   *5*
    Strug'ling on th' hook.

    Now is the season
Now the great combat of our flesh and reason:
    Oh help my God!
    See, they break in   *10*
Disbanded humors, sorrow's troops of Sin
    Each with his rod.

    Lord, make thy Blood
Convert and color all the other flood
    And streams of grief   *15*
    That they may be
Julips and Cordials[6] when we call on thee
    For some relief.

PERSEVERANCE

My God, the poor expressions of my Love
Which warm these lines, and serve them up to thee
Are so, as for the present, I did move
    Or rather as thou movedst me.

---

5. *wishly.* Wistfully.
6. *Julips and cordials.* Medicinal drinks.

But what shall issue, whither these my words   *5*
Shall help another, but my judgment be;
As a burst fouling-piece doth save the birds
     But kill the man, is seal'd with thee.

For who can tell, though thou hast died to win
And wed my soul in glorious paradise;   *10*
Whether my many crimes and use of sin
     May yet forbid the banes[7] and bliss.

Only my soul hangs on thy promises
With face and hands clinging unto thy breast,
Clinging and crying, crying without cease   *15*
     Thou art my rock, thou art my rest.

[SONNET (I)]

My God, where is that ancient heat towards thee,
     Wherewith whole shoals of *Martyrs* once did burn,
     Besides their other flames? Doth Poetry
Wear *Venus'* Livery? only serve her turn?
Why are not *Sonnets* made of thee? and lays   *5*
     Upon thine Altar burnt? Cannot thy love
     Heighten a spirit to sound out thy praise
As well as any she? Cannot thy *Dove*
Outstrip their *Cupid* easily in flight?
     Or, since thy ways are deep, and still the same,   *10*
     Will not a verse run smooth that bears thy name?
Why doth that fire, which by thy power and might
     Each breast does feel, no braver fuel choose
     Than that, which one day, Worms, may chance refuse?

---

7. *banes.* Banns of marriage.

[SONNET (II)]

Sure Lord, there is enough in thee to dry
  Oceans of *Ink;* for, as the Deluge did
  Cover the Earth, so doth thy Majesty:
Each Cloud distills thy praise, and doth forbid
Poets to turn it to another use.   *5*
  Roses and *Lilies* speak thee; and to make
  A pair of Cheeks of them, is thy abuse.
Why should I *Women's eyes* for Crystal take?
Such poor invention burns in their low mind,
  Whose fire is wild, and doth not upward go   *10*
  To praise, and on thee Lord, some *Ink* bestow.
Open the bones, and you shall nothing find
  In the best *face* but *filth,* when Lord, in thee
  The *beauty* lies, in the *discovery.*

TO MY SUCCESSOR

  If thou chance for to find
  A new House to thy mind,
And built without thy Cost:
  Be good to the Poor,
  As God gives thee store,   *5*
And then, my Labor's not lost.

BIBLIOGRAPHY

In recent years, there has been a strong revival of interest in Herbert. What follows is in no sense inclusive, but instead an annotated guide to the works referred to in the text, as well as those I have found particularly helpful in coming to grips with Herbert's life and works. For a fuller listing of studies relating to Herbert, see John R. Roberts, *George Herbert: An Annotated Bibliography of Modern Criticism, 1905–1974* (Columbia: University of Missouri Press, 1978). See also Jerry Leath Mills, "Recent Studies in Herbert," *English Literary Renaissance* 6 (1976): 105–18; Samuel and Dorothy Tannenbaum, *George Herbert: A Concise Bibliography* (New York: Tannenbaum, 1946); and *The New Cambridge Bibliography of English Literature*, Vol. I, ed. George Watson (Cambridge: Cambridge University Press, 1974), cols. 1201–06.

BIOGRAPHY

The standard biography is now that of Amy Charles, *A Life of George Herbert* (Ithaca, N. Y.: Cornell University Press, 1977). See also Marchette Chute, *Two Gentle Men: The Lives of George Herbert and Robert Herrick* (London: Secker & Warburg, 1960); and Joseph Summers, *George Herbert: His Religion and Art* (Cambridge: Harvard University Press, 1968). Early biographies include Barnabas Oley's Preface to *Herbert's Remains* (London: For Timothy Garthwait, 1652); and Izaac Walton's *Life* (1670; reprinted Oxford: Oxford University Press, 1973). Studies of Herbert's biography include Robert E. Reiter, "George Herbert and his Biographers," *Cithara*, 9 (1970); 18–31; and David Novarr, *The Making of Walton's Lives* (Ithaca, N. Y.: Cornell University Press, 1958).

GEORGE HERBERT

TEXT

The standard edition of Herbert is that of F. E. Hutchinson, *The Works of George Herbert* (Oxford: Claredon, 1941). Useful editions of *The Temple* include that of C. A. Patrides (London: Dent, 1974) and Barbara K. Lewalski and Andrew J. Sabol, in *Major Poets of the Earlier Seventeenth Century* (New York: Odyssey, 1973). The Williams manuscript of *The Temple* is available in a facsimile edition prepared by Amy Charles (Delmar, N. Y.: Scholars' Facsimilies & Reprints, 1977); facsimile editions of the 1633 *Temple* (1968) and the 1652 *Remains* (1970) are available from London's Scholar Press. Hutchinson's editorial decisions have been found wanting by J. Max Patrick, in "Critical Problems in Editing George Herbert's *The Temple*," in *The Editor as Critic and the Critic as Editor*, ed. Murray Krieger (Los Angeles: Clark Memorial Library, 1973). Patrick's edition of Herbert's *Works*, coedited with John R. Muldur, is forthcoming. A *Concordance* to the works of Herbert has been prepared by Mario A. Di Cesare and Rigo Mignani (Ithaca, N. Y.: Cornell University Press, 1977).

GENERAL STUDIES

The modern revival of interest in Herbert was sparked by Rosemond Tuve's *A Reading of George Herbert* (Chicago: University of Chicago Press, 1952), which stresses Herbert's use of traditional liturgical forms in his poetry. The best general study of Herbert is still Joseph Summers' *George Herbert: His Religion and Art* (Cambridge: Harvard University Press, 1954), which surveys all of Herbert's major work with attention to biographical, theological, and artistic backgrounds. Margaret Bottrall's *George Herbert* (London: John Murry, 1954) also surveys the major works in light of seventeenth-century religious and literary developments. The most recent full-length reading of Herbert's poetry is Helen Vendler's *The Poetry of George Herbert* (Cambridge: Harvard University Press, 1975), a study that provides a useful guide to the intricacies of Herbert's lyrics. Herbert's poetic style has been the subject of three major studies, chief among them Arnold Stein's *George Herbert's Lyrics* (Baltimore: Johns Hopkins Press, 1968). The impact of the metrical translations of the Psalms on Herbert's style is the subject of Coburn Freer's *Music for a King* (Baltimore: Johns Hopkins Press, 1972). Mary Ellen Rickey traces the development of Herbert's style in

BIBLIOGRAPHY

Utmost Art: Complexity in the Verse of George Herbert (Lexington: University of Kentucky Press, 1966). The most provocative recent studies of Herbert are two by Stanley E. Fish, "Letting Go: The Dialectic of the Self in George Herbert's Poetry," in *Self-Consuming Artifacts* (Berkeley: University of California Press, 1972), pp. 156–223, and *The Living Temple: George Herbert and Catechizing* (Berkeley: University of California Press, 1978). A helpful introduction to seventeenth-century religious poetry is Anthony Low's *Love's Architecture: Devotional Modes in Seventeenth-Century English Poetry* (New York: New York University Press, 1978). Two appreciative essays that are always worthy of our attention are that of Austin Warren in *Rage for Order: Essays in Criticism* (Chicago: University of Chicago Press, 1948) and T. S. Eliot's slim volume on Herbert in the Writers and their Work series, no. 152 (London: Longmans, Green, 1962). For discussion of the spiritual and theological dimensions of Herbert's poetry, see Sister Maria Thekla, *George Herbert: Idea and Image* (Buckinghamshire, England: Greek Orthodox Monastery of the Assumption, 1974).

BACKGROUNDS

Louis L. Martz, in his monumental *The Poetry of Meditation: A Study in English Religious Literature of the Seventeenth Century* (New Haven: Yale University Press, 1954), sees Herbert from the context of Counter-Reformation meditative practices. A contrasting view, noting Herbert's use of a distinctively Protestant theory of meditation and biblical poetry, is Barbara K. Lewalski's *Protestant Poetics and the Seventeenth-Century Religious Lyric* (Princeton: Princeton University Press, 1979). Herbert's place in the Pauline and Augustinian tradition of spirituality is traced in William H. Halewood's *The Poetry of Grace: Reformation Themes and Structures in English Seventeenth-Century Poetry* (New Haven: Yale University Press, 1970) and Patrick Grant's *The Transformation of Sin: Studies in Donne, Herbert, Vaughan, and Traherne* (Amherst: University of Massachusetts Press, 1974). Herbert's debt, or lack of it, to the tradition of Christian humanism is discussed in M. M. Mahood's *Poetry and Humanism* (1950; reprinted New York: Norton, 1970) and Malcolm Ross, *Poetry and Dogma* (New Brunswick, N. J.: Rutgers University Press, 1954). Two early studies of Christian mysticism in Herbert's poetry are Helen C. White's *The Metaphysical Poets: A Study in Religious Experience* (1936; reprinted New York: Collier, 1962) and Itrat Husain's *The Mystical Element in the Metaphysical Poets of Seventeenth Century* (London: Oliver and Boyd, 1948). Herbert's relationship to Counter-Reformation spirituality is surveyed in Richard Strier, "Herbert and Tears," *ELH* 46 (1979): 221–47. Studies of the liturgical context of Herbert's poetry include John E. Booty, "George Herbert: *The Temple* and *The Book of Common Prayer*," *Mosaic* 12 (1979): 75–90; Mary Paynter, " 'Sinne and Love': Thematic Patterns in George Herbert's Lyrics," *Yearbook of English Studies* 3 (1973): 85–93; Gregory Ziegelmajer, "Liturgical Symbol and Reality in the Poetry of George Herbert," *American Benedictine Review* 18 (1967): 344–53; and William J. McGill, Jr., "George Herbert's View of the Eucharist," *Lock Haven Review* 8 (1966): 16–24. Herbert's use of the Psalms for models of divine address is the subject of Heather Asals, "The Voice of George Herbert's 'The Church,' " *ELH* 36 (1969): 511–28.

SPECIAL TOPICS

For discussions of the unity of the three parts of *The Temple*, see Elizabeth Stambler, "The Unity of Herbert's 'Temple,' " *Cross Currents* 10 (1960): 251–66; John David Walker, "The Architectonics of George Herbert's *The Temple*," *ELH* 29 (1962): 289–305; Annabel Endicott, "The Structure of George Herbert's *Temple*: A Reconsideration," *University of Toronto Quarterly* 34 (1965): 226–37; Sara William Hanley, C.S.J., "Temples in *The Temple*: Design and Methodology," *Studies in English Literature* 8 (1968): 121–35; and Elizabeth McLaughlin and Gail Thomas, "Communion in *The Temple*," *Studies in English Literature* 15 (1975): 111–24. Other studies of special interest include Stanley Stewart, "Time and *The Temple*," *Studies in English Literature* 6 (1966): 97–110; Ira Clark, " 'Lord, in thee the *Beauty* lies in the *Discovery*': 'Love Unknown' and Reading Herbert," *ELH* 39 (1972): 560–84; Robert Higbie, "Images of Enclosure in George Herbert's *The Temple*," *Texas Studies in Literature and Language* 15 (1974): 627–38; Barbara Leah Harman, "George Herbert's 'Affliction (I)': The Limits of Representation," *ELH* 44 (1977): 267–85; and "The Fiction of Coherence: George Herbert's 'The Collar,' " *PMLA* 93 (1978): 865–77. A number of important essays on Herbert are reprinted in John R. Roberts, *Essential Articles for the Study of George Herbert* (Hamden, Conn.: Archon, 1979). For an account of Herbert's use of imagery, see Fredson Bowers, "Herbert's Sequential Imagery: 'The Temper,' " *Modern Philology*, 59 (1962): 202–13. For discussions of Herbert's use of "shaped verse," see Rosemary Freeman, *English Emblem Books* (London: Chatto and Windus, 1948; rpt. 1967); and Peter Daly, *Literature in Light of the Emblem* (Toronto: University Press, 1979).

INDEX TO PREFACE,
INTRODUCTION AND NOTES

INDEX

INDEX

Humility, 4, 5, 26, 27, 34, 35, 47.
Hutchinson, F.E., 19, 21, 48, 49, 51, 59, 61, 74, 79, 83, 86, 108, 151, 164, 168, 209, 250, 314.

Israel, 39, 46, 145, 317.

Jacob, 120, 151.
James I, 10, 16, 21, 22, 70.
Jardine, Lisa, 29.
Jerusalem, New, 10.
Jews, 277.
Johnson, Samuel, 54.
Joseph, 284.
Josephus, 108.
Judas, 140.

Krieger, Murray, 14, 49.

Laban, 121.
Laud, Archbishop, 8, 10, 23.
Lennox, Duke of, 21.
Leicester, Earl of, 9–10.
Lewalski, Barbara K., 29, 38, 41, 49, 51.
Life, Christian, xi, 5, 6, 10, 11, 12, 14, 17, 18, 20, 23, 24, 25, 26, 28, 31, 35, 36, 38, 42, 43, 44, 45, 47; of Church, xiii, 6, 17, 18, 24, 25, 26, 35, 42, 44, 45, 46, 47; conduct of, 28, 97; reformation of, 32; religious, 6, 7, 11; spiritual, 4, 6, 10.
Life of George Herbert, cf. under Walton, Izaak.
Liturgy, xiii, 24.
Luther, Martin, xii.

Macarius, 318.
Maria Thekla, Sister, 29.
Martin, L.C., 1, 11.
Martz, Louis L., 9, 29.
Mason, Kenneth, xiv.
Maycock, A.L., 23.
McGee, J. Sears, 10.
Melchizedek, 247.
Milton, John, 9.
Miner, Earl, 41.

Ministry, xiii, xiv, 28, 86, 110.
Mohammed, 321.
Moses, 39, 144, 218, 252.

Nathan, 31, 76.
Nethersole, Sir Francis, 19.
Noah, 216, 250, 251, 317.
Novarr, David, 1.

O'Hara-May, Jane, 89.
Oley, Barnabas, xx, 48.
Ong, Walter J., S.J., 29.
Osborne, James, 10, 20.
Ovid, 150.

Pandora, 284.
Parliament, 2, 12, 13, 18, 19, 20, 22, 23, 24, 25, 26, 70, 103.
Patrick, J. Max, 14, 24, 49, 151, 152, 291.
Patrides, C.A., 1, 51.
Paul, Saint, 31, 141, 151.
Pebworth, Ted-Larry, 16.
Pembroke, Earl of, 310.
Prayer, and Church, xiii, 6, 7, 20, 23, 28, 35, 42, 47; and Herbert, xii, xvi, 7, 20, 23, 135.
Preaching, xiii, 6, 27, 30, 31, 32, 33, 34, 35.
Priesthood, xiv, 2, 4, 5, 6, 26, 27, 28, 30, 32, 33, 34, 35, 41, 42, 47, 110; of Christ, xiv.
Puritans, 8, 10, 11, 22, 36, 64, 110, 119.
Puttenham, George, 29.

Rebekah, 218.
Reformation, xii, 8, 9, 12, 20.
Renaissance, xii, 25, 322.
Rhetoric, 28–30, 33, 35, 42.
Rickey, Mary Ellen, 26, 46.
Rohde, C.S., 89.

Sabol, Andrew J., 49, 51.
Sacraments, xiii, xiv, xv, 4, 40, 42, 43, 110, 148.
Salvation, xiv, 10, 11, 27, 32, 35, 37, 39, 40, 42, 43, 45, 46, 47.

INDEX

INDEX TO TEXTS
AND SCRIPTURE REFERENCES

INDEX

INDEX

INDEX

INDEX

INDEX

Vanity, 134, 152, 203.
Venus, 332.
Vice, 57, 68, 91–94.
Virgil, 107.
Virginity, 66–67.
Virtue, 66, 68, 72, 82, 92, 94, 105, 137, 179, 186, 189, 206, 220, 240, 248, 302.

Wealth, 127, 149, 231, 289.
Whitsuntide, 86, 174.
Wisdom, 88, 128–129, 132, 133, 202, 214, 240, 258, 268, 284.

Wisdom, 8:1, 237.
Wit, 129–130, 131, 132, 134, 150, 169, 196, 207, 208, 231, 237, 257, 280, 329.
Works (Deeds), of charity, 72, 77, 89; of creation, 149; of darkness, 57; of God, 251; good, 67, 68, 69, 72, 76; of healing, 75; of man, 177, 180; and Parson, 59, 333.

Zechariah, 4:12, 175; 7:12, 139.

351

INDEX TO POEMS

INDEX

353

INDEX